OMAI

The Prince Who Never Was

ALSO BY RICHARD CONNAUGHTON

Rising Sun and Tumbling Bear: Russia's War with Japan

The Republic of the Ushakovka: Admiral Kolchak and the Allied Intervention in Siberia 1918–1920

Military Intervention in the 1990s: A New Logic for War

Shrouded Secrets: Japan's War on Mainland Australia 1942–1944

Celebration of Victory: V-E Day 1945

The Nature of Future Conflict

Descent into Chaos: The Doomed Expedition into Low's Gully

The Battle for Manila (with John Pimlott and Duncan Anderson)

MacArthur and Defeat in the Philippines

Military Intervention and Peacekeeping: The Reality

OMAI

The Prince Who Never Was

RICHARD CONNAUGHTON

TIMEWELL
PRESS

First published in Great Britain in 2005 by
Timewell Press Limited
10 Porchester Terrace, London W2 3TL

ISBN 1 85725 205 5

Typeset by Antony Gray
Printed and bound in Great Britain by
Biddles Ltd, King's Lynn

for
DR ERIC GROVE
*friend, pre-eminent
naval historian,
enthusiast.*

Contents

List of Illustrations

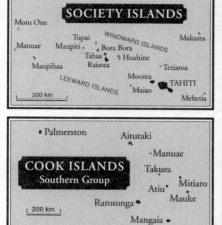

SOCIETY ISLANDS

Motu One

Manuae

Tupai
Maupiti
WINDWARD ISLANDS
Bora Bora
Tahaa
Raiatea
Huahine

Makatea

Maupihaa

Moorea

Tetiaroa

TAHITI

LEEWARD ISLANDS
Maiao

Mehetia

200 km

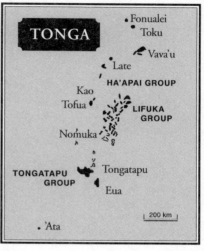

TONGA

Fonualei
Toku
Vava'u

Late

HA'APAI GROUP

Kao
Tofua

LIFUKA GROUP

Nomuka

TONGATAPU GROUP

Tongatapu
Eua

'Ata

200 km

Palmerston

Aitutaki

Manuae

COOK ISLANDS
Southern Group

Takuea

Atiu

Mitiaro

Mauke

Rarotonga

Mangaia

200 km

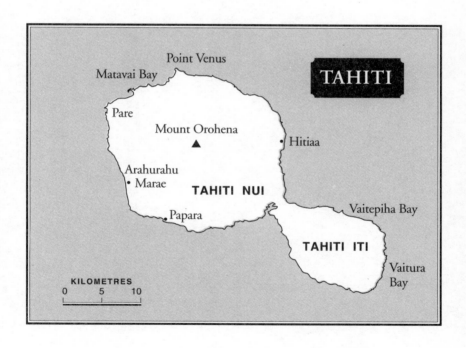

Point Venus

Matavai Bay

Pare

Mount Orohena
▲

Hitiaa

Arahurahu
Marae

TAHITI NUI

Papara

Vaitepiha Bay

TAHITI

TAHITI ITI

Vaitura Bay

KILOMETRES
0   5   10

Introduction

If a face can launch a thousand ships, it is not unreasonable that a portrait can be responsible for the launch of a book – this book. The portrait in question is Sir Joshua Reynolds's *Omai*, a superb, full-length, romanticised painting of Omai, a young South Sea islander who came to England in 1774 aboard Tobias Furneaux's HMS *Adventure*. Nevertheless, the problem with the Reynolds painting is that it represents a deception, a masquerade in which Omai was positively acquiescent. The white toga in which he is dressed is the clothing of Tahiti's aristocracy: but Omai was a commoner, not an aristocrat. It is out of this, apparently trivial, misrepresentation that the tragedy of Omai is founded.

This does not, of course, detract from the quality of a portrait exhibited to great acclaim at the Royal Academy in 1776. Omai had taken England by storm. His arrival in England coincided with a long-running intellectual debate, stimulated by the French philosopher Jean-Jacques Rousseau as to whether man in his natural state was superior to civilised man. To the curious, Omai epitomised the 'noble savage': the embodiment of an anthropological experiment to observe and to learn how a savage might behave in a civilised environment. No one quite knew what to expect and society appears to have been divided equally between those who believed there was something to be learned from Omai and what he represented, and those who were certain the contrary was true. Omai's story went beyond anything Rousseau may have imagined.

The Omai portrait, considered to be one of Reynolds's finest, became one of the artist's favourites, and he kept it to himself in his studio until his death. Acquired by an agent, the painting came into the possession of the Howards of Castle Howard where it remained until 2001, when it was sold at Sotheby's for £10.3 million. The purchaser was the London dealer, Guy Morrison, thought to be acting on behalf of Irish bloodstock magnate John Magnier.

The British government placed an export licence deferral on the portrait, then valued at £12.5 million. Meanwhile, steps were taken to raise the funds to save *Omai* for the nation. A fundamental difference existed between the portrait and the other national treasures, which had also been placed on the 'at risk' list. *Omai* was a portrait of English significance by an English artist. Attractive (and wickedly expensive) as Reubens's *Massacre of the Innocents* and Raphael's *Madonna of the Pinks* may have been, they had no specific national significance. Fortunately, the portrait was within the budget of one generous, anonymous donor who provided Tate Britain with the requisite amount should the new owner be willing to sell. Nevertheless, at the time of writing the owner is not willing to sell and, as the painting has been refused an export licence, it remains in the country.

It is not commonly known that the portrait is a representation of the tragedy that befell the young man whose image has been captured so magnificently on canvas. On 18 December 2002, *The Times* carried the portrait on its front page, depicting 'a Tahitian Prince who took fashionable society by storm in the 1770s'. But Omai was not a prince but a commoner. His sponsors inflated his status to that of either priest or prince. He went along with the ruse, regarding it as harmless, having his ego progressively inflated over the two years he spent being lionised in England.

It was always the intention of George III that Omai should return home, but his home was a place where there existed a formally structured aristocracy closer to the French than the British model. He returned home with the airs and graces, possessions and wealth of an aristocrat but was unable to become what he was not. The English experience had spoilt him. He went on to antagonise the chiefs, giving to people highly prized gifts which the chiefs themselves coveted. He became a sad and lonely figure, dying in his late twenties, possibly of a throat infection from a germ introduced to the islands by Spanish colonisers.

I came to know the true story of Omai through a book I was preparing on the 1796 missionary voyage of a Thames riverboat, the *Duff*, to Tahiti. A great deal of new history owes its revelation to serendipity. The story of the *Duff* falls into this category. I discovered a book published in Fleet Street in 1799, *A Missionary Voyage to the Southern Pacific Ocean performed in the years 1796, 1797, 1798, in the ship Duff commanded by Captain James Wilson compiled from the journals of the officers and the missionaries*. The leadership of the Missionary Society criticised the Admiralty for neglecting the opportunity to teach Omai English in order that he might become their evangelist. Practically, the idea would not have worked because Omai appeared incapable of learning anything more than a few words of English.

The fragments of the Omai story are widely scattered. The task has been simplified by a number of outstanding academic works, but this book was always destined for a lighter touch than the scholarly treatment of Cook and Omai found in books by J. C. Beaglehole and E. H. McCormick.

In selecting the material to support my case, I have been generously assisted by a large number of individuals and institutions. I am grateful to John Montagu, Earl of Sandwich, for directing me towards Omai material within the fourth Earl's papers; to Lord Harmsworth, chairman of Dr Johnson's House Trust, who read and commented upon the draft; and to Lady Juliet Townsend, a descendant of Tobias Furneaux. To Richard Aylmer of the Joshua Reynolds Society, Rosemary Best for reading the drafts, the Dorset Library Service for finding rare books and making available a microfilm reading facility, to Jan Prince of the Tahiti Beach Press, to Michelle Hetherington and Sylvia Carr of the National Library of Australia, Canberra, to Tim Lovell-Smith and Kevin Stewart of the Alexander Turnbull Library, Wellington, the Mitchell and Dixson Libraries in Sydney, Gerry

McCormack, my invaluable researcher in Sydney, the British Library, the National Portrait Gallery, London, Dr Howard Roscoe of the British Antarctic Survey, Kiri Ross-Jones of the National Maritime Museum, London, the Royal Society Library and Archives, the National Archives, Kew, the Museé de Tahiti et ses Îles, to Tate Britain and to cartographer Giles Dearlove, I extend my thanks and gratitude.

Grateful thanks are also due to all those who assisted and advised while we were researching in Sydney, Canberra, Auckland, Wellington, Cook Islands, Moorea, Raiatea, Huahine and Tahiti – a memorable experience. I am particularly grateful to long-established resident of Tahiti and restaurateur, Roger Gowen; to Henri Theureau, linguist and translator resident on Raiatea; and to anthropologist and archaeologist Mark Eddowes met on Huahine. I am deeply appreciative of these various additional skeins of colour with which to embroider the tapestry of this, the story of Omai and his tragedy. Having said all this, the responsibility for conclusions drawn is mine. And finally, to Georgina: this book could not, as usual, have been put together without your mastery of technology and word processing which still remain entirely beyond my competence and understanding.

Richard Connaughton
Nettlecombe, Dorset, 2005

OMAI

The Prince Who Never Was

CHAPTER 1

Fiction and Fact

The Theatre Royal, Covent Garden, the evening of Tuesday 20 December, 1785. As streams of theatre-goers flowed out along the dark corridors leading away from the brightness of the Adam auditorium, the noise of animated conversation signified their enjoyment of the first-night performance. A nearby gilt-framed billboard revealed there to have been two plays for the audience's enjoyment. The first, *The Tragedy of Jane Shore*, had been followed by the Christmas pantomime *Omai, or a Trip Round the World* by the playwright John O'Keefe. So popular would the pantomime prove to be that it ran a full Christmas season of fifty performances, including a royal command performance, and was repeated in the following two years. While the reviews of *Jane Shore* had been lukewarm, the Omai pantomime was enthusiastically received: 'A spectacle abounding with such variety of uncommonly beautiful scenery never before was seen from the stage of a theatre; nor was there ever . . . a more rich treat for the lovers of music.'

The show employed all the theatrical skills available in contemporary stagecraft, offering a colourful, exciting, romantic and extravagant portrayal of life as it was imagined to be on the Pacific island of Tahiti. The hero, Omai, was not a fictitious character. He had come to England from Tahiti, becoming a well-known figure. He knew King George III and was much in demand at society functions. It had been the King who eventually told Omai to return home. He travelled under the care of Captain Cook on the latter's third and fateful voyage into the Pacific.

At the same time as the first members of the well-wrapped audience had begun to emerge into the carriage-lined street, others who had been in the front stalls had barely left the auditorium. Up in David Garrick's former box above them lingered Fanny Burney, renowned author of *Evelina,* and the other literati she had taken to the performance as her guests. The famous artist Joshua Reynolds had sat in the orchestra. His personal interest lay not simply in having known Omai and painted his portrait, but also in the stage scenery, for which he 'expressed the utmost satisfaction at all the landscape scenes'. Fanny's countenance appeared strangely at odds with the happy faces surrounding her. Tears began to well in her eyes. Fanny and her sailor brother James (Jem) had both known Omai well and she recognised that while the pantomime was a type of show where liberties were both expected and taken, it was nevertheless far removed from reality. She, more than most, knew that Omai's story was not a tale of fun and amusement but one of tragedy; a tragedy founded upon man's inability or unwillingness to consider fully the effects and consequences upon others when behaving out of self-interest. Omai played out the role of both victim and, in respect of two New Zealand Maoris he took as his servants to Tahiti, villain. This particular story had its beginning on another stage, halfway round the world, on 18 June 1767.

Tahiti is one of thousands of islands dotted across the Pacific, the world's largest geographical feature covering almost half the world's surface yet containing approximately only eight hundred inhabited islands. Indeed, 'Polynesia' means *many islands* and lies to the east of Micronesia and Melanesia, all three of which together comprise Oceania. Tahiti comprises two conjoined volcanic islands of unequal size 33 miles across – big Tahiti, *Tahiti Nui* and little Tahiti, *Tahiti Iti* – and is also linked by virtue of proximity to the island of Eimeo, later called Moorea. Polynesian legend has it that Moorea was formed as the second dorsal fin of the fish that became Tahiti. There is historical speculation that Tahiti was first discovered in 1606 by the Spaniard Pedro Fernandez de Quiros but the lack of precision navigation instruments at that time and the fact that Tahitians did not have a written form of their language means that there is no corroborative evidence. The first certain discovery of Tahiti by non-Polynesians occurred at dusk on 18 June 1767 by the thirty-eight-year-old Samuel Wallis commanding the fast, 32-gun, copper-bottomed frigate HMS *Dolphin*. The nine-year-old *Dolphin* was a ship of some pedigree, having already taken John Byron on his unsuccessful attempt to find the North-West Passage into the Atlantic from the Pacific. The quest to discover the North-West Passage was one of two prevailing fixations shared by a number of countries. The second quest focused upon the southern hemisphere – the search for the non-existent Terra Australis Incognita.

Wallis had been sent into these waters by the Admiralty to find Terra Australis Incognita, the unknown Southern Land, a mythical land mass believed since ancient Greek times to be in the southern hemisphere, the counterbalance to the land mass of the northern temperate zone. Terra Australis should not be confused with Australia which had been discovered and was then known as New Holland. Wallis was a good sailor but not a dedicated explorer; he was content to go through the motions. He had been severely affected by biliousness on this voyage which, like so many of its time, demanded a great deal of frail human bodies. His officers and crew, which numbered one hundred and thirty-one, not the most harmonious group of people, were desperate to go ashore to find fresh food and uncontaminated water. It was almost a year to the day since they had sailed from Plymouth on 19 June 1766. As if to answer their prayers, the tops of the cloud-shrouded, 7000-feet high, deep purple, jagged peaks of Tahiti were seen 70 to 80 miles away. Wallis anchored the *Dolphin* off the island to see what daylight would reveal. Could this be the southern continent?

A long coral reef lay between *Dolphin* and the island, the narrow gaps in the reef defined by the absence of breaking waves. From their side of the reef, the crew stared across to the island, wondering about its nature and its people. The visible land ran back a few miles from the beaches through cultivated fields. They observed, beyond the coconut palms, a profusion of trees of a type they did not recognise. The green circular fruit of this tree, the size of a Cantaloupe melon, was the islanders' staple diet – breadfruit, *arto-carpus*. Numerous houses with neat thatched roofs and open on all four sides could be seen between the palms. Deeper inland the lush green terrain and tropical forests ascended mountain peaks to the sides of which lay deep, beautiful valleys. The mystery for sailors coming from a country of defined seasons was that, in what for Tahiti should have been the winter, everything should appear so verdant and luxurious.

In the early morning Wallis ordered the anchor raised and sailed parallel to the reef to locate a suitable place to put victualling parties ashore and ultimately to find a safe anchorage. This activity was observed by crowds of natives who had been drawn by curiosity on to the black sandy beaches to stare in amazement at the enormous *canoe*, which was the *Dolphin*. It was a sight beyond their experience and comprehension. Friend or foe they knew not but they were wise enough to treat the apparition as hostile until evidence to the contrary became available.

The Tahitians, Samoans, Maoris and Hawaiians are of the same race which three and a half thousand years ago set out from South East Asia, Indonesia and Malaysia, the probable starting points of Polynesian migrations. The separate civilisations that developed meant that cultural differences would inevitably arise. The surprise is that those differences are not profound. For example, records show that in the eighteenth century they all indulged in surfing on makeshift surfboards, the only variation being in Hawaii where the surfers stood up. The botanist Joseph Banks, who came to the island on Cook's first voyage, enjoyed sitting on the volcanic black sand on and around Matavai beach watching the natives surfing: 'their chief amusement was being carried on by an old canoe; with this before them they swam out as far as the outermost beach, then one or two would get into it, and opposing the blunt end to the breaking wave, were hurried in with incredible swiftness.' Where there were gaps in the reef, the surf became more challenging. Among other recreational activities, the Tahitians also engaged in kite flying.

Tribes were rarely at peace with one another. In warfare there was a preference for the certainty of a hand-held club and the confirmation of effect by virtue of the sound of a cracking skull. Wars were not infrequent but the number of casualties arising in domestic land warfare were usually few. When there were exceptions to that rule, the loss of life was great. Inter-island maritime warfare was far more dangerous and costly in lives and injuries. Bows and arrows were used on Tahiti, the bow being 6-feet long and strung with local flax. A competent archer could send an arrow over 300 yards but the bow was used in sport, not in combat. Even then, they sought distance rather than accuracy. They had slings and lances but concurrent with the *Dolphin's* reconnaissance, battle canoes were in the process of being loaded with nothing more serious or long-ranged than hand-sized rocks. The natives launched dozens of canoes from the beaches in the dawn mist and headed out for the *Dolphin*.

Over the years, Polynesian canoes – the *va'a* or *waka* – were adapted to the new requirement of island-hopping rather than long voyages of exploration over thousands of miles. Most sea-going canoes were not outriggers proper but double-hulled, catamaran-type vessels. The need for the *va'a* to fulfil a migratory function having passed, the requirement for the uniquely shaped canoe as a means of communication remained. If there was a Polynesian standard canoe design it lay in low bows and high, ornate sterns rising up to 24 feet, from which long and colourful streamers were hung. Lateen sails harnessed the wind. The Tahitian war canoe differed from the virtually standard Polynesian model in so far as it was the bow which was raised and the stern which was low. Assembled behind the high bow and taking advantage of its limited protection could be up to fifty sling- or lance-wielding troops. In times of conflict there were a thousand war canoes available to the chiefs.

There were, of course, smaller commuting canoes and outriggers. The chiefs' canoes might also carry a small shelter where the chief would sit. Fairness of skin denoted aristocracy and the chiefs took great care to shelter from the sun. The initial influx of Europeans and North Americans, as heralded by the *Dolphin*, was in general tolerably well received because of the visitors' fair complexions. The milkiness of their skin fascinated the Tahitians to the extent that they would attempt to undo the many layers of clothing worn by officers and crew to touch pale skin unsullied by the sun.

The natives paddled round the ship, satisfying their enormous curiosity but offering no violence. The crew discerned from the behaviour in the canoes that the cheerful natives offered only friendship. One chief stood up and, after a speech of fifteen minutes – not one word of which had been understood on board – threw plantain branches into the sea, symbolising peace. For their part, the *Dolphin*'s crew held aloft the usual baubles of little intrinsic value that had traditionally pacified and won over potential enemies. Holding in one hand coarse cloth, knives, ribbons and beads, they pointed shorewards and, using the lingua franca of the farmyard, grunted or crowed like the pigs or cocks they desired in exchange. One by one, the islanders came on board, eyes wide with amazement at everything they saw. All seemed to be progressing smoothly until the *Dolphin*'s goat, spotting an obvious foreigner, butted him in the rear. Severely shaken, the injured party screamed and dived overboard followed by all the visitors, one of whom snatched the gold braid hat off Midshipman Henry Ibbot's head in a single move from deck to sea. That one act of common theft had greater significance than would have been apparent to the crew at the time.

Because it was they who had discovered Tahiti, the crew of the *Dolphin* arrived with no preconceptions regarding the island, its people or their customs. En route, they had anchored at Tierra del Fuego whose population they found to be backward and unprepossessing: 'perhaps', as Cook would write, 'as miserable a set of people as are this day upon earth'. The first encounter with the Tahitians left a very favourable impression upon the *Dolphin*'s crew, one which would be embellished on their return to England, so much so that when later explorers reached Tahiti they found it some way short of paradise and the people not as alluring as they had been led to believe. In 1797, a missionary wrote: 'Neither could we see aught of that elegance and beauty in their women for which they had been so greatly celebrated.' There was some artifice in their looks, created when they were infants when skulls were soft and malleable. Pressure put on the skull with hands widened the face, distended the mouth and flattened the nose and forehead. But this was all superficial for there are accounts that examined the female and her form in the round:

> They possess eminent female graces: their faces are never darkened with a scowl, or covered with a cloud of sullenness or suspicion. Their manners are affable and engaging; their step easy, firm, and graceful; their behaviour free and unguarded; always boundless in generosity to each other, and to strangers; their tempers mild, gentle and unaffected; slow to take offence, easily pacified, and seldom retaining resentment or revenge, whatever provocation they may have received.

The observation concludes with a very revealing sentence: 'Many are true and tender wives.' That sentence says a great deal of the tolerance of the Tahitian woman who, on her husband's whim, could be sent to a male friend or stranger to satisfy his desires. The inferiority of the female was ingrained in Tahitian society: they were so low as not to be considered even worthy of sacrifice.

The natives did change lifetime habits over a short period and it was contact with an increasing number of sailors, dropouts and beach-combers that shifted their life's emphasis away from spiritualism towards materialism. At that first meeting the islanders were found to be taller and fitter than the English explorers. Men who might be described as working men as opposed to the chiefs wore very little – a cloth belt wrapped around the waist and pulled through between the legs. The lower classes of women wore skirts made from leaves. Further up the social scale, bark (*tapa*) cloth was worn, perhaps made into a poncho. The most sought-after *tapa* came from the bark of the mulberry tree. White *tapa*, the highest quality, was reserved for the chiefs, the wives of chiefs and other notables. Wallis and the visitors observed a class structure in place in Tahiti with a clearly defined social order and aristocracy. The monochrome dark tattoos seen to varying degrees on male and female bodies also served as badges of rank. Sailors brought the idea of the tattoo home with them where colour was introduced to an imaginative catalogue of designs. The Royal Society's Joseph Banks also returned to England with a tattoo on the inside of one arm.

Finding the Tahitians reasonably amenable, the *Dolphin's* officers felt it safe to send the master and his mate in two boats to take soundings between the gaps in the coral. In a short while the two rowing boats had been surrounded by two hundred canoes, half the occupants of which appeared friendly, the other half hostile. On more than one occasion the absence of unanimity was observed among the Tahitians. This could have been due to the influence of different priests and chiefs. At any one time there were up to ten regional high chiefs descended from the gods on Tahiti. Known as the *arii*, they took precedence over the priests.

When an attempt was made by the natives to leap into the leading boat, the master ordered two marines to fire. The shock of the discharge of the muskets could be seen in the reaction of the Tahitians, a physical reaction to the jolt, a collective shudder of bodies, then inquisitiveness – what was the noise? – and finally the association of the marines with the noise, and one dead and one wounded Tahitian. The discharge of those two weapons, as much as the arrival of the *Dolphin*, had a volcanic effect on the history of the Pacific. The canoes dispersed, their crews contemplating their experience and considering precisely how their friends had been struck down without there having been visible contact. The next day, when another attempt was made to pass through the coral, the Tahitian canoes held back.

This new expedition was not bravado on the part of the *Dolphin's* crew. They urgently needed fresh water. One of the *Dolphin's* boats approached sufficiently close to the beach to hurl ashore a number of shells of the calabash tree, used on board as water receptacles. Luck was on the sailors' side for these were good-natured Tahitians who, understanding the requirement, filled the containers and swam out to the boats to deliver the water. Their generosity extended further for they brought on to the beach and up to the water line a bevy of half-naked, dark-haired, giggling women and, using gestures universally understood, made it perfectly clear to the men in the boat what was on offer. The men were mightily tempted but with extreme reluctance obeyed the mate's orders to row back to the *Dolphin.* They could see the women taunting them, questioning their sexuality.

The next day the amiable natives returned in their canoes in numbers with pigs, chickens and fruit to barter. They also brought in each canoe a young girl with dark eyes and sleek black hair down over her shoulders. Again these women used sign language which required no translation for what they had in mind. The sailors brought out their cheap trinkets to exchange for fresh food, only to find the natives unimpressed. The axes were useful and mirrors fascinating but what they wanted most were iron nails. There could be no certain explanation for the importance or knowledge of nails since there had been no contact across the two cultures. They would fashion the nails into fish hooks, iron being preferred to shells and human bones, materials which had been in use for centuries. The common iron nail became currency with a high rate of conversion.

After four days of probing, HMS *Dolphin* came upon a natural harbour free of coral and protected by a spit on the eastern side. The opening had been created by a 12-yard-wide river, the Vaipopoo, whose fresh water kept the coral at bay. (A flow of fresh water creates a gap in a coral reef, which is why it is easier to approach high islands than atolls.) The water of the Matavai River descended from the high mountains then meandered through the valley before entering the sea close to what would become known as Point Venus. Vital fresh water also ran behind the black sandy beach. This was Matavai Bay where Cook and the London Missionary Society's men in black also set up temporary residence. Named Port Royal Bay, the curving, 2-mile-long anchorage came to be regarded as a safe haven except between December and March when the northwest and westerly winds blew. With a depth of between 6 and 18 fathoms, Matavai Bay became a busy harbour and market in the eighteenth century. War canoes came and went and canoes of various types were built along the shoreline. The industry attracted people and this area had become one of the most heavily populated on the island.

Some embarrassment did arise when the *Dolphin* ran aground while attempting to move to her anchorage in the harbour. It would have been dangerous if the natives had decided then to attack in force. There is a shoal at the entrance to the harbour, named Dolphin Bank by those who came later. Although this grounding was unintended, ships were frequently beached deliberately to be scraped and caulked. Centuries of scouring by the river meant that the *Dolphin* could anchor close to shore, which she did on 23 June.

The next morning, following breakfast, bartering was well under way, there being five hundred canoes with up to four thousand men in very close proximity to the *Dolphin*. Sentries on board observed a large catamaran leaving the shore and standing off so that she could be seen by the canoes' occupants. A signal appears to have been given from aboard the catamaran which had the reported effect of bringing about a complete change in the nature of the Tahitians. No longer were they happy-go-lucky traders but opponents intent upon the capture of the *Dolphin*. Stone throwing proved to be little more than an irritant because it was patently difficult to throw stones weighing 2lb upwards on to the deck. Although a number of the crew were struck, the sun awning fixed across the length of the deck kept the majority of the missiles away. Nevertheless, the crew suffered minor cuts and injuries. Warning musket fire had no effect. As a precaution, the ship's guns had been loaded with grape shot – each round comprising seventy musket balls – and iron cannon balls. Wallis gave the order to fire into the serried ranks of canoes. This display of firepower wreaked havoc among the terrified Tahitians, killing up to three dozen, and left the *Dolphin*'s sailors with a sense of shame for their disproportionate response. 'To attempt to say what these poor ignorant creatures thought of us, would be taking more upon me than I am able to perform', wrote the master, Robertson. The large catamaran which was thought to have initiated the attack took a direct hit from a cannon ball. Clearly a chief of some rank was on board as others paddled through the gunfire to rescue the warriors and crew. The *Dolphin's* sailors appreciated, recognised and applauded this display of bravery.

The voyagers contemplated the mixed messages of natives who pretended to want to trade but who very suddenly had become aggressive, attempting to seize and neutralise the apparition in their harbour. The *Dolphin's* broadsides had served their purpose. The display of power both impressed and worried the islanders. For two days the Tahitians held back until their entrepreneurial spirit and quest for nails overcame their natural caution. Another floating bazaar began its tentative progress across the bay towards the *Dolphin.* Unsure of their intentions, the *Dolphin* again opened fire on the closing canoes but also, this time, upon the groups of people assembled on One Tree Hill projecting out into the sea above the eastern extremity of the bay. (The hill was not formally described as One Tree Hill until 1769 when so named by Captain James Cook.) The solitary tree had bright red and orange flowers, *erythrina indica.* It is long gone but had once proved to be a valuable navigational reference point. Among those injured ashore was a young man named Omai. In reality his name was Mai. The prefix O simply means *it is,* as in Otaheite and Oberea, the *queen* of Matavai territory. In English usage the O in Otaheite was later dropped. Despite being named otherwise separately and in close succession by the British, French and Spanish, Tahiti was generally referred to as Otaheite or Tahiti.

The Tahitians were very proud of their canoes and kept them in immaculate condition. Approximately eighty of these examples of naval craftsmanship and design were drawn up on Matavai beach, a threat to no one. Wallis rose from his sick bed and, on seeing the 50-feet-long cream of Tahiti's navy assembled on the beach a few yards from the *Dolphin,* ordered his crew ashore to destroy them. In a matter of hours, the results of many years of dedicated labour had been destroyed in a frenzy of wanton destruction. It had been a malicious and pointless gesture, for over 90 per cent of the available war canoes were beached elsewhere on the island. Thereafter, the crew were put on their guard against retaliation, which fortunately did not materialise.

Of the three senior officers, the second lieutenant, thirty-year-old Lieutenant Tobias Furneaux, was the fittest and the most popular officer among the ship's company. He was sent ashore, protected by a large squad of marines, to lay formal claim to Tahiti. He stood on the beach between the river and the sea where he planted a pole bearing a Union Jack pennant and formally declared Tahiti to be King George's Land. Two natives watched all, unaware that they had just become part of Britain's fledgling empire. The green plantains they carried indicated that they had come in peace. Among the food and gifts they offered were two dogs, their hind legs tied together. It is not clear whether Furneaux was aware that these dogs, raised on vegetables, were considered a delicacy; he cut their bonds and they raced off along the beach to live another day. Dogs later presented to Cook did not have the benefit of such consideration. Cook declared South Sea dog to be 'next to an English lamb'. Assuming the flag to be a gift, it was taken to the chief's quarters, to be seen again by Cook two years later in use as the chief's belt.

As contact developed between crew and islanders, so too did sexual conquest, although a more willing party would be difficult to imagine. Under normal circumstances favours might have been freely given but there was an element here of pimp and prostitute in so far as the girl handed over to her husband the fee for her services. The fixed price was initially a 6-inch iron nail until inflation took hold and the price jumped 50 per cent to a 9-inch nail. The first crew member to avail himself of the service was a marine of Irish parentage who had been so keen to establish himself as the first that he performed in a public place. He received 'a severe thrashing for the liberty'. By European standards what he had done was unacceptable but the girls gave the crew every encouragement to perform wherever and whenever the mood took them. The French Captain de Bougainville, who arrived in Tahiti eight months after HMS *Dolphin*'s departure, wrote of his crew's confusion at being invited to copulate in public. But he did admit: 'I would not answer for it that every one of our men found it impossible to conquer his repugnance and conform to the customs of the country.' The *Dolphin*'s officers were sufficiently concerned about the dangers of introducing European diseases to a people with no real defence mechanisms to ask the surgeon whether the crew might release venereal disease among the community. The surgeon assured the officers that there was no venereal disease aboard the *Dolphin*.

The writing of George Robertson, the master of the *Dolphin*, stands out from many other naval records in his breadth of description and grammatical exactitude. The Royal Navy may have been able to fight and sail their ships but their writing and spelling were almost universally execrable. Robertson's eye for details proved especially beneficial within the context of the emerging debate over Rousseau's concept of the noble savage. Robertson observed in the Tahitians characteristics which were equally apparent in contemporary England, as true today as they were then.

An unsuspecting crew member, possibly a petty officer, responded to having been given the eye by a local beauty by putting a pair of nails in his pocket and following her into the wood. From time to time she turned her head to reassure the poor matelot that his journey would prove worthwhile. After a short distance the young woman stopped in front of a hut and made it clear that the sailor would not be dissatisfied with the return on his two iron nails. Then, inexplicably, a well-built man appeared, a carpenter by trade and a man of some importance, the woman's husband. The woman disappeared into the house and returned carrying a chicken. She explained to her husband that the sailor's offer of two nails for this chicken had been so generous that she felt it a bargain but first desired her husband's consent. The upshot was that the happy carpenter received two nails and an extremely irritated sailor returned to the ship with a chicken under his arm.

A few days later the woman came on board the *Dolphin* accompanied by her husband who immediately became fascinated by the *Dolphin's* method of construction. The frustrated sailor of two days previous seized the opportunity to lead the wife into a cabin while the husband was professionally engaged. He, however, noted his wife's disappearance and followed her in order to discover what else of interest might be revealed. The husband's arrival therefore obliged the sailor to show him everything of interest in the cabin; he was given a suit and a shirt for his wife.

By now the wife's interest had become aroused. She leapt into their canoe which she cast off from the gun-room port, calling out to her husband to save her. Hearing the cries of his distressed wife, the poor carpenter ran to the ship's side with a view to plunging into the sea to save both wife and canoe. However, his progress was arrested by the would-be lover who shouted to the master to send a boat to rescue the woman adrift in the canoe. Before George Robertson could react, the carpenter had slipped through the grasp of the sailor and dived into the sea. No sooner was he in the water than his wife paddled back to the *Dolphin*, made straight for the designated cabin and taking hold of the would-be lover's coat, pulled him in, slamming the door. Robertson described how, while she was 'enjoying the reward of her art and cunning', there were fears for the safety of the cuckolded carpenter out in the deep water. In ten minutes he arrived safely back at the ship, coming aboard at the gun-room. By this time, his wife was there to greet him and give him a few nails. 'This greatly pleased the good man, as he knowed nothing of the way and manner the nails were procured.'

When Wallis heard of the trade in nails he called his carpenter to account for his supply. All were accounted for. Then, one by one, the crew forsook their hammocks and began sleeping upon the hard deck, there being no nails upon which to fasten the hammocks. During a ship's inspection, it became apparent that the cleats to which the rigging was fastened were loose. As an expedient to prevent the ship from disintegration, Wallis ordered that no man other than 'wooders and waterers, with their guards should be permitted to go on shore'. This was an order the surgeon persuaded the skipper to retract in order that the men with scurvy might continue their recuperation ashore.

The *Dolphin* had been in Tahiti for almost a month, during which period there had been no contact with the local chief of Matavai. Since it seemed possible that the chief might have been killed in the naval action, it was thought best to ask no questions. On 11 July 1767, however, the self-declared Queen Oberea, in a fleet of canoes, made an official, ceremonial visit to HMS *Dolphin*. Oberea was not the chief since she had a husband named Amo. He had once been chief but according to local tradition the title had passed to the first-born, now five years old. Oberea acted as regent with the consent of her weak husband. She had been unaware of the appearance of the *Dolphin*, returning home to Matavai as soon as she received word. There was no doubt that her word was law. She was described as being about 5 feet 10 inches tall, approximately forty-five-years-old, and having 'a pleasing countenance and majestic deportment'. It is probable that she was younger than forty-five. The teenaged Midshipman Ibbot had no reason to temper his youthful impression that 'she was the stoutest woman I ever saw there and had a very commanding aspect, but not handsome, being upon the decline'. Wallis was unavailable to meet Oberea, being confined to his cabin with recurring illness. His two lieutenants deputed for him, entertaining Oberea and her entourage although, according to custom, she refused to eat and drink with the visitors. It proved to be a good-natured, even raucous event. On leaving, Oberea hoped Wallis might be able to call upon her in the morning.

Wallis awoke the next day feeling sufficiently well to repay the courtesy, taking with him his first lieutenant, the irritable William Clarke (not to be confused with Cook's Charles Clerke), the surgeon, the purser and a marine protection party. They made rendezvous on the beach, where Oberea ordered one of the men to carry the weak Captain Wallis to their meeting place. At one point Oberea insisted that she would carry Wallis for part of the way. The place where they halted was not Oberea's home but what might have been a council building or place of entertainment, over 100 yards long. Once there, four young girls were called forward to undress the captain, first lieutenant and purser, all of whom had been ill, and to begin massaging away their aches and pains. The surgeon took himself off for a long walk to explore the surrounding area. On his return, hot and discomfited, he was surprised to find the massage session still in progress. Then, abruptly, it stopped. Aware that something untoward had occurred, Wallis looked up and noted that the surgeon had removed his wig. 'Every eye was fixed upon the prodigy', he wrote, 'and every operation was suspended: the whole assembly stood some time motionless, in silent astonishment, which could not have been more strongly expressed if they discovered that our friend's limbs had been screwed on to the trunk.'

From this point Wallis, enchanted by Oberea, visited almost on a daily basis until it became clear that in the interest of naval law and order he would soon have to take ship and crew away from Tahiti and its many temptations. One morning Oberea, accompanied by the usual entourage, arrived off the *Dolphin* at breakfast time. They were invited aboard. The habits of the English were a never-ending source of amazement to the Tahitians whose curiosity could land them in trouble, sometimes over the most innocuous events. One of the minor priests observed the surgeon replenishing the teapot from the urn on the table by turning the tap at its base. The native did the same, only to pour scalding water over his hand. He screamed, leaping around the cabin in agonising pain, to the bemusement and embarrassment of those who had accompanied him but who were at a loss to comprehend this apparent instantaneous onset of madness.

The farewell was genuinely heartfelt and moving as the great queen wept as though she was bidding farewell to husband or children. Wallis also admitted to having a tear in his eye. As a farewell present he gave the queen two turkeys, two geese, three guinea fowl and a large pregnant cat.

There is some irony in Oberea's posthumous representation on the London stage as an enchantress. In the pantomime *Omai*, a prince and heir to the Tahitian throne, is advised by a prophet to go to London to woo and marry an English girl by the name of Londina. Londina falls for her dusky suitor and together they travel to Tahiti where Omai outwits the sorceress Oberea and is enthroned as King of Tahiti. In the moving finale the English sailors sing a rousing tribute to the late Captain Cook whose portrait is slowly lowered from the ceiling. It was a very romantic, emotional portrayal of absolute fiction. In reality, the performance was a double requiem, for both Cook and Omai were already dead.

Although there was no apparent connection between low-born Omai and Queen Oberea, there was a connection through association with a priest by the name of Tupia. Omai was not a Tahitian but came from a family living on Raiatea approximately 130 miles to the north-west of Tahiti. The ancient Polynesians first chose to settle on Raiatea which became the cradle of their civilisation. In the eighteenth century, the Mai tribe is known to have had a presence on Bora Bora, Tahiti, Huahine and Raiatea. With no written language, an accurate genealogy of such a far-flung tribe is virtually impossible to construct. It is from British sources, however, that it is possible to follow Omai's antecedents, his birth on Raiatea to his untimely death on the island of Huahine. Warring tribesmen from Bora Bora (there is no 'b' in Tahitian, hence the small island is actually Pora Pora, or even Popora, but the European spelling appears to have been established since the American occupation of the island during the Second World War) attacked the family home, killed Omai's father and dispossessed the family of its land. In 1762 Omai, a smouldering, embittered refugee, sought sanctuary in Tahiti in the company of the high-born priest, similarly dispossessed, Tupia. Twenty-four-year-old Tupia took pity on the young Omai, employing him as his religious assistant. Henceforth, the driving force in Omai's life became a determination to exact revenge upon those who had killed his father and to recover the family's land.

Tupia was an impressive, charismatic man who soon caught the attention of Oberea. She appointed him priest in charge of a temple, or *marae*, she had built in 1767 at Papara and which was the largest on the island. It was not long before they became lovers. On the basis of this relationship and the respect the natives showed to him, an invitation from the *Dolphin* requested Tupia's presence at a dinner held in the gun-room. They gave him the Christian name Jonathan and after dinner showed him a miniature of an English lady. So impressed was he that he kissed the painting twenty times. 'I really believe', wrote the master, 'that he would have come to England for her had we been more willing to take him with us and his friends content to let him go.' Oberea was evidently one of those not content to let him go, for when the time came for the *Dolphin* to weigh anchor on 27 July, Tupia was not there to bid farewell and his absence was noted in pained surprise by those aboard. 'We never saw nor heard anything more of him', wrote the master. 'We supposed the young man's friends were afraid of his going off with us and had ordered him back into the country to prevent him.' Tupia's time would come, but the experience and ending would prove to be far from happy.

HMS *Dolphin* anchored off the Downs on 20 May 1768. A briefing note released from the ship a few days later told the world that while Terra Australis had not been found, they had found an idyllic island and then went on to describe Tahiti's attributes: 'a large, fertile and extremely populous island in the south seas . . . ' The account was necessarily abbreviated due to Wallis's lack of curiosity as to what lay on the other side of the island; the only reconnaissance into the interior being of one day's duration. The letter set a ball in motion. Wallis took the precaution of confiscating all records and the diaries of the officers and crew, yet one crew member managed to sell his diary to the Spanish, thus revealing the coordinates of Tahiti's position in the Pacific. Among those to become positively interested were the Spanish government, the Royal Society's Joseph Banks and Calvinist clergy who pondered the possibility of forsaking the well-worn missionary paths into India and China in favour of crossing the Pacific to introduce the recently discovered heathen to Christianity. These were competing interests which could not all be reconciled. There were, however, those such as Dr Johnson and Horace Walpole who remained unimpressed and unexcited by the news of the discovery of a remarkably happy-go-lucky, uninhibited people. The chance discovery of Tahiti by HMS *Dolphin* meant that the Tahitians' way of life would never be the same again and that change would be rapid and pronounced.

In nautical terms, the *Dolphin's* achievement had been record breaking: the first ship to circumnavigate the world twice. Inside Truro Cathedral there is a simple memorial plaque which reads:

> To the Glory of God and in honoured memory of Samuel Wallis, Captain RN and the members of his crew who circumnavigated the world in HMS Dolphin 26 July 1766 – 10 June 1768 and discovered Tahiti.

CHAPTER 2

Omai's World

When Tupia and Omai arrived as refugees in Tahiti, their respective places in Tahitian society were preordained. An analogy would be of military men posted from one place to another: it is their rank that determines precisely where they fit into the new environment. Islanders' tattoos served as their badges of rank. Tupia, a priest in Raiatea, was therefore able to resume living as a priest among Tahiti's powerful priesthood, the source of spiritual power. It was not possible for him to be promoted to chief, or *arii*, because chiefs who held political power were born into the position. Omai, who had originally been among the yeoman class on Raiatea, the *raatira*, was demoted to the *manahune* or lower class on the loss of the family land. He therefore became a warrior or commoner on Tahiti. The warrior's place was one of total submission to his chief, to provide food and labour and to obey the chief's call to arms. Warriors from the lower classes were valued for their ferocity in conflict; the greater the ferocity the more assured the chief's success.

The chiefs were educated men but the lower orders had no education. Their function was to do as they were told. Above them was a class structure not dissimilar to that which existed in England but it was more rigid, less flexible, the chiefs being jealous of their position and privileges. The taboo, the regulatory mechanism that determined what was and was not permitted, was precisely delineated. Moreover, the nature of taboos was fully understood by all. Although the structure of Tahiti's hierarchy would have been recognised in England, the rigidity of its day-to-day routine was more akin to that of the pre-revolutionary French Court than the relatively relaxed regime of Britain's George III. 'Few people in the history of the world', wrote Bengt Danielsson, 'have had such an aristocratic social organisation as the Polynesians, and the class differences were so great that one can almost call it a caste system of the Indian type.'

In the future, territorial chiefs would make way for a paramount chief or king. Their authority was derived from their god, Oro, who came to prominence by superseding the supreme god Taaroa and the intermediate gods: Tu, god of war, Rongo, god of the harvest and Tane, god of light. Quite simply, war, harvest and light were rolled into one god, and he was Oro. All this came about not on the principal island of Tahiti but at their spiritual home, the nearby island of Raiatea, Omai's birthplace. Oro enjoyed his earthly manifestation in the *marae* of Taputapuatea, at Opoa on Raiatea, the most sacred *marae* in Polynesia. The name means 'sacrifices from abroad' and it was to this place that the heads of victims slain in battle were brought and stacked in rows upon the steps of the temple. All other sacred temples traced their lineage back to Taputapuatea, their sacred foundation stone having come from the original temple on Raiatea or from other temples similarly qualified by virtue of having gone through this process. There are temples which took the name Taputapuatea as far distant as New Zealand and Rarotonga. From Raiatea, Oro made his great pronouncements and it was here that the principal ceremonies in his honour were held. Unlike the Christian god who is invisible, Oro could be seen, being represented over a period of time in different forms. He could be fought over and possessed. Anything out of the ordinary which happened in Tahiti was attributed to a command or message from Oro. An eclipse of the moon was not without its meaning and sometimes implied a significant event yet to come.

So liberated and egalitarian was Oro that instead of marrying another god he sent two of his elder brothers to earth to find him a mortal wife. This they did, and he was delighted with their selection. As a means of visiting his wife he chose a cloud-shrouded rainbow but the remainder of his family, worried and intrigued by his frequent disappearances, sent his younger brothers to earth after him, where they found him with his wife. The two young brothers, although celibate, were overwhelmed by the beauty of Oro's earthly wife and, as a sign of their approval, turned themselves temporarily into a fat hog and a bunch of red feathers. Delighted by their display of support, Oro promoted the young brothers to gods in their own right and pondered upon the manner in which their status should be recognised. His solution was to establish a special society of which they would be the patrons.

Thus began the *arioi* society, a large, unique and powerful religious secret sect of males and females, not confined to Tahiti but having lodges throughout neighbouring islands. The members' habit of placing red feathers and a hog on Oro's altar and practising infanticide became the hallmarks of this influential society. It is from this custom that red feathers, signifying blood and fecundity, became such valuable possessions for use as adornment. Wearing the rare red feathers became the prerogative of the chiefs. Even the possession of feathers outside the circle of chiefs was considered to be presumptuous. Feather cloaks were also worn but only by chiefs. In earlier times canoes were sent to Rarotonga, a direct round trip of 1416 miles (2284 km), for the express purpose of collecting the feathers of Rarotonga's understandably now extinct red parakeet. A number of ornithologists doubted the existence of a red parakeet on Rarotonga even in the mid-eighteenth century, insisting that it must have been the red lorikeet* which is still found on Rimatara in the Tubuai or Austral Islands. The absence here of the black rat, *rattus rattus*, provides some protection from nest predation.

The *arioi* practised infanticide, strangling their own progeny born within the society. Only the children of the most senior members were permitted to live. The *arioi* justified this barbarity on the grounds that there were 'too many children and too many men' for the island to support, though they were permitted to sleep with anyone within their group.

---

* Today there are plans to reintroduce the red lorikeet, *vini kuhlii*, into Rarotonga where it has been extinct for one hundred and fifty years, by way of Atiu, the famed land of birds.

The *arioi* performed a number of useful functions, one being to maintain the line of succession and another to act as a bonding agent, giving the Tahitians a sense of nationhood. A problem common to all royal houses is that there can be only one chief. The question so often is, what can the lesser royals do that is constructive, keeps them above criticism and allows them some freedom of expression? In England at the time, junior members of the nobility went into the army or the church. This might explain the closeness of the priesthood to the chiefs on Tahiti. Certainly, in England, rectories were often the grandest buildings in their community.

In the same way that the *arioi* society provided the lesser gods with an outlet, it also fulfilled a similar function for subordinate royalty. There were seven ranks within the society, denoted by something quintessentially Polynesian and first observed in 1769 by Captain Cook during a visit to Tahiti – tattoos. The principal chief of Raiatea was the senior *arioi* and he and other leaders were known as Painted Legs. Each had one leg tattooed so thickly that it gave the appearance of having been painted. The technique of tattooing, which symbolised the arrival of puberty, remained within the bailiwick of the priests and was conducted by a tattoo artist, a craftsman in his own right. The composition of tattoos was of inestimable importance. Omai's status, for example, could easily be determined by reference to his tattoos. It was not unknown for a bride to reject her suitor because his tattoos did not support his claimed status.

The tattoo was a symbol of manhood and rank but this does not mean tattooing was confined to men. The word *tattoo* comes from the Tahitian word *tatau* which means to be hit repeatedly, because the traditional technique was to puncture the skin lightly by means of a shark tooth mounted on a stick which was lightly tapped with a mallet before ink was applied to the wound. These inky designs confirmed the individual's place in the pecking order. They were important because in Tahiti great care had to be taken in selecting a wife. A high-born male dared not marry beneath him and arranged marriages were common among the upper classes. The daughters of chiefs were obliged to be virgins when they married and some form of guarantee was often expected. Given that it was believed there were no virgins on Tahiti above the age of eight, the chiefs' daughters were considered to be exceptional examples of restraint. Marriage was often a ploy or convenience whereby scheming natives could optimise their landholding and social ambition. Unlike some other places in the South Seas where polygamy did not exist, on Tahiti the senior chiefs had a principal wife and the opportunity to maintain a bevy of concubines. Divorce was straightforward. Before Omai left Tahiti for England he was said to have been living with his fourth wife. He had abandoned the previous three because they were barren. No thought appears to have been given to the possibility that the problem might have been on Omai's side.

The *arioi* membership expressed themselves through entertaining and dancing. More often than not they chose to arrive in a village in a fleet of up to one hundred and fifty double-hulled canoes sporting yellow sails and flying coloured streamers. They came in their thousands and occupied the *arioi* house, a large, open building up to 400 feet long, which served as the centre for entertainment. The house where Captain Wallis received his beneficial massage fits this description. The *arioi* have been likened to the strolling players and minstrels in England, but their repertoire was decidedly different. In Tahiti, there would be the strumming and drumming of countless instruments, supported by enthusiastic songs and dancing ranging from the visually pleasing, melodic and rhythmical, to something downright lewd. Cook wrote of the *Timorodee* in which eight to ten young dancers sang 'the most indecent songs and using most indecent actions in the practice of which they were brought up from their earliest childhood'.

On arrival, the *arioi* would be greeted with mixed emotions. Certainly the music was enjoyed but the impoverishing tax associated with what was often three days of non-stop merriment was less welcome. Only the commoners paid for the three days of excess. Some villagers simply got up and moved away from the catchment area of their nearest *arioi* house. Maintaining the *arioi* in the expected manner had become a test of the chiefs' prestige. The withdrawal or denial of food for the *arioi* was the most prevalent reason for Tahitians being sent into exile.

New recruits to the *arioi* community dressed in yellow and red leaves and dyed their bodies red. They were obliged to act as though mad as part of the initiation process. A condition to be satisfied prior to admission to the order was to kill their own sons and daughters and to undertake the killing of any subsequent children. It was only within the *arioi* that women were accepted as the equals of men.

That the *arioi* society had definite religious overtones was confirmed by the behaviour of the group on their arrival at a village. Their first act was to go to the local *marae* where they presented gifts and prayers to Oro. After the religious preparations, they bathed in readiness for the mandatory feast furnished by the local chief. Then followed the dancing. It was only the younger representatives of the lower ranks who performed; their seniors engaged in the less energetic acts of organisation and choreography, or – for the painted legs – they were treated as respected guests. Of all the Tahitian dances, the *heiva* was the most extreme, lending credence to the belief that it was associated with agricultural fertility. Surprisingly, the Tahitians are exceedingly coy about nakedness, even when bathing. Thus the *heiva* – involving suggestive gestures, interventions by elders giving the young the benefit of their advice, leading to a finale of public copulation – was entirely out of character.

Despite their negative points, the *arioi* represented the only organisation that encouraged nationwide bonding on Tahiti. The availability within their ranks of fit young warriors made it in part a territorial volunteer army. They also maintained, for better or for worse, the cultural traditions of Tahiti and, within this autocracy, enjoyed the privilege, through their entertainment and sketches, of criticising authority.

There was no written Tahitian code of law and order; rather, right and wrong were represented by a state or situation known as *taboo*.

Taboo is an old Polynesian word which has since become universal, yet its common interpretation as something forbidden is too narrow. It also had deeply religious overtones, embracing both the sacred and the unclean. As the descendants of the gods, the chiefs were sacred people, as were their relatives to a declining degree. It was this religious association which gave the chiefs and priests a reason for their imperious behaviour.

Among the ten or so most important chiefs, the *arii*, there were three or four senior chiefs, the *arii rahi*, who were accorded total subservience. If a drop of chiefly blood fell on an object, the owner was obliged to present it to the chief. If a chief entered the house of one of his subjects, that house had to be burnt. If a chief stood on ground belonging to one of his subjects, that ground passed automatically into the ownership of the chief. It is for that reason that when a chief visited his territory he was carried on the shoulders of a bearer. The bearer might also be employed as the chief's feeder, he being unable by convention to feed himself.

Men and women were divided into two distinct classes -- the clean and the unclean. Men cooked their own food and dared not risk eating with women lest they or their food be sullied by the unclean. The relationship between gods and chiefs, the clean and the unclean, and other fixed ideas (for example, a man's head was never touched lest he be weakened), were examples of real, permanent taboos. Woe betide any man or woman who broke a taboo. The death penalty was available for serious breaches but more often than not a public rebuke by a priest and the automatic bestowal of public disgrace served its purpose. The suggestion that the death penalty was automatically passed on those who broke taboos is an exaggeration. There were countless taboos and, from time to time, everyone broke them unintentionally.

There were also temporary prohibitions, known as *rahui*. If a person wished to protect his property, he would persuade a priest to put a *rahui* on the object (a house, a canoe, a fruit tree) and the presence of the temporary restriction was denoted by a piece of cloth tied to the object. It may seem implausible but fish were also subject to a *rahui*, the no-fishing zone being marked by flagpoles stuck out on the reefs.

Where precisely the natives who first occupied New Zealand came from is not known. The Maori speak of their ancestral home as Hawaiki (not Hawaii), an undefined place to the east of New Zealand. That homeland will vary according to the tribe under consideration and in which canoes their forebears travelled. A consensus would have it that the original settlers came from Tahiti and its neighbouring islands while others support the claims of Rarotonga. It comes down to a question of timing. What is not disputed is that the first settlers brought with them their traditions and customs, including the *taboo* and *rahui*.

The coastal town of Kaikoura between Queen Charlotte Sound and Christchurch on New Zealand's South Island has revealed archaeological evidence of the earliest period of human occupation nine hundred years ago. The name Kaikoura means 'eat crayfish', which were then found in abundance in the surrounding sea. When Cook passed this way, hostile natives in canoes left him with the clearest impression of their wishes that he should sail on by. Today, there is confirmation of the origins of the first explorers, from either Tahiti or Rarotonga, in the form of a *rahui* on a post forbidding all forms of fishing or the collection of pebbles, seaweed and driftwood within the designated exclusion zone.

The *marae* was the Tahitians' temple, a meeting place where they worshipped their god, held services for dead chiefs and conducted human sacrifice. Ceremonies in the *marae* revolved around the chief because he was the living representative of the god. A number of Tahiti's *marae* date back to the eighth century but many were constructed in a spate of building during the thirteenth century. The Papara *marae*, the largest in Polynesia, under Tupia's charge had taken over a year to construct. The whole community had been dragooned into the workforce and administration, the former despatched into the mountains and lagoons to collect materials and the latter to ensure that food was regularly available to sustain the workforce. Once all the material had been assembled at the site, construction began. Cook knew the Papara *marae* as did successive visitors until a later generation of missionaries took it down and dispersed much of the stonework throughout the island. After Joseph Banks had examined the structure he wrote: 'It is almost beyond belief that Indians could raise so large a structure without the assistance of iron tools.'

The *marae* was shaped like a pyramid based upon a parallelogram. It had a flight of ten steps on each side, the first of which was six feet from the ground, each of the other steps being of five feet. The steps were composed partly of regular rows of squared coral stones about eighteen inches high and partly with round, bluish-coloured pebble stones of a harder texture and in a natural unhewn state. The base of the Papara *marae* was 270 feet by 94 feet, tapering to the top which was 180 feet by 6 feet. The inside was filled with stones of irregular size. One observer contemplated the time and effort required to bring all these stones to one place, and particularly to square the coral of the steps with the limited tools they had, since the *marae* had been built prior to their iron age. 'As they were ignorant of mortar, or cement, it required all the care they have taken to fit the stones regularly to each other, that it might stand.'

When Banks had visited, there had been a bird carved in wood at the top and, nearby, a stone fish, both of which subsequently disappeared. Not everyone appreciated the building of Oberea's large *marae* at Papara. It became involved in a bitter struggle with the supporters of the sacred *marae* at Arahurahu, the rightful home of the image of Oro since its introduction into Tahiti from Raiatea. The Arahurahu *marae* also adopted the name Taputapuatea from the Raiatean *marae*, becoming in effect a *fare marae*, a centre for the dissemination of Oro's influence. The Arahurahu *marae* stands on level ground just over a mile from the beach but today differs from its historic description. Around the group of buildings ran a square wooden fence, the length of each side being approximately one 120 feet. Inside the fence there was a paved area covering about half the interior. In the centre, on the pavement, stood an altar or sacrificial table built upon sixteen pillars about 8 feet high. On top of the pillars lay thick matting, overhanging on each side. Upon this matting a visitor saw whole hogs, a turtle, large fish, plantains and young coconuts, all of which were in a state of putrefaction. Wars had been fought for the custodianship of Oro's *marae*. Near the altar were a house and two sheds for the use of Oro's guardian; *maraes* have traditionally had an appointed caretaker. Inside the house stood the ark of the god, a small hut similar in size to those the chiefs used in their canoes to shelter from the sun. The god Oro, then the *objet de culte*, resembled a sailor's hammock, lashed up and in two parts. The larger part was the length of the hut and the smaller about half that size. At each end were fastened small bunches of red and yellow feathers, the offerings of the wealthy. Oro did not remain consistently the same shape. In other descriptions he was 'a billet of wood' or symbolised by a stick carved out of casuarina, wrapped in plaited coconut fibre and decorated with red feathers. String had been used to sketch out the form of a human face. The Tahitians knew casuarina as the 'warrior of wood', so hard that it did not float.

A visitor observed within the *marae* the corpse of Orepiah, a recently departed chief. His body, wrapped in cloth, with its feet protruding, lay on a platform or *tupapow*, above which was a thatched roof. Plantains and breadfruit had been put out on the nearby trees for his use. Nearby lived his attendant. In order to unwrap the body the attendant drew the corpse out on to the open stage and removed a number of layers of cloth, all the while laughing, and raised the desiccated body to a sitting position. The skin, unbroken, clung to the skeleton like oilcloth. There was little or no odour as the body had been eviscerated as part of the preservation process. The corpse had been washed through as if cleaning a gutted fish and then rubbed on a daily basis, inside and out, with coconut oil until the flesh became dry. In that condition, despite the heat, it remained intact for some time.

Access to food was rarely a problem in Tahiti. The coconut grows well here, its tall palms producing both a food and a refreshing drink. Many streams flowed from the high mountains bringing plentiful supplies of clean, fresh water. When something stronger to drink was needed there was *kava*, an intoxicating beverage prepared from the chewed or pounded aromatic roots of the Polynesian shrub *piper methysticum*. During his first visit, Cook observed: 'These people may almost be said to be exempt from the curse of our forefathers, scarcely can it be said that they earn their bread with the sweat of their brow, benevolent nature has not only supplied them with necessaries but with abundance of superfluities.' Future wars and the demands of an increasing number of visiting ships would mean the natives would have to work harder to find their food.

The most important food on Tahiti was the breadfruit that produced two or three crops a year. Nearly fifty varieties of breadfruit were found on Tahiti, and its availability was more or less guaranteed for ten months of the year, June and July being potentially difficult months. The most common method of preparation was, and still is, to peel the large fruit and roast, boil, bake or even stew the flesh. The natives laid down stocks of fruit for fermentation when it was abundant, drawing upon stocks when supplies were less plentiful. The breadfruit was first baked and then pounded into a paste before being wrapped in leaves and laid in the ground to ferment and become *mahei*. It could keep for months but by then was possessed of a distinctive odour all of its own. Once the fermentation process had been completed, the *mahei* was removed and cooked to produce hard brickettes called *poi*. It is fair to say that breadfruit was an acquired taste, mostly due to the fact that it stank. Westerners had some difficulty with the food as did West Indians. Following up a recommendation by Joseph Banks, the Lords Commissioners of the Admiralty sent Lieutenant William Bligh aboard HMS *Bounty* to Tahiti to collect breadfruit plants to take to the Caribbean with a view to the cultivation of breadfruit for plantation workers. The story of the mutiny and Bligh's epic experience in an open rowing boat is well known, but when Bligh eventually returned to England, the Admiralty sent him back to Tahiti to complete his task.

When the breadfruit was eventually delivered to the Caribbean, it was found not to be to West Indian taste. They preferred bananas.

There was also, of course, an abundant supply of fish in Tahiti's waters. Fishermen were easily distinguishable from indolent farmers who did not have to over-exert themselves to gather the produce of the land. Fishermen's skin was black from the sun. The sea was a never-empty larder. Fish was one of the natives' favourite foods, often eaten raw or, even when cooked, rare by western standards. There were many methods employed to catch fish, including long seine nets, angling and two- or three-pronged weapons. The men were impressively skilful. They could manoeuvre shoals of fish into the shallows as sheepdogs would guide sheep. At night, torches set out on the reefs and along the shoreline lured the fish into the shallow water where they became ensnared in the nets. The main reef, about half a mile from shore, was inhabited by shellfish of almost every kind imaginable – clams, whelks, cockles, crayfish, crabs and mussels. It was out on the reef that women were likely to be found – they rarely ventured out in canoes – and here they spent the best part of the day, waist deep in the sea. One of the taboos forbade them the use of fishhooks and line. Ninety per cent of Tahiti's population lived off fish and local produce as meat was reserved for the higher castes. All women were forbidden from eating pork.

The natives made fire by cutting a groove in a piece of wood and setting a second piece inside the groove. The friction caused by rubbing the two together produced a spark which ignited the tinder – usually a bundle of grass. The conventional method for cooking meat was called the *ahimaa*. A pit was dug, into the bottom of which the fire was set. Large stones were placed on to the fire until they became white hot. The meat, wrapped in banana leaves, was placed on the stones and the whole pit covered in earth. In a few hours the meat would be cooked to perfection. For larger pieces of meat such as hogs, which were slaughtered by strangulation with a piece of rope, hot stones might also be placed inside the animal's stomach before it was covered in green leaves and the pit opening sealed with earth. Pork, provided it was not too old, was reputed to have been excellent but the chickens, possibly for the want of a corn-fed diet, were said to be stringy and tough.

The crew of *Dolphin* found the Tahitian insistence upon cleanliness commendable. They bathed as frequently as twice or thrice daily, preferring to wash in fresh water rather than in the sea. By contrast, the natives found the body odours of the overdressed sailors unpleasant. Much time was devoted to arranging their glossy, jet-black hair, and for this purpose they applied coconut oil and sandalwood perfume. The chiefs demonstrated their superiority over their subjects by using shell lime to keep their hair a light brown colour. The introduction of scissors and mirrors from the *Dolphin* proved very popular in the grooming processes. An inordinate amount of time was spent on self-examination and grooming. When Tupia saw a mirror for the first time, at dinner aboard the *Dolphin*, he automatically sought to pluck hair from his chin. With the exception of the head, men and women alike would not allow a hair on their upper bodies.

Unlike in other South Sea islands such as Fiji and also in New Zealand, cannibalism was not practised on Tahiti at this time. It had been the custom in Eastern Polynesia to eat an enemy in order to emphasise his total humiliation, yet it was taboo to eat one's own relatives. On Tahiti, there had been so much inter-marriage that it was impossible to be certain that opponents were not also relatives. Polynesian society came from such a limited gene pool that virtually everyone was family. It is perhaps for this reason that the practice had died out on Tahiti.

The palm-thatched dwellings in which the natives lived had no subdivisions, being entirely open to the elements on all sides. When the weather did turn rough, it was the custom to cover the weather side of the house with two or three layers of matting woven from coconut fronds. On the floor, there might be grass to a depth of three or four inches. People slept on the floor either on grass or mats. As a European observed: 'Moreover they had but a sleeping cloth about the loins each and no nightgowns or pyjamas.' What was most striking was the absence of personal possessions. Theft of neighbours' property was a grave offence, yet it was a rare occurrence since the Tahitians were barely a property-owing community. Theft of their property by natives became a major problem for the *Dolphin* and those who were to follow. The obvious question was asked: 'Why do they not steal from their own but so freely from us?' The answer is that the natives had little of value worth the trouble of stealing whereas the procession of visitors from abroad had much of interest and novelty well worth acquiring.

This, then, is a summary of the environment from which Omai came. A starker contrast with eighteenth-century England could not be imagined. Tahiti was where he performed his obligations as a commoner, available as a warrior when called upon by the chief in whose area he had taken refuge. Call-outs were frequent because conflict between the competing chiefs was regular and sustained. There appear to have been two reasons for the apparent state of perpetual conflict among island chieftains. First, steady attrition was an essential counterbalance to the impact a free lifestyle had upon the size of the population. The island could not support a population left free to find its own level. Secondly, the men appear to have enjoyed battle. Moreover, in a structured, class-oriented society, just about the only way the common man could improve his lot was through the display of outstanding valour on the battlefield. Recognition of bravery might bring the hero a plot of land and the praise of his peers and betters. More important was the prospect of being remembered by those left on earth after his death and of spending the afterlife in a warriors' paradise.

Warriors spent a great deal of time on military and naval exercises. There were precise tactics, one of which involved the employment of canoes either as part of an enveloping attack or as a means of engaging the enemy's fleet. In the latter case, canoes were tied together end to end with a view to meeting the enemy head-on in a bloody naval contest. These maritime battles were almost always conducted within the reefs where the sea was calm. The opposing sides closed on one another in a formation known as the *api*, a tactic intended to prevent both the line being broken and flight during the battle. Hostilities commenced with a mandatory phase during which insults were exchanged. Once tempers were sufficiently aroused, the embarked foot soldiers, among whom might have been Omai, used their slings until the lines closed, opposing canoes lashed together and lances reached for. With opposing canoes so tightly interlocked there was no room for manoeuvre, which is why the sea engagement as opposed to the majority of land engagements proved to be so deadly; it was a question of kill or be killed. The slaughter would be horrific as men fought in wild desperation. Fighting only came to a standstill through attrition and exhaustion. The victors took prisoners as slaves and the more fortunate among the vanquished returned to their villages to lick their wounds, comfort the dying and bury their dead. The Tahitians treated infected wounds with the application of a concentrated poultice made from the grated nut of the hutu tree, *barringtonia asiatica*. The hutu nut had multiple medicinal uses as well as being used in all the Polynesian islands to poison fish. (So effective was the narcotic effect that fish would become neutralised in less than ten minutes, at which point they were gathered up, their flesh none the worse for the poisoning.)

Land battles also had set procedures. Tribal champions advanced towards the lines of their enemy, all of them hurling threats and insults. The atmosphere of this moment is captured in the Maori *haka* war dance as displayed by the All Blacks rugby team, although the *haka* is more to do with conditioning the Maori warriors for war. All the while, emotions and tempers were being stoked to breaking point. Each set of champions screamed out their personal attributes and warrior credentials to lend support to their threats; they introduced themselves, their family lineage, outlined their achievements in battles past, foretold the disaster about to overwhelm the opposition and wound up with the invitation 'come and get me'.

The first man to fall would be greeted with a great cry of enthusiasm by his slayers, intended to discourage the opposition. To the victors came the spoils of war and invariably a transfer of land. Occasionally, when a dignitary's body was found among those of the enemy, a ceremony known as *tipouta taata* would be held to emphasise the victors' dominance. Clubs were used to pummel the corpse until it became flat. A hole was then cut through the abdomen, the contents eviscerated and the hole extended through the victim's back. One of the victors then lifted the corpse, inserted his head through the hole in the body and wore this ghastly poncho, the body bent in two, head to the front, feet to the rear. Tahiti's warriors were no shrinking violets. In battle they employed extreme, uncompromising violence.

CHAPTER 3

The Noble Savage

In the century prior to Cook's great voyages, the English poet John Dryden first wrote of the noble savage in *The Conquest of Granada*:

> I am as free as nature first made man,
> Ere the base laws of servitude began,
> When wild in woods the noble savage ran.

The difficulty with the idea of the noble savage is the inherent problem in accepting the compatibility of nobility on the one hand and savagery on the other. Among the islanders there were certainly those who could be described as noble, being of high rank, belonging to the nobility and decidedly high-minded, but these were a small minority. As a people, the South Pacific islanders could behave with extreme savagery – that is, with brutality, ferocity and cruelty. Words change their meanings over the centuries and although today *noble* does not sit easily as an all-embracing word with which to describe eighteenth-century islanders, the word *savage* can only be applied sporadically to the native population subject to the influences of time, place and circumstance. Tupia was noble but could not be described as savage. Then there is Omai who was not noble yet while in England took all steps possible to ensure his behaviour could not be described as anything other than genteel. In his own natural environment, however, he could behave as the most savage of the savage. The term 'noble savage' therefore was neither useful nor accurate in collectively describing the people of the Society Islands. Some would claim that such an argument is to test Dryden's poetry in a way which the poetry itself cannot sustain. In more recent years, an effort has been made to define the noble savage as 'any free and wild being who draws directly from nature virtues which raise doubts about the value of civilisation'. In short, Dryden was exercising poetic licence. Such an argument could be upheld, for the existence of an actual state of Arcady was not then in anyone's living memory.

Jean-Jacques Rousseau developed the theme of the noble savage in three published Discourses between 1749 and 1762. Rousseau applauded the noble savage in his undiscovered state where food was plentiful, sleep came easily and women were available and willing. To Rousseau, man in his natural state was in an infinitely preferable situation to civilised man. All that the subsequent advances intended to perfect and enlighten these people achieved, so the argument went, were rapid advances towards the decay of the species. What civilisation and the suppression of primitive simplicity introduced among a good and happy race was evil, pure and simple. The problem so often with philosophy and philosophers is that they describe the world not as it is but how they believe it should be – the gulf that so often exists between realism and idealism. However, in the matter of Tahiti, here, as illuminated by early discoveries, was a place which appeared to match Rousseau's model and where men were not everywhere in chains. Although Wallis brought back to Europe the news of the discovery of Tahiti, it did not have the same dramatic impact as the news released by the next European to visit the island, the thirty-seven-year-old Frenchman, Louis-Antoine de Bougainville.

De Bougainville was a soldier, sailor, statesman, explorer and mathematician, one of the most interesting characters of the eighteenth century. He became a friend of Napoleon and spent the last years of his life growing roses. Originally a diplomat in France's embassy in London where his thesis on the internal calculus earned him membership of the Royal Society, he went on to become General Montcalm's aide-de-camp fighting the British in Quebec. That his name today is more readily recognised than it might otherwise have been is due to his discovery in South America of the *Bougainvillea.* This is a genus of eighteen species of shrubby, climbing, deciduous plants whose flowers are of little consequence. The glory of the bougainvillea and what accounts for its wide popularity in hot climates are the brilliantly coloured, crimson, scarlet and purple, papery bracts which enjoy a long season.

Aboard the frigate *La Boudeuse* with the store ship *Étoile* following, de Bougainville passed through the Magellan Straits into the Pacific on the same mission which had brought Wallis and the *Dolphin* ahead of him – to find Terra Australis Incognita. He too found Tahiti by accident and after some difficulty finding a gap through the coral reefs, the *Passe de la Boudeuse*, anchored on 4 April 1768 at Hitiaa on the eastern coast. The first impression of the scenery before him set a standard that would never fail to excite throughout the ten days' duration of the French visit. The surprise is that the French were able to learn as much as they did about the island in so short a time. The mountains impressed de Bougainville, for nowhere could bare rock be seen underneath the greenery: 'We could hardly believe our eyes when we saw a peak crowned with trees to its isolated summit.' His record of the landscape might well have been that penned by the *Dolphin's* diarist. At the lower levels he saw grassland and woods and at the foot of the mountains along the sea's edge, 'it was there in the midst of banana and coconut groves and other fruit trees that we saw the houses of the islanders'.

Before the ships had anchored they became surrounded by canoes carrying goods for barter and girls whose availability was signified by the same lewd gestures the *Dolphin's* crew had experienced. These people had probably never seen the *Dolphin*, but although they may have heard of her it is difficult to account for the French reception being precisely the same as that experienced by the first English visitors. De Bougainville's policy was to maintain a *cordon sanitaire* between his people and the natives. Certainly they would trade but initially no natives were to come aboard and no crew were to go ashore.

In the autobiographical account of his travels, *Voyage Autour du Monde*, de Bougainville revealed fascinating glimpses of 1768 Tahiti. The reason his accounts have attracted considerable attention, more so than Wallis's, may be due to his romantic, sometimes lascivious narrative, first published in France in 1771, and in an English version, translated by the acidic academic Johann Reinhold Forster, in 1772. Here he describes what happened when one woman did manage to scramble aboard *Boudeuse*:

> The canoes were filled with women, who in the charm of their features conceded nothing to most European females, and who in beauty of form could easily rival them all. Most of these nymphs were naked, for the men and old women who were with them had taken off the loin cloths which they usually wore . . . The men, either more simply or more freely, soon made matters quite clear, pressing us to choose a woman and follow her on land, their unequivocal gestures making it obvious in what manner we were to form her acquaintance. I ask you – how, in the midst of such a spectacle could one keep at work four hundred French men, young, sailors, and who had not seen any woman for six months? In spite of all our precautions, a young girl came aboard and stood on the quarterdeck, by one of the hatchways above the capstan; this hatchway was open to provide air for those who were winding it. The young girl negligently let fall a loin-cloth that covered her and appeared to all eyes as Venus revealed herself to the Phrygian shepherd; she had the same celestial form. Sailors and soldiers pressed forward to the hatchway and never was the capstan wound with such keenness.

De Bougainville was wrong to believe that all his sailors and soldiers had not seen a woman for six months. The crew of the *Étoile* saw a woman on a daily basis, a fact of which neither captain nor crew were aware. Such a situation had come about due to the deviousness of the ship's surgeon-botanist Philibert de Commerçon and his need for home comforts. His 'assistant' on the voyage was twenty-eight-year-old Mademoiselle Baré. Tahitians immediately recognised that she was a woman, the first European woman to go ashore on Tahiti. Since native men and women wore much the same clothing, they saw nothing exceptional in seeing a French female dressed in men's clothing. According to an English account, 'they conceived mean ideas of European beauty from her countenance'.

The crew of the *Étoile* had harboured only some suspicions, based upon the fact that she slept in Commerçon's cabin, had a high-pitched voice, a beardless chin and paid scrupulous attention to not changing her clothes or making 'natural discharges' in the presence of others. In those days, the urinal was over the ship's side, so it was no mean subterfuge. When the natives encountered Mlle Baré gathering plant specimens ashore, they 'wanted to do her the honours customary in the isle'.

One French sailor disobeyed orders and swam to the shore, undoubtedly to claim to have been the first to land, but his reception was not as he imagined. Curious natives surrounded him, prodded at him and his parts. They wanted to know whether he was equipped in the same way as they were. It is possible that while in the process of being fingered and undressed it might have dawned upon the over-hasty Frenchman that he was among cannibals. Reassured that this was an exact white replica of themselves, the natives, who meant the man no harm, returned his clothes and brought forward a young girl. The natives did not disperse but stayed to witness what would happen next, but so terrified was the Frenchman that he was in no position to raise interest. The man was de Bougainville's cook, a good reason to extricate him from his predicament on the beach. Called before de Bougainville, the cook said he deserved to be punished in whatever manner de Bougainville thought fit. De Bougainville sent him away. 'I could never frighten him so much as he had just now been frightened on shore.'

De Bougainville wrote considerably more about Tahitian women, *vahine*, than about Tahitian men, *tane*. He was particularly interested in the influence promiscuity had upon girls' marriage prospects:

Everything invites her to follow the inclination of her heart, or the instinct of her sensuality; and public applause honours her defeat: nor does it appear, that how great soever the number of her previous lovers may have been, it should prove an obstacle to her meeting with a husband afterwards. Then wherefore should she resist the influence of the climate or the seduction of examples? The very air that the people breathe, their songs, their dances, almost certainly attended with indecent postures, all conspire to bring to mind the sweets of love, all engage to give up to them.

Of the men, there appeared to be two categories. In the top grade were those of whom de Bougainville said he had 'never met men better built or proportioned; to depict Hercules or Mars one would find nowhere finer models'. This was the stock of the *bon sauvage*. Below them was a less presentable group that had 'frizzled hair as hard as bristles, and both in colour and features they differ but little from mulatoes'. De Bougainville was less discriminatory in his argument as to why legislators and philosophers should go to Tahiti 'to see as an established fact what they had not even dreamed of – a thronging populace of handsome men and beautiful women living together in health, plenty and ordered amity'.

In due course de Bougainville decided the time was right to assemble a party to go ashore to pay a courtesy call on the chief. The French believed the chief to be called Ereti. He had a brother called Aoutourou who, over the next week, proved to be ubiquitous. 'The zeal of this islander to follow us everywhere was unfeigned', wrote de Bougainville. After the formalities, the chief took his visitors back to his own home where he fed them fruit and fish. It was while eating that one of the French officers discovered some light-fingered relative had taken his pistol from his pocket. De Bougainville did his best without the benefit of language to express to the chief his disappointment. The chief appeared to be fully contrite and receptive to the complaint and next day appeared off the frigate in his canoe bearing gifts and the missing pistol. It may be that the Tahitians never stole among their own circle but they were unlikely to have become so accomplished at thievery without having had practice.

After the first week, an onshore wind started to build in intensity. The ships within the reef began to slip anchor and their cables began to chafe upon the coral until, after three days, eight cables had been cut through. While de Bougainville had one eye on the weather, he also had to keep an eye on what was happening ashore. An English account found much to criticise in the behaviour of de Bougainville's men: 'Sensuality seems to have been practised with still greater indecency than before, and several murders were privately committed by the French sailors notwithstanding the hospitality with which they were entertained.' The French had bayoneted and killed three Tahitians but the potential for more serious trouble was nipped in the bud by de Bougainville's diligent attempts to find the killers.

The chief and his tribe left their villages for fear that the French would kill them; they were found a few miles inland, and after many smiles and much encouragement were persuaded that the French intended them no harm. The situation returned to normal: the good men brought the French an ever-increasing amount of food and the thieves continued to circulate among the unwary sailors.

The wind strengthened and sea conditions worsened. A different gap to leeward was found through the reef and through that gap the *Étoile* reached open sea. *La Boudeuse* waited for the next day's high tide but while in the process of negotiating the narrow gap the wind suddenly failed and the risk of the frigate being wrecked upon the reef appeared real. De Bougainville believed the sea to be so rough that 'the best swimmers could hardly have saved their lives', but suddenly a westerly breeze sprang up and carried the frigate beyond the reef.

The chief saw with alarm his new-found friends making for the open sea. He jumped into a single canoe and paddled through the rough sea to the frigate. With the by now customary tears in his eyes he bade each officer adieu. When Ereti finally came to bid de Bougainville farewell he spoke in a language which the Frenchman obviously did not comprehend yet the sentiment was perfectly clear:

'He feared that the arrival of a new race of men would trouble these happy days which he had spent in peace.' Meanwhile the chief's personal canoe came alongside with more gifts, his sobbing wives and brother Aoutourou. The latter intimated to de Bougainville that he wished to accompany him. De Bougainville looked at Aoutourou, a man of approximately thirty years. He was one of the 'frizzy' kind: not the best of specimens to represent Tahiti in Paris. Given the circumstances in which he found himself, the captain had little choice but to agree, thinking that what Aoutourou lacked in beauty he possessed in understanding. He might be helpful in guiding the French explorers through Polynesia and be a useful ambassador when he eventually returned to Tahiti. The chief's brother bade goodbye to a girl left in the canoe. He took three pearl earrings from his ears, gave them to her, gave her a final kiss and went aboard. *La Boudeuse* left the two canoes in her wake. It was 15 April.

De Bougainville exercised his seniority over Commerçon who wanted to call Tahiti *Utopie* and became upset and temperamental when his wish did not prevail. De Bougainville called Tahiti *La Nouvelle Cythère* after the small island off the coast of southern Greece which, in Greek mythology, provided a sanctuary for Aphrodite, goddess of love, and the place where the gods enjoyed sybaritic interludes. Having also been a diplomat, de Bougainville gave Tahiti an alternative name: *Isles de Bourbon.*

Several weeks into the voyage de Bougainville discovered a number of the crew to be infected with venereal disease. 'I do not know whether the Tahitians, along with their knowledge of iron', wrote de Bougainville, 'also owe to the English that of venereal disease which we already found there.' The English had not visited the east coast so the infection would have had to have spread rapidly from Matavai Bay. As mentioned, the *Dolphin's* doctor 'affirmed upon his honour that no man on board was affected by any sort of disorder that they could communicate to the natives of this beautiful island'. De Bougainville ordered the examination of Aoutourou and he was found to be 'quite ruined' by the disease.

There is no record of Aoutourou being seasick but there is evidence that he was homesick and not clear in his own mind precisely what he had undertaken. He attempted to persuade the helmsman to steer for a nearby island. After a polite rebuttal he settled into the voyage, amusing himself, despite his condition, in a serious attempt to seduce Mlle Baré. De Bougainville arranged for Aoutourou to have French language lessons throughout the eleven-month voyage. His teachers believed him to be exceedingly unintelligent, a situation that was not helped by an apparent speech impediment. He did, however, assist de Bougainville in the preparation of a Tahitian dictionary of two hundred and fifty words which was eventually published, but to everyone's disappointment by the time he reached Paris, in March 1769, he could speak just ten words of French.

Aoutourou's difficulties with language applied to a lesser degree to Omai whose command of English would prove to be only marginally better. The problem for Tahitians learning a European language was that in their language there is no b, c, d, g, j, q or s, w, x y and z so that these sounds had to be learnt before inroads could be made into languages richer and more sophisticated than their own. The cultural gap was so broad that Tahitians found it a problem to visualise concepts that lay beyond their experience. It would be wrong, however, to pretend that Europeans found the learning of the Tahitian language a simple matter, although a few did find they had an aptitude for it. In Tahitian, every consonant has to be followed by a vowel and there are no silent letters. The first English missionaries had been persuaded that a corporal of marines had become fluent in a short period, yet it was their inability to communicate, to preach the Gospel, which undermined their first mission on Tahiti.

On Wednesday, 3 April 1776, the Rousseau-phile James Boswell and Samuel Johnson discussed this very subject of communication and understanding:

BOSWELL: I gave him an account of a conversation which had passed between me and Captain Cook, the day before, at dinner at

Sir John Pringle's; and he was much pleased with the conscientious accuracy of that celebrated circumnavigator, who set me right as to many of the exaggerated accounts given by Dr Hawkesworth of his voyages. I told him that while I was with the Captain, I caught the enthusiasm of curiosity and adventure, and felt a strong inclination to go with him on the next voyage.

JOHNSON: Why, sir, a man *does* feel so, till he considers how very little he can learn from such voyages.

BOSWELL: But one is carried away with the general grand and indistinct notion of A Voyage Round the World.

JOHNSON: Yes, sir, but a man is to guard himself against taking a thing in general.

BOSWELL: I said I was certain that a great part of what we are told by the travellers to the South Seas must be conjecture, because they had not enough of the language of those countries to understand so much as they have related. Objects falling under the observation of the senses might be clearly known; but everything intellectual, everything abstract – politics, morals and religion, must be darkly guessed.

Dr Johnson was of the same opinion. Upon another occasion, when a friend mentioned to him several extraordinary facts, as communicated to him by the circumnavigators, he slyly observed: 'Sir, I never before knew how much I was respected by these gentlemen; they told me none of these things.'

Intellectual French society found the basic, unprepossessing Aoutourou to be a novelty but to have nothing else of interest to offer. De Bougainville made his noble savage available to his friends La Condamine and Pereire to examine in two intensive interviews. They tested among other things his linguistic ability and found he had none, attributing this to Tahiti's isolation. He was introduced to Louis XV at Versailles but, overall, observers found his absence of interest and enquiry a disappointment. Rousseau never met him but Denis Diderot, who wrote the radical *Supplément au Voyage de*

Bougainville, did. Diderot found himself attracted to the concept of raw nature, shunning Christian morality and avoiding answering questions beginning to arise regarding the suspect morality and infanticide reported to be prevalent in the land of the noble savage. Diderot railed against the Christian presumption that there was a duty to intervene in the pagan world to introduce Christian values. He forecast that one day the Christians would come 'with crucifix in one hand and the dagger in the other to cut your throats or to force you to accept their customs and opinions; one day under their rule you will be almost as unhappy as they are'. When the timid Spanish Franciscans came with their crucifixes they dared not come close to the natives to be in any position to cut their throats. When members of the London Missionary Society arrived on the island in 1797, they tried their utmost to encourage the natives to accept their customs and opinions. The natives went along with the missionaries' wishes until they exhausted their supply of guns and presents.

Aoutourou was soon ignored and destined to live a lonely life in Paris, unable to communicate with those around him. De Bougainville tried to reassure himself that all was going reasonably well: 'Though Aoutourou could hardly blabber some words of our language, yet he went out by himself every day, and passed through the whole town without missing or losing his way.' Curiously, de Bougainville wrote of the visitor's enthusiasm for opera, 'for he was excessively fond of dancing', and how he would take his place in the gallery behind the boxes. De Bougainville's claim that all was well was not shared by Forster, the English translator of *Voyage Autour du Monde*:

> He was one of the most stupid fellows; which not only has been found by Englishmen who saw him at Paris, during his stay there, and whose testimony would be decisive with the public, were I at liberty to name them: but the very countrymen of Aoutourou were, without exception, all of the same opinion, that he had very moderate parts, if any at all.

The first trophy out of Tahiti, their first noble savage, was therefore a failure. The idea had not been thought through to a proper conclusion, nor had Aoutourou been protected from his impulsiveness in wanting to escape from familiar territory where he had been at liberty to roam wild in the woods. After a year, de Bougainville accepted that the experiment had failed. He paid £1500, allegedly one third of his fortune, to a shipping agent who undertook to return Aoutourou to Tahiti. Aoutourou arrived at the island of Mauritius aboard *Le Brisson* from where he was taken homewards in an eastbound vessel, *Le Mascarin*. At Réunion he died of smallpox.

CHAPTER 4

Two Kinds of Venus

The official foundation date of the Royal Society is 28 November 1660. On that day a group of scientists, the foremost being Christopher Wren, decided to found 'a college for the promotion of physico-mathematical learning'. After securing the patronage of Charles II, two Royal Charters followed in 1661 and 1663 when the Society became known as 'The Royal Society of London for Improving Natural Knowledge'. One hundred years later saw the Society in its own accommodation in two houses in Crane Court, off the Strand. The Fellowship, comprising working scientists and wealthy amateurs, reflected the cosmopolitan nature of a wider society increasingly inquisitive and curious to learn of the mysteries that continued to unfold in the world in which they lived.

In 1768, abiding British scientific interest continued to focus on the creation of an expedition to the South Seas to observe the 1769 transit of the planet Venus across the face of the sun, an event which would not be repeated for over one hundred years. Venus has been described as the Earth's twin sister in so far as they are of similar size, mass and composition and are both situated in the inner solar system. The dissimilarities, however, are marked. Venus is shrouded in dense clouds of sulphur and sulphuric acid, its atmospheric pressure is ninety times that of Earth and its maximum temperature can rise to 450°C. Venus orbits the sun closer than does the Earth but different planes of orbit mean that Venus's transit across the face of the sun is a phenomenon rarely seen from Earth. Since 1631, transits have occurred in cycles of 8, 121.5, 8 and then 105.5 years, a pattern which will continue until 2984. The passage of Venus seen from Earth on 8 June 2004 had never previously been seen by any living person, having last occurred 121.5 years before.

As a result of the proposed 1769 observation, it should have been possible, in theory, to measure the distance of Venus from Earth. The first man to attempt to do so was a twenty-year-old British scientist named Jeremiah Horrocks. On 24 November 1639 Horrocks estimated, inaccurately, that the sun was 59 million miles from Earth. An appeal to the Society's patron, George III, brought to the sovereign's attention the preparations already in hand in France, Spain, Denmark, Sweden and Russia for simultaneous observation of this phenomenon. In the opinion of the Fellowship, Britain should also contribute to a project of international scientific significance:

> That the passage of the planet Venus over the disc of the sun which will happen on 3rd of June in the year 1769, is a phenomenon that must, if the same be accurately observed in proper places, contribute greatly to the improvement of Astronomy on which navigation so much depends . . . the British nation has been justly celebrated in the learned world, for their knowledge of astronomy, in which they are inferior to no nation upon earth ancient or modern.

George III agreed and granted the Society the £4000 they requested, a sum over and above the cost of the ship and crew to be provided by the Admiralty. There were to be two points of observation, the first at Prince of Wales Island in Hudson's Bay and the second, probably in the Pacific, to be confirmed. The Admiralty was happy to mount this expedition, the opportunity for further discovery in the Pacific was not lost upon its Lords.

By Easter 1768, there was within the Admiralty and the Royal Society a sense of urgency about agreeing on the civil component, for which the Society was responsible, and the selection of captain and crew of a suitable ship, for which the Admiralty was responsible. James Cook's first long-distance voyage brought together the otherwise unlikely personalities of Cook and Joseph Banks, both of whom would have important roles in the unfolding story of Omai. Another person who became important in the lives of all three was a family friend and neighbour of Banks, John Montagu, fourth Earl of Sandwich. 'He [Sandwich] is a tall, stout man and looks as weather-proof as any sailor in the navy', wrote Fanny Burney. Little is remembered today of the fourth Earl's achievements, notorieties even. The islands which took his family name were later to be renamed Hawaii but the name *has* survived, breaching even sturdy language barriers to be included in the *lingua franca*. The Earl's habit of eating sliced beef between slices of toasted bread so as not to interrupt hunting or card games became widely copied in the form of food which bears his name – the sandwich.

Banks struggled at Harrow School and was moved to Eton College where he fared better. By the time he went up to Oxford, he was already deeply interested in botany. When he discovered there was no botany tutor at Oxford, he found one in Cambridge and paid the academic a great deal of money to switch universities. Banks left Oxford in 1763 with an insatiable appetite to learn as much as was possible about botany. Money was not a matter of great concern. His Lincolnshire estate generated an annual income of £6000 – a truly substantial sum. Banks used his influence over the Earl of Sandwich, now the Admiralty's First Lord, to allow him to join a fishery protection vessel off Newfoundland where by chance Cook was surveying. Banks possessed great powers of persuasion although that is not to say he was always right. He was a keen proponent of the idea of there being a southern continent, Terra Australis Incognita, principally because he insisted that only fresh water could freeze. When he returned to London and heard of the plans to observe the passage of Venus, the twenty-five-year-old Banks used his membership of the Society as his *entrée* to the expedition – not simply as a member but as the civilian leader. Banks had no interest in astronomy or mathematics; for him the expedition was a means to an end, namely to discover and identify new plants. Wallis had not yet returned from Tahiti so the final destination for the expedition had not yet been determined. Banks is said to have guaranteed his place by contributing £10,000 to the venture.

The Society appointed the professional astronomer Charles Green to what was undoubtedly the key post on the expedition. Green was formerly of the Royal Navy where he adopted the habit of drinking to excess, a common feature among the Navy's personnel at that time. The Admiralty cannot be held blameless for this undesirable state of affairs since the daily rum ration was a pint. A fee of 200 guineas was agreed for Green and on 19 May Cook, nominated as an observer, accepted 100 guineas as his fee. On 20 May, Wallis's HMS *Dolphin* anchored off the Downs and in so doing opened up a whole raft of possibilities.

Banks chose as his companion and deputy the eminent Swedish botanist Dr Daniel Carl Solander. Two Scottish artists were selected, Sydney Parkinson, who would be responsible for natural history, and Alexander Buchan, chosen to paint figures and landscapes. Solander recommended a fellow Swede, Herman Diedrich Spöring, to be expedition secretary and manager. As befitted his status, Banks had four servants and two greyhounds included on the manifest. The arrangements had all been made before the Society communicated with the Admiralty on 9 June:

Joseph Banks Esq, Fellow of this Society, a gentleman of large fortune, who is well versed in natural history, being desirous of undertaking the same voyage the Council very earnestly request their Lordships, that in regard to Mr Banks's great personal merit, and for the advancement of useful knowledge, he also, together with his entourage, being seven persons more, that is, eight persons in all, together with their baggage, be received on board the ship, under the command of Captain Cook.

There is a discrepancy of one person because Dr Solander was yet to volunteer. The Admiralty took six weeks to consider its position before finally and reluctantly agreeing.

The Admiralty stopped James Cook from returning to the New-foundland survey, appointing him instead in early April to command

His Majesty's Bark the *Endeavour*. HMS *Endeavour* was formerly the 106-feet long, eighteen-man, three-masted collier *The Earl of Pembroke*, purchased in March for £2800. The *Endeavour* had been built three years and nine months previously at the Yorkshire port of Whitby. Between working as a farmer's boy and grocer's assistant and joining the Royal Navy at the age of twenty-seven, Cook had been at sea in the Whitby coal trade. He was therefore very familiar with the collier type of ship known as a cat, with a flat bottom and shallow draught.

The etymology of the word *cat* is not known. The ships were local trade colliers which also carried timber. The idea that the name might be derived from *coal and timber* fails because acronyms were not used in the eighteenth century. The term *cat-built ship* was in use at that time but was obsolete by the nineteenth century. Interestingly, the word *cat* was never used in Whitby, the centre of construction and operation of ships of this type.

Cook did not personally select the *Endeavour*. That was done by the Navy Board one month before his appointment, but he was not dissatisfied with the choice. The *Endeavour* needed urgent modification for the perilous journey she was about to undertake. The major work was to protect the hull by fitting so many large, flat-headed nails as to provide a virtually armoured outer shell.

Within four weeks of HMS *Dolphin* returning to England, an American-born lieutenant named John Gore, Robert Molyneux the master, and two mates, joined the crew of the *Endeavour*. A thought might be spared for the *Dolphin's* infamous goat, deserving of green pastures after circumnavigating the world, but reassigned to the *Endeavour* for the purpose of providing the officers with fresh milk. (The existence of this famous goat was so well known as to warrant an obituary in the *General Evening Post* of 3 April 1772.) By early August the eighteen-man collier had a complement of eighty-five including a section of twelve marines.

The news the *Dolphin* brought back had a decided influence upon the *Endeavour's* mission. The prospect of confirming the delights of

Tahiti appealed to many but it was the fact that the island's longitude had been determined by purser John Harrison meant that it could be confirmed as sitting within the zone recommended for optimum observation of the passage of Venus. While on Tahiti, Harrison had taken advantage of an eclipse of the sun to determine the position of Matavai Bay as 17°30'S, 150°W. With access to more precise instruments, Cook was later able to refine these figures to 17°29'15"S, 149°32'30"W. Tahiti therefore became the obvious location for the Society's observatory. The Admiralty's interest had also been held by an enticing report from the *Dolphin* that a number of those on board believed they had seen a land mass to the south of Tahiti. Cook's mission therefore could be seen to be satisfying the interests of both the Royal Society and the Royal Navy. He was to support the Royal Society's scientific enterprise. 'When this service is performed you are to put to sea without loss of time, and carry into execution the additional instructions contained in the enclosed sealed packet.' In short, he was to look for Terra Australis Incognita and, if that expedition were to prove nugatory, he was to 'fall in with the eastern side of the land discovered by Tasman and now called New Zealand'.

On 14 August, Cook invited Banks and Solander to join the ship at Plymouth, sailing on 25 August. There is no record of Cook and Banks having met previously. There was every prospect that the influential, clever rather than intelligent, occasionally arrogant, self-publicist Banks might clash with the dour James Cook, but opposites can at times attract. In reality, what Cook wanted on board happened. Responsibility for the safety of the entire complement and the difficult act of navigating an insignificant little coastal ship over thousands of sea miles and arriving precisely at a chosen speck of land rested with Cook and Cook alone. They not only tolerated but actively enjoyed each other's company. Their cabins were adjacent. Officers, young gentlemen and civilians messed together in the Great Cabin that was built of necessity over the stern. Between mealtimes, Banks and his suite used the cabin for the identification and cataloguing of fauna and flora. There were too many men living too closely together to allow relationships to sour. They lived cheek-by-jowl, most of the ship's capacity taken up by a cavernous hold in which two years' supplies and stores were stacked. That the *Endeavour* looked out of the ordinary may not have occurred to those on board but it was an impression which forcibly struck Portugal's Viceroy at Rio de Janeiro, Don Antonio Rolim de Moura, Conde de Azambuja.

Before him in the harbour on 13 November lay a small, former, English coastal collier which would normally have attracted a crew of eighteen. As a soldier, he was unaware that the Royal Navy employed colliers as warships. This little ship flew the Royal Navy's Admiral of the Red's red ensign, was armed with twelve swivel guns, had embarked infantry among the crew and also had civilians on board. The Viceroy was convinced the *Endeavour* was an armed merchantman masquerading as a ship of the Royal Navy and engaged in smuggling. James Cook reported to the Viceroy who had earlier refused to receive a junior officer. When Cook explained to Don Antonio that the *Endeavour* was *en route* for a Polynesian island, the name of which the Viceroy had never heard, to watch a planet track across the face of the sun, he wondered what kind of fool Cook took him for. Then there were the civilians. Banks in particular was assumed to be a spy. The Portuguese, Britain's allies for fifty years, placed stringent restrictions on the comings and goings to and from the ship. Revictualled at last, Banks wrote in his diary on 2 December, 'thank God we have got all we want from these illiterate impolite gentry'. Five days later the heavily laden ship took a southerly course for Tierra del Fuego and Cape Horn, cutting links with civilisation. There would be more room on the return journey. Over one-third of those on board would die between this point and the ship's return to England.

Cook dipped into two bodies of work to help in the drawing up of orders to regulate behaviour ashore in Tahiti. The first, an humanitarian *aide mémoire* or 'hints', had been prepared by the Earl of Morton, President of the Royal Society, and the second was an account of Captain Wallis's experience of Tahiti. The orders were applicable not only to officers and crew but were 'to be observed by every person in or belonging to His Majesty's Bark the Endeavour, for the better establishing a regular and uniform trade for provisions etc, with the inhabitants of Georges Island'. There were five basic rules. The first was formulated upon an honest hearts-and-minds policy: 'To endeavour by every fair means to cultivate a friendship with the natives and to treat them with all imaginable humanity.' The second rule restricted the right to trade for provisions to Cook's own appointees. The third reflected that he had fully absorbed what Wallis had told him of the natives' thievery. If a man 'by neglect looseth any of his arms or working tools or suffers them to be stolen, the full value thereof will be charged against his pay according to the custom of the Navy and he shall receive such further punishment as the nature of the offence may deserve'. The fourth rule provided for the application of similar punishment to those who misappropriated ship's stores. The fifth rule was designed to prevent the disappearance of items of iron from aboard the *Endeavour* in return for sexual favours, thereby devaluing the metal as a currency for trade: 'No sort of iron, or anything that is made of iron, or any sort of cloth or other useful or necessary articles are to be given in exchange for anything but provisions.' At 7 a.m. on Thursday, 13 April, after having been at sea for almost eight months, the *Endeavour* anchored in Matavai Bay.

Their reception proved to be a happy event without any show of hostility. The assembly of natives at Matavai Bay, normally the island's hub of activity, appeared relatively thin on the ground. That much was observed by those who had served aboard *Dolphin*, notably Molyneux, the master, who boasted of having had a special relationship with Oberea. But she was not in evidence on this the first day ashore and, over successive days, Cook remained unclear as to precisely who was the chief in charge. Apparently there had been a war six months previously when the inhabitants of little Tahiti rampaged through big Tahiti. An unusually large battle had been fought close to Oberea's *marae* at Papara, the building of which had caused so much offence throughout the island. There was a strong possibility that the prestige

Oberea derived through her close association with the *Dolphin* had inflated her ego and ambition to such an extent that others may have felt the time had come to cut her down to size. The consequence of all this was a shift of population westward, away from Matavai, and although Oberea remained queen, her position had been weakened and the new pecking order had not been finally resolved. Food, particularly hogs, was in short supply.

On Friday, 14 April 1769, news of the *Endeavour's* arrival brought out natives in large numbers both in canoes and on shore. They pressed forwards, surrounding the visitors, with pickpockets among them: Dr Solander lost his telescope, Dr Monkhouse, the surgeon, his snuff box. When Banks heard of these thefts he was seated at a welcoming banquet with a pretty girl 'with fire in her eyes' beside him. There was no doubt in his mind which course of action to take. Standing up, he took his musket and demanded the return of the stolen goods. His action cleared the hall and embarrassed the chief who immediately attempted to pacify the botanist by giving him a free hand to take whatever he wished from among the bales of cloth set out in a nearby store. Banks would have none of it, he meant business, maintaining his threatening position until the items were returned and friendship providentially restored.

The natives could not help but rise to the challenge of relieving the visitors of their possessions. This was a game to them, an equal and opposite response to the importance the visitors placed upon their personal belongings. The natives did not, could not, understand the reaction, sometimes over-reaction, to their efforts to equalise the ownership of fascinating goods beyond their experience. Theft exasperated the visitors. Cook had his stockings stolen from under his pillow while still awake. It depends by what standard the natives are judged. Both Britain and France claimed Tahiti as their possession. Spain had not done so because it was still in the haphazard process of organising its claim. Is that not also theft?

By the next day, the 15th, Cook had decided where to establish his observatory, to be named Fort Venus after the planet not the goddess of love. The site selected, Point Venus, lay close to the *Endeavour*'s anchorage in an area at the north-western end of Matavai Bay where there were no native huts, the sea on one side, the Vaipopoo river on the other. A working party accompanied by a number of marines set out to put up a tent and mark out the area to be fortified – the natives were not to be allowed to interfere with a mission that had brought the *Endeavour* halfway round the world. While the labouring went ahead, representatives of the non-labouring class – Cook, Banks, Solander and Green – set off on a walk to orientate themselves, followed by a large number of inquisitive natives. They had not gone far when a flight of ducks flew over. Banks took aim, fired a shot and three ducks fell dead to the ground. Turning around, the visitors were surprised to see that the majority of the natives had also fallen to the ground as if dead. Suddenly they heard the sound of firing coming from the direction of the site of Fort Venus. A native had snatched a musket from a sentry's hand and made off with it.

A good proportion of the literate, early explorers in the Pacific kept diaries or records of their experiences. This gave the authorities headaches when expeditions returned with different people having different stories to tell. In that respect, little has changed. Records of Cook's voyages are spread widely, principally between library and museum shelves in London, Canberra, Sydney and Wellington, New Zealand. Shared history of this importance will always be sought after for acquisition by provincial or national collections. Cook, Banks and the artist Sydney Parkinson all made mention of the events at Fort Venus on 15 April. The latter had no axe to grind, no position to protect, but what he has to tell is the story how, within a mere two days, Cook's first rule – to treat the natives with all imaginable humanity – had been broken in the profoundest of ways. 'A boy, a midshipman, was the commanding officer, and, giving orders to fire, they obeyed with the greatest glee imaginable, as if they had been shooting at wild ducks, killed one stout man and wounded many others. What a pity that such brutality should be exercised by civilised people upon unarmed ignorant Indians.'

The lost weapon was recovered and in time cordial relations were restored.

Elsewhere, while the business of the shooting had been going on, the expedition's only artist of recognition, Alexander Buchan, had an epileptic fit, and after two days in a coma, died. This was bad news for the expedition, particularly for Banks who had already reflected in his mind's eye his triumphal homecoming: 'His loss to me is irretrievable, my airy dreams of entertaining my friends with scenes I am to see here have vanished.' Ever inventive, through a series of consequences, Banks believed that he might be able to compensate for the loss of his artist by producing a noble savage to set before his friends. The conduit through whom that goal might be achieved was Tupia, who had seemed intent on returning with the *Dolphin* to England. It was thought that he had been prevented from so doing by his mistress Oberea. But now Oberea had another young man by the name of Obadee who, by chance, had been found *in flagrante* with her by Banks. Tupia and Banks established a formal friendship, becoming *tayos*. Although Banks invariably set up shop in front of Fort Venus from where he traded beads for flora, he would also walk into the hinterland. There could be none better than a priest to advise him whether *taboos* or *rahui* applied to specimens he wished to collect. One of the ship's officers, Dr Monkhouse, created serious difficulties when he removed a flower from a tree close to a *marae*. Tupia now found his association with Oberea's *marae* to be life-threatening, which seemed as good a reason as any to consider visiting the land of Cook and Banks.

Banks rated Tupia as the most intelligent of the natives. It does seem likely that Omai may also have attempted to ingratiate himself with Cook and Banks. That he would have been overlooked would have been due not only to his relative youth – he would have been in his late teens – but also to the fact that, compared with Tupia, he would have been a poor specimen. The problem was that Cook felt disinclined to return to England with any natives at all because there was no guarantee they could be returned to Tahiti. But Banks persuaded him that Tupia would prove to be a useful interpreter and pilot on the return voyage. That did prove to be the case. Banks had his own selfish reason: 'Thank heaven I have a sufficiency and I do not know why I may not keep him as a curiosity, as well as some of my neighbours do lions and tigers at a larger expense than he will ever put me to; the amusement I shall have in his future conversations and the benefit he will be of to this ship, as well as what he may be if another should be sent into these seas, will I think fully repay me.'

An interesting characteristic of the Tahitians revealed itself within the first week. In terms of behaviour this characteristic appeared odd, an apparently artificial reaction, but it is worth recording for it was also emblematic of Omai's future behaviour. The woman to whom Henry Jeffs, the ship's butcher, had the misfortune to offer violence in order to steal her stone axe, happened to be the wife of one of the transitional chiefs. Both were in the process of leaving a reception hosted by Cook. The chief, in high dudgeon, returned to Cook, highly voluble and effusive in his complaints. Jeffs was apprehended and duly flogged the next day, fastened to the ship's rigging, in front of the chief and his wife. His back became shredded, the volume of blood scattering around increasing with every bite of the whip. They cried 'enough' but Cook would not listen. Their reaction proved surprising for a people so barbarous in conflict. They wailed and screamed and wanted to see no more, for this was not part of their experience. Cook preferred psychology to flogging but where the crime was serious, the cat o' nine tails came into play. He even had a midshipman, one of the young gentlemen, flogged for a serious misdemeanour.

In a matter of two weeks, forty-five members of the crew produced a mini-fortress to a standard which would have impressed Todleben. A combination of banks, ditches, palisades, guns both ashore and mounted in the *Endeavour*, and armed guards, seemed to promise the observation of Venus would proceed as intended in all but the unlikely event of a concerted, major attack by hundreds of natives. With the defences ready, the quadrant and other astronomical equipment were transferred from the safety of the ship to the supposed safety of Fort Venus. 'I now', wrote Cook, 'thought myself perfectly secure from anything these people could attempt.' During the night, someone stole the astronomical quadrant, without which the passage of Venus could not be observed. For the natives, this was an extension of their great game. They could see the reverential protection being given to the quadrant and could not resist the challenge of its removal, even though they did not know how it might be used. Threats to imprison the chiefs and destroy their boats saw the eventual return of the quadrant so that the mission could proceed. Once the task had been completed (it had not been a success), Cook showed no urgent inclination to leave Tahiti to undertake the second part of his orders, to head south into the freezing waters where Terra Australis Incognita was believed to lie. The *Endeavour* required complete refurbishment and cleaning, meanwhile Banks found sufficient tasks to occupy himself and his staff.

The longer the explorers stayed, the more they were appreciated by the natives and the more the crew appreciated the women. In a language devoid of so much, the best representation the natives could make of Cook's and Banks's names were Toote and Tapane. As time passed, relationships intensified. Cook, happily married, never permitted himself to be tempted although his voluntary abstinence was the subject of measured jibes from the natives. The same could not be said of Joseph Banks who, though unmarried, had a fiancée at home, Miss Harriet Blosset. It was clear to the natives that this young, debonair, handsome man was a member of Britain's aristocracy. Oberea made a play for him and it has been said that Banks stayed overnight with her, a fact which might not have become known had not someone stolen all his clothes except his trousers during the night. A lampoon did the rounds in London:

'Rise Oberea, rise my Queen', you said,
'Something has stolen my breeches from my head.'

Rumours in London had it that the popular queen had a child by him. But this formidable woman, whom he had described as 'about forty, tall and very lusty, her skin white and her eyes full of meaning; she might have been handsome when young but now few or no traces of it were left', was not his type. For Banks, she was a means to an end: access to the young handmaidens surrounding her. Mindful of the devoted Miss Blosset waiting patiently at home, Banks wrote: 'I am at present otherwise engaged; indeed was I free as air, her majesty's person is not the most desirable.' The energetic competition between Banks and the ship's surgeon to seduce these young girls was duly recorded and published in London.

Shortly after the *Endeavour's* return, stories of Banks's sexual escapades began to do the rounds in London. It is unlikely that this was the cause of the breakdown in Mr Banks's engagement to Miss Harriet Blosset. It is more likely that the freedom which he enjoyed in Tahiti and the ability to come and go as a free agent in the pursuit of his interests were privileges he was not yet prepared to forfeit to marriage. Unfortunately, this was a decision that he appears not to have had the courage to share with Miss Blosset who, during his absence, had been busy embroidering a number of his waistcoats. Banks made no effort to contact his fiancée after his return home. She, having apparently been abandoned, sought out Banks in high dudgeon demanding an explanation. The couple spent twelve hours discussing their future. Banks insisted he was ready for marriage but she could see his heart was not in it. She suggested they should allow two weeks to elapse before coming to a decision. Only three or four days were required for Banks to decide to break off the engagement. Hugely embarrassed and worried about his reputation, Banks agreed the sum of £5000 as the price for ending the engagement. Miss Blosset did rather well from the deal, for with £5000 in the bank she remained an attractive catch without having had to marry someone who would be a constant cause for concern. Many of the stories of Banks's conduct in Tahiti were untrue: though some were true.

One early morning in mid-May found Banks seated as usual outside the fort gates with Tupia nearby, both engaged in trading. The attention of those surrounding Banks was taken by the appearance of a chief's double canoe of a quality to suggest that the man and two women under its shelter were aristocrats from elsewhere on the island. Tupia advised Banks he should stand to receive the important visitors. The visitors walked towards Banks and Tupia carrying approximately a dozen plantains (bananas) and some other plants. These they placed on the ground about 20 feet from Banks. The spectators moved back so as to make a lane between the visitors and Banks. When this was done the man, apparently a servant, brought the plantains one at a time with some of the other plants which he gave to Banks. After each individual presentation the man said a few words until there were no plants remaining. He then brought forward two pieces of cloth which he laid out on the ground. One of the young women, the senior woman, came forward, stepped upon the cloth and with an air of complete innocence allowed her clothes to slip from the waist downwards, 'quickly', in Banks's words, 'unveiling all her charms'. She began to turn slowly once or twice, revealing her lower body before stepping off the cloth and out of her remaining clothes. The other girl came forward, more cloth was spread out and she performed precisely as her friend had done. When she had finished, the cloth was rolled up and presented to Banks, whereupon the girls came forward and put their arms around him. Taking one of the girls by the hand, Banks led her into his tent, followed by the other. Inside, presents were exchanged but, in the words of Banks, 'I could not prevail upon them to stay more than an hour'.

It had been to Cook's everlasting regret that a native had been shot and killed in front of the fort for taking a musket, something seen as very serious by the visitors but at that particular time not something the native who stole the musket would have recognised as being life-threatening. Cook wished to be seen as an humane man. He tried to be even-handed in the exercise of justice whether dealing with the ship's butcher or a light-fingered native. Arguably he became less humane over the years but here, on his first voyage, he tried to be fair and just. He foresaw the possibility that his men might bring venereal disease to Tahiti and infect the islanders. A month before landing, he had the ship's surgeon inspect every one of them. All were said to be clear of infection. Abstinence could have been argued as being preferable to the cure, namely being injected with arsenic, but these young men found the young women irresistible. It was not always lust since many of the sailors found genuine love. Cook described how he did all in his power to prevent the disease's progress, 'but all I could do was to little purpose for I may safely say that I was not assisted by any one person in the ship'. One-third of his men contracted the disease.

In due course the natives reassured Cook that his men had not brought the 'venereal distemper' to the island. They said that two ships which had called at Hitiaa had been responsible for the infection. Cook invited the senior chief aboard the *Endeavour* to look through pictures of coloured flags to identify the nation of the culprits responsible. The chief would not have understood this since he would have assumed the explorers were the same people from the same place. Nevertheless, he pointed to the Spanish flag as having been flown by *La Boudeuse* and *Étoile*. Not until they called at Batavia would Cook discover the French connection.

Before leaving on 26 June, Cook and Banks accompanied by Tupia and oarsmen took the pinnace to journey round the island, Cook sketching it as they were rowed. When they came to Ahui on little Tahiti they went ashore and found fifteen human jawbones fastened to the end of a house, trophies from the battle against Oberea's men. They also discovered a goose and a turkey-cock, part of Wallis's gift to Oberea. When they reached Papara and looked in amazement at Oberea's *marae*, the sea, littered with human bones, proved testament to the implications of the Queen's overweening ambition. As time of departure drew near, two marines deserted. They had 'wives' ashore. Thoughts of the unfavourable comparison between life on Tahiti where they would want for nothing, where the climate was so favourable, and some dreary, depressing hovel in a naval port, can generate nothing but sympathy. The deserters had to be found and although Cook's arrest of five chiefs including Oberea proved to be excessive in so far as they had not been party to the desertions, it did mean that the natives turned the absconders in. Cook did not punish the marines for he knew that it was 'the spring that caused these commotions'. Many on board the *Endeavour* were of the same frame of mind. Cook took the *Endeavour* out to sea, thereby nipping in the bud any lingering talk of desertion.

Bligh of the *Bounty* did not have the luxury of choosing the appropriate time for his departure. The assumption that he had been delayed because the harvesting of breadfruit had not been finished is incorrect. The store of breadfruit plants was apparently completed (1,015 thriving shoots, 309 more than planned) long before the *Bounty* sailed away from Tahiti. Bligh delayed his departure mainly because January and February meant northerly winds and bad weather. His orders were to sail westwards to the Torres Straits and the Dutch East Indies: he could not risk the reefs in bad weather.

Oberea wept as the *Endeavour* moved out into the open sea. Tupia could be seen at the topmast, standing with his patron Banks, 'where we stood a long time waving to the canoes as they went off'. Below them on the deck, looking wistful and lost, was a native boy, Tayeto, servant to Tupia. The crew found Tayeto to be a charming lad, 'of a mild and docile disposition, ready to do any kind of office for the meanest in the ship, and never complaining, but always pleased'. The crew became fascinated by Tayeto's music, played on a flute through his nostril. They enthused less with Tupia for although many represented the lowest in a broad English yeomen class, they could not accept the native's airs and graces and thought themselves belittled 'by bending to an Indian'. Tupia was a 'shrewd, sensible, ingenious man', wrote Cook, 'but proud and obstinate which often made his situation on board both disagreeable to himself and those about him, and tended much to promote the diseases which put a period to his life'. He refused to comply with the dietary regime as ordered by Cook, a consequence of which was his early contraction of scurvy.

After sailing from Tahiti, Cook did not immediately sail south in accordance with his orders to attempt to discover Terra Australis Incognita. First he put in at Huahine, one of the Society Islands, so named by Cook due to their proximity one to another and not to any association with London's Royal Society. The Windward Islands within the Society group include Tahiti and Moorea while the Leeward Islands include Huahine, Raiatea, Tahaa and Bora Bora. Eventually, reluctantly, he took the *Endeavour* deep into the Southern Ocean but no further than his precise orders required. The reversal of course northwards proved a relief for all aboard whose long stay at Tahiti had served to intensify the cold and their discomfort. They sailed past New Zealand, Australia and New Guinea, exploring new land, to arrive in October at Batavia in the Dutch East Indies, aware that all was not well with the hull of the *Endeavour*. There were competent craftsmen available at Batavia but repairs take time, which meant the crew had to languish in a port notorious for its pernicious climate and endemic tropical diseases. Aoutourou had also passed this way, describing Batavia, built on a swamp, as 'the place that kills'. Dysentery and malaria soon made an unwelcome appearance.

Tupia had begun to show signs of growing stronger, so much so that his and Tayeto's curiosity were drawn to go out and inspect Batavia, the first town of its kind they had seen. On one occasion, when Tupia was in the company of Banks, a man rushed out of a house and asked Tupia whether he had been in Batavia before. When he replied in the negative, his interrogator told him that he was not the first, that one of his countrymen, obviously Aoutourou, had recently passed through Batavia aboard a French ship. The news interested Cook for it was clear that the visitors who had called at Tahiti between the visits of the *Dolphin* and the *Endeavour* had been French, not Spanish.

Tayeto's illness was brief. His sudden death exerted a dreadful strain upon the weakened body of Tupia. It was as though he had lost the desire to live. He 'gave himself up to grief' and he too died, three days later. Deprived of paintings, Banks had now been deprived of the noble savage he had intended to use to impress his friends. Banks had not stayed in town but had moved outside with his friend Solander. This may have saved them. Among those who did not return were Cook's first lieutenant, the surgeon, Molyneux the master, Green the astronomer, Spöring the secretary and Parkinson the artist who were among thirty-eight in all to die.

CHAPTER 5

The Second Voyage

The nature of the homecoming of Lieutenant Cook and Mr Banks reflected the public response to the achievements of these two central characters who had shared the *Endeavour* experience. After his duty call at the Admiralty, Cook made his way to a quiet family reunion with his wife Elizabeth and their children at their home in Mile End Road in the unfashionable East End of London. There was no metaphorical sidelining for Joseph Banks, whose home in New Burlington Street was at the heart of London society. To Banks and Solander came the public accolades. Both fed readily on the public adulation. Oxford awarded them honorary doctorates because the voyage of the *Endeavour* was seen by the public as *their* achievement. Some take the view that the botanists over-egged what they had done and had not given due recognition to Cook, without whom their successes would not have been possible.

Self-publicity is a difficult act to manage but already the botanists had turned their thoughts to a second voyage so that it was not unreasonable for them to milk the publicity for as long as the exploits of the *Endeavour* remained newsworthy. Banks had been prominent in justifying the voyage to Tahiti and he had also been generous in offsetting costs. It is indisputable that he and his team also made significant new discoveries, in the pursuit of which they had risked their health and well-being, undertaking a voyage which lasted for three years. It was precisely because they were civilians that separated them from Cook, his officers and crew. Servicemen tend not to be applauded by the public for doing what can be described in basic terms as what they do. Although the press remained essentially silent about Cook and focused upon the botanists, Cook did not go unrewarded or unrecognised. He had an audience with the King and was promoted by the Admiralty.

The empathy between Banks and the Earl of Sandwich arose through their social life rather than through having grown up together – Banks was twenty-eight and Sandwich already in his fifties. It was to Banks that Sandwich intimated his thoughts of a second voyage to determine once and for all whether Terra Australis Incognita existed. Upon that principal aim it was, of course, possible to superimpose subordinate missions such as a return to Polynesian waters, to use Tahiti as a base. Cook heard of the First Lord's thinking from Banks, for much strategic decision-making came from within social circles.

Lord Sandwich had his country seat at Hinchingbrooke, Huntingdonshire. The musical events he held there were renowned. The Earl, a competent percussionist, brought world-class performers to a home somewhat removed from the beaten track. It was here that the second voyage was discussed with Banks and Cook and where connections and opportunism became exercised to their fullest extent. One of Sandwich's musical friends was Fanny Burney's father Charles, a famous musicologist and historian. Charles Burney's twenty-one-year-old son James (Jem) had been in the Navy from the age of ten and intended to make it his career. Again, an active old-boy network saw Charles and Jem Burney travel to Hinchingbrooke to meet James Cook. It was quite normal in the eighteenth century for a Royal Navy ship's captain to take under his wing boys from the age of ten to act as captain's servants. The permitted quota was one boy for every hundred members of crew. Appointments were made as a result of parental lobbying. The boy served out his apprenticeship doing chores and batting for his captain until he entered his early teens when, if successful, he became known as a young gentleman or midshipman. With the support of the First Lord and the expedition commander, Jem Burney's place on the second voyage became accordingly assured.

On 25 September, the Admiralty authorised the purchase of two suitable ships, not the rumoured three, for a voyage towards the South

Pole: 'We do hereby desire and direct you to purchase upon the best or cheapest terms you can for His Majesty, two proper vessels of about 400 tons burthen each to be employed upon service in remote parts.'

The doubling-up of ships can be explained by the recognition that there is safety in numbers. Although Cook had not been consulted in the selection of the *Endeavour* he was, for the second voyage, invited to propose the type of ship he thought best and with which he would be most content. The *Endeavour* was unavailable, for after repair she had been sent to the Falkland Islands in the South Atlantic. Had she been available, she would have been one of the two choices for, although slow, she was sure and her shallow draught reduced the prospect of officers and crew becoming marooned upon some distant, unreachable reef. Cook relied upon the builders of the *Endeavour* to supply him with the next generation of ships. The *Marquis of Granby*, 462 tons, and the *Marquis of Rockingham*, 340 tons, were both former colliers built at Whitby's Fishburn Yard less than two years previously. The ships became registered as the sloops HMS *Drake* and HMS *Raleigh*. Technically, neither was a sloop since a sloop is a single-masted sailing vessel, rigged fore and aft. After some contemplation, a feeling developed in royal circles that these two names might prove too provocative to the Spanish (who in any event went on to declare war against Britain in 1779). After Lord Rochford, a Secretary of State, conveyed the broadest of hints that *Drake* and *Raleigh* were not the most diplomatic of names, Sandwich replied: 'The names pitched upon for the two discovery ships are the *Resolution* and *Adventure*.' Both ships went into naval dockyards at Deptford and Woolwich to be fitted-out for the voyage and the taking on of complements not previously imagined – one hundred and twelve men and twelve guns, and eighty-one men and ten guns respectively.

Concurrent with the preparation of the two ships was the planning of the scientific side led by Joseph Banks whose ego had become alarmingly inflated. His suite on this occasion numbered fifteen for the conduct of scientific examination upon an expedition whose rationale was geographic. In terms of priority, therefore, there was potential for a disconnection between Cook and his orders and Banks and his aspirations. There had been no major conflict of interest between Cook and Banks on the *Endeavour* voyage, but according to the newspapers this, the second voyage, was Banks's voyage and he made the fatal mistake of believing what he read in the newspapers.

In the conviction that he was the *de facto* leader of the expedition, Banks thought it right and proper that he should be consulted about all decisions. The first major problem was that he insisted that the *Resolution* was too small to accommodate his requirements and, through his connections with Sandwich, he arranged for the ship to be altered to accommodate passengers; namely, he had a whole new deck of cabins added so that members of his entourage might be accommodated with due deference to their rank. It was so arranged that Banks and his followers would take over the entire new deck, including the captain's cabin. Provision was made for Cook by building an additional cabin above Banks's deck. Cook took all this in his stride while Banks insisted that he should have his own way on every point. If anyone questioned the wisdom of his way, he threatened the ultimate and dangerous sanction of withdrawing from the expedition. Cook thought the high-rise plan to be nonsense but bided his time in the hope that, despite his strong reservations, it all, somehow, might just work out. Cook understood the importance of not opening up a divide between the separate interests of scientists and geographers before the voyage even began. In the meantime, the opportunity for a March sailing had passed.

Many were the curious who came to Deptford to examine the ugly duckling. The First Lord visited on a number of occasions, an exceptional event for such a senior naval person to show so much interest in a ship of such unexceptional size. Banks entertained the French ambassador and other personal guests including Sandwich on board prior to sea trials on 14 May. No one was to be left in any doubt that this was *his* voyage and Cook, whom he liked and respected, was none the less a subordinate who had his place. The problem was that Cook knew about ships while Banks did not. If

Cook had been less concerned with the niceties of diplomacy, much time and money might have been saved. Even before sea trials proper could begin, the pilot aboard *Resolution* refused to take her any further down the Thames from the Nore because she was too unstable. Immediately after the sea trials on 14 May, Cook sent a note to Sandwich: 'This morning I received the inclosed letter from Lieutenant Cooper informing me that the ship is so exceedingly crank that he thinks it unsafe to proceed with her any further than the Nore.' Cook informed the Admiralty that the cabin deck would have to be removed. *Resolution* put into Sheerness and into the hands of the yard's master builder who said that if he had been 'directed to build a ship for the purpose for which *Resolution* is intended', he would have 'constructed her exactly with the same [original] body and dimensions'.

Midshipman John Elliott was at Sheerness when Banks arrived in response to a request that he examine the restored *Resolution* to confirm whether or not she could accommodate his retinue. 'When he saw the ship and the alterations that were made, he swore and stamped upon the wharf like a madman; and instantly ordered his servants and all things out of the ship.'

Banks sat down and wrote a long, unwise, letter to Sandwich. He questioned how it was possible that the Navy Board could have purchased a ship without first consulting him and questioned Cook's abilities. He did not like the Whitby cat class ship. To his mind it was too slow and ponderous. Might not his Lordship make HMS *Launceston*, a 44-gun ship of the line, available? Within the letter lay an implied threat that Banks would go public. There is no doubt that press sympathies lay with Banks, fuelled by what might have been planted letters questioning how it was possible that public employees in the Navy were able to frustrate the wishes of the King and Mr Banks. If Banks had gone public, there is little doubt that an uninformed public would have sided with him, but Sandwich's exquisitely crafted reply three days later took the wind out of Banks's sails.

Sandwich's rejoinder, 'more urbane but more deadly', was intended as his Lordship's emergency contingency plan, to be sent anonymously to the press in the event that his friend Banks caused trouble. The First Lord told Banks precisely what he intended to do, 'for it is a heavy charge against the Board to suppose that they mean to send a number of men to sea in an unhealthy ship'. Banks recognised that he had been outmanoeuvred and could not win. He then went ahead and chartered a brig, the *Sir Laurence*, at a cost of £100 a month, taking his followers off on a far less exciting voyage to explore Iceland.

HMS *Adventure* had required little alteration and waited at Plymouth for the *Resolution* to appear. Two months had been lost through the Banks fiasco. Cook must have reflected that, on balance, his was a bad decision to accommodate Banks's wishes. The skipper of the *Adventure* was Tobias Furneaux, sometime of HMS *Dolphin* and planter of the Union flag on Matavai beach, claiming Tahiti in the name of the King. The thirty-seven-year-old Furneaux remained a popular officer although Cook believed him to be somewhat lax on discipline. The *Adventure* also carried a ship's astronomer, William Bayly, who, as the exception to rule, was unable to strike up a friendly relationship with the captain.

Cook's astronomer, William Wales, had been the astronomer on Prince of Wales Island, monitoring of the passage of Venus, and was the more gifted and gregarious of the two. Both astronomers were of importance because one of the expedition's aims was to test an instrument with which it was hoped to calculate longitude. The loss of Banks and Solander was keenly felt in their replacements. Johann Reinhold Forster, translator of de Bougainville's partly salacious *A Voyage Round the World*, was a botanist who brought a new meaning to the word 'difficult'. His remuneration for this expedition at £4000 compared very favourably to Wales's £400. He brought with him his teenage son whose abilities some ranked superior to those of the father and who was certainly more agreeable company. Among the ship's officers were Cook's deputies, Lieutenants Cooper and Clerke, the interesting Jem Burney and a fifteen-year-old midshipman who would go on to survey the north west coast of America. His name was George Vancouver.

As the time drew nearer to the commencement of the delayed voyage, the number of desertions increased – fifty-eight from the *Resolution* and thirty-seven from the *Adventure*. The numbers discharged were twenty-nine and eleven respectively. A long voyage such as this, requiring three or more years away from home, was rarely popular. A number of these losses were made up but there was always an excess of provision among the crew on voyages such as this in order to compensate for projected losses due to sickness or accident. No one could have objected to sailing with less than the intended complement for reasons based on simple ergonomics, a problem eased by one-third of the ship's company being on duty at any one time. Late to join the ship was a young man responsible for providing a permanent image of late eighteenth-century Polynesia. His name was William Hodges, the landscape artist.

Cook's orders were dated 25 June and contained no surprises. He had been fully consulted 'and nothing was inserted that I did not fully comprehend and approve of'. Only Cook knew what was intended on a voyage which would take them to Madeira to take on wine, to the Cape of Good Hope to revictual and then southwards among the ice in the attempt to find the elusive Terra Australis Incognita. Furneaux was not informed of the mission until some days into the voyage but was forbidden to publicise the Admiralty's intentions. There was provision in the orders after the discovery or otherwise of the elusive continent to make for some known place, a base to the north. It may already have been Cook's intention that that special place would be Tahiti which he held in such high regard and knew would compensate the crew for the rigours and monotony of time spent among the icebergs. At 6 a.m. on 13 July 1772, HMS *Resolution* and *Adventure* sailed from Plymouth.

The ships arrived at Cape Town in October where they spent almost a month recovering and preparing for the next leg into the inhospitable frozen south. Progress through the icy waters was slow, so much so that drinking water had almost run out. It was as a consequence of this problem that Banks's association of sea ice with land came to be disproven. Work parties from both ships went on to the ice floes where they cut blocks of ice to be taken aboard and melted into the empty water casks. The water was indeed fresh, but of land there was no sign.

When sea water begins to freeze, its ice contains just over half the salt of sea water. This proportion continues for as long as there is plenty of sea water remaining. Most sea ice is normally brackish and just about drinkable when it is fresh. Then it inevitably becomes covered in fresh snow as there are frequent snow and sleet falls in the Southern Ocean. If, therefore, the top is scraped off older sea ice, it can be used as fresh water or in coffee with no detrimental effect. Shackleton's crew did this for their winter camped out on the sea ice in 1915 and until modern desalination plants existed, ships would put alongside sea ice and shovel it into their water tanks.

On 8 February 1773, in high seas and poor visibility, the two ships lost contact. According to their agreed standing operating procedures, Furneaux spent three days criss-crossing the point where contact was lost, firing guns in an attempt to attract attention. When that proved fruitless, he embarked upon the next step in the plan which was to make rendezvous in Queen Charlotte Sound, New Zealand. Queen Charlotte Sound is a bay in the north of South Island, opening up into Cook Strait which separates the main North and South Islands. The *Adventure* anchored in Queen Charlotte South on 7 April and found evidence that the *Resolution* had been there, but it was not until 18 May 1773 that both ships regained contact in the Sound. Winter was now upon them so the decision was made to pass into the warmer climate of the east and north Pacific before ending that phase of exploration at Tahiti.

Not for nothing is the ocean called pacific. Sometimes it is. It may have been Wales the astronomer or Hodges the artist, perhaps both, who told the story of this voyage to Samuel Taylor Coleridge, author of *The Rime of the Ancient Mariner*:

Day after day, day after day,
We stuck, nor breath nor motion
As idle as a painted ship
Upon a painted ocean.

On those occasions when the ships were becalmed, officers would be rowed from one to the other. It was by this means that Cook became gravely aware of the severe impact of scurvy upon the crew of the *Adventure*. Their cook had died and twenty of the crew were suffering the effects of this the most prevalent of nautical diseases. Scurvy, a killer, is a dietary disease caused by a lack of vitamin C. In 1741, Lord Anson lost 620 dead from his crews of 961 men. In an attempt to alleviate the vitamin C deficiency, British sailors off the North American coast drank the citric juice of limes procured in the Caribbean, hence the pejorative term 'limeys' used by Americans to describe the British. There was no way that Cook could have kept South African citrus fruit fresh. Instead, there were vegetables used as anti-scorbutics which included *sauerkraut,* and something new on this voyage, also a German recipe, yellow carrot marmalade. These, however, were of little value because of their poor vitamin C content. What many anti-scorbutics had in common was their sharp, often unappetising taste. A drink made from the juice of wort and beer proved to be more popular. Cook used psychology to ensure the lower deck took the medicine. He told his officers they would be seen to eat their anti-scorbutics and declare how much they enjoyed the food. When the lower deck heard that anti-scorbutics were the most popular food in the wardroom, the men too wanted their share. The effect of scurvy on board the *Resolution* was therefore very much less than it might otherwise have been and far less severe than it was on the *Adventure* where the command was more lax and less imaginative.

On Sunday 15 August 1773 the mountains of Tahiti were seen to the west. Cook sent reinforcements to the *Adventure* where the scurvy was so bad that some of those affected could not walk. So parlous was the ship's condition that he decided to anchor at Vaitepiha Bay on the east coast of the island rather than make for the favoured Matavai Bay.

Both ships were barely under control for a twelve-hour period and risked collision and running aground on the reef. Cook, who was unwell at the time, went to bed, leaving the ship under the command of the officer of the watch. When he awoke, he found the ship on the wrong course and barely half a league from the reef. He ordered the ship to be steered northwards but no sooner had he given the order than the wind dropped and the tide carried both ships towards the reef. Sheer muscle and seamanship averted disaster, allowing the *Resolution* and the *Adventure* to pass through the gap in the reef and to anchor with one of their few remaining anchors. Despite being in the midst of crisis, the local people came on board to trade or to thieve. It was difficult to keep an eye on them when the ships were in danger. What was not brought on board was what the explorers most required, hogs and poultry. Recent wars meant these meats were in short supply and under the personal control of Chief Vehiatua. There was an abundant supply of fruit. When the chief saw the two ships arrive, he assumed they were on a visit of retribution for his having fought friends from the north and west of the island. Consequently he had gone inland to hide and therefore there was no one available to authorise the release of fresh meat.

The next day, the sick were sent ashore to begin their recuperation while salvage crews went out on to the reef in an attempt to recover lost anchors. The friendly natives recognised Cook and asked after Mr Banks but it was only two days later that any enquiry was made of Tupia. They heard of his death in a matter-of-fact way and appeared uninterested in the death off Madagascar of the local man Aoutourou. The natives conveyed some intelligence of another ship having called after the *Endeavour*, news which was borne out by the sighting by sailors of a Caucasian beyond the tree line. The fresh fruit and vegetables had such a miraculous effect upon the sick that Cook decided that when the wind became favourable he would take the ships through and beyond the dangerous reef and make for Matavai in the hope of securing unrationed meat.

While waiting for the wind to change, Cook received a message from Vehiatua that he would be welcome to call upon the chief. The chief turned out to be a youth whom Cook remembered as a boy when he had come this way on his tour of the island. After the presentation of better quality baubles appropriate for a chief, Vehiatua reciprocated with the gift of several hogs. The chief regretted there were not more but, if Cook chose to wait a few days, more would be forthcoming. Cook did not believe the young chief and said he had to depart the next day, 24 August, but would leave the cutter to bring on the promised meat. The chief honoured his promise for when the cutter under Lieutenant Pickersgill made rendezvous with the *Resolution* it was laden with hogs. The oarsmen had spent one night at Hitiaa with Ereti, brother of Aoutourou, on their way northwards. Ereti made no enquiry of Aoutourou and likewise appeared uninterested when the sailors informed him of his fate.

Cook or 'Toote' found himself warmly welcomed by the Tahitians at Matavai who came aboard with bolts of coloured cloth which they insisted on winding around him so that when they had finished, he stood sweltering on his quarterdeck like an untidily packaged mummy. A minor chief also came on board with his wife, promising to take Cook the next day to meet the victor of the struggle for local supremacy among the chieftains. Cook, Furneaux and the minor chief with wife found Tu or Otoo sitting on the ground with his family among subjects who were totally naked, thereby demonstrating their subservience. He was a man of impressive stature, in his early to mid-thirties and over 6 feet tall. The better quality baubles again came out and were presented to Tu. He offered Cook some cloth in exchange, but this Cook declined saying that his presents had been given to his *tayo* in friendship. There was clearly a shortage of animals on the island – a sure indication of recurring conflict: 'This fine island, which in the years 1767 and 1768 swarmed, as it were, with hogs and fowls, is now so scarce of these animals that hardly anything will induce the owners to part with them.'

Cook, Furneaux and the minor chief and his wife returned to the beach where they were met by Lieutenant John Edgcumbe, Officer Commanding, Royal Marines, who saw the two captains to their boats which took them back to their ships. Inexplicably, the chief and his wife dallied, the wife making her intentions perfectly clear to the smartly uniformed young subaltern. 'This lady', he wrote, 'wanted neither youth nor beauty, nor was she wanting in using those charms which nature had given her to the most advantage. She bestowed her caresses on me with the utmost profusion, and before I could get clear of her I was obliged to satisfy all her demands, after which both she and her husband went away.'

Tu's refusal to accept Cook's offer of hospitality aboard the *Resolution* left Cook perplexed. Tu was, after all, the victor of a series of bloody local wars yet he refused to go on board because of a fear of guns. Cook regarded him as 'a timorous prince'. Overnight Tu reflected upon his apparent ingratitude and weakness and decided after all to accept Cook's offer. He arrived bringing fish, fruit and cloth but, significantly, only one hog. The dire shortage of meat did not augur well for the revictualling of the British ships for the continuation of their anticipated long and arduous voyage. The British devoured greater quantities of meat than the *arioi*. However, in the meantime, Furneaux presented Tu with two of his remaining goats but Cook's efforts to put a broadsword round the chief's waist terrified the man and he insisted it be removed. Otherwise, all seemed to be well until a run ashore on 30 August went badly wrong, proving once again that the men had an incredible knack of letting their officers down. An armed shore party was sent to bring back and put in irons those responsible for the disturbances. It appears that drink – too much – had been at the heart of the problem, and the sailors had attempted to rape Tahitian women. The next morning, while Cook went ashore to apologise, the miscreants were flogged.

Oberea had thus far been conspicuous by her absence but by chance an officer on a foraging mission encountered her in her district of Papara. She had been sidelined in the recent power struggle, having to concede to her nephew Tu. She said she felt unable to visit the ship since she had nothing to bring and did not wish to appear a scrounger dependent upon handouts.

While at Matavai Cook heard of the visit of yet another ship, the same size as the *Resolution*, whose commander was named Opeppe. Cook assumed the ship to be French but she was not, she was the Spanish frigate *Aguila*. The origin of the *Aguila*'s voyage can be found in a memo dated 9 July 1766 from Spain's Minister of State to the Secretary of State for the Indies:

> The Prince de Masserano [ambassador in London] has forwarded to the King the accompanying journal, which he has been good enough to procure, kept by one of the English aboard the vessel called the *Dolphin*, which has just been round the world; her business to recommend, as there are good grounds for suspecting, some place suitable for an English settlement; which may prove very prejudicial to ourselves.

In due course, news of the voyage of the *Endeavour* and the success of '*el famoso capitán Santiago Cok*' gave rise to concern in Madrid and the Spanish vice-regency in Lima, Peru.

A despatch dated 9 October 1771 from the Spanish Secretary of State to the Viceroy gave details of the *Endeavour*'s voyage and ordered him to 'at once make suitable preparations in connection with the exploration being carried out in those seas, for searching out by any practicable means the island of Otaheite'. Spain remained jealous of its sovereignty, having sparred with France and Britain over the ownership of the Falkland Islands in the South Atlantic, an area far less important to Spanish interests than the Pacific, the so-called Spanish Lake. Spain's problem in this region was that although it may well have entertained the intention of dominating its imagined sphere of influence, it lacked the capability. Before the solitary *Aguila* could embark upon a long voyage, she needed a refit and, since the Viceroy's coffers were empty, the money had to be raised from among Lima's business community.

Opeppe was in fact Commander Don Domingo de Boenechea

who left El Callao, Lima, as captain of the *Aguila* on 26 September 1772. Among the *Aguila's* complement of 231 persons were two priests who were to report back on what they found with a view to founding the first Christian mission on Tahiti. The voyage carried strong religious overtones, for the Viceroy had suggested that:

> It will not be difficult, using tact and persuasion, to recruit four or five lads from amongst those who may seem the smartest with the object of bringing them to this capital and of instructing them not only in the Spanish language, but chiefly in the rudiments of our holy religion; because this might count for much hereafter towards inseminating the Christian Faith among these hapless folk.

The *Aguila* arrived off Tahiti on 19 November 1772, anchoring in Vaiurua harbour, and remained until 20 December. De Boenechea's journal, signed at the port of Valparaiso on 8 March 1773, is a detailed and encouraging document. If the Spaniards did experience any 'sensuality', it remained their secret. The most risqué revelation that de Boenechea was prepared to reveal to his devout superiors was the information that some of the women 'go entirely nude from the waist upwards', which was due to 'their individual poverty'.

What de Boenechea did not know is that he brought to Tahiti a virulent form of gastric influenza against which the natives had no immunity. The complaint affected the head, throat and stomach and was sometimes fatal. His journal included a small vocabulary and translation of the numbers one to ten: 'They do not count farther than up to ten, but from thence they begin over again.' Four Tahitian natives accompanied the *Aguila* on her return voyage. One died at Valparaiso. The remainder reached the capital and were found accommodation in the royal palace where another died.

There are reports of Spaniards being executed for misdemeanours committed while on Tahiti and of a number of desertions. De Boenechea did what Wallis and de Bougainville had both done before him: laid claim to the island and its unsuspecting natives in the name of his state. For the Spanish, Tahiti became 'Isla d'Amat' after

Manuel de Amat, Viceroy of Peru. It all had a certain predictability about it, a process which Cook would find deeply unsatisfactory.

On 1 September the *Resolution* and the *Adventure* sailed from Tahiti to nearby islands to restock the sea food-store with hogs and poultry which had been found to be in short supply on Tahiti. Taken on board was a native by the name of Poreo who, Cook explained, 'might be of service to us on some occasion'. While it is probably true that at this juncture in the second voyage Cook neither liked nor respected paramount chief Tu, the same was not true of Oree, principal chief of Huahine, whom he had come to know on the first voyage. The old man gave Cook the warmest of welcomes to his island which, fortuitously, unlike Tahiti, was positively groaning under the weight of provisions. When the two sloops did eventually weigh anchor, having bad farewell, they each carried 300 hogs in their sea food-stores.

Cook's arrival at Raiatea prompted a suggestion from the natives that he consider harnessing his firepower to attack their Bora Bora enemy occupying Raiatea. This was an idea with which Omai was entirely sympathetic, it being his abiding intention to eject the Bora Borans from his family land. Although he was not prominent among the proponents, that is not to say he had not stirred them up. Oree would not countenance an attack against Raiatea and, since Cook would never contemplate intervention on one side against the other, the initiative failed through lack of interest.

Omai took the first available opportunity to approach Tobias Furneaux with the request that he be allowed aboard the *Adventure* and taken to England. Omai had more sense than to approach Cook. For both Furneaux and Omai, the timing proved serendipitous. Before the *Adventure* had sailed from England, Banks had privately approached Furneaux saying that if the Captain brought back with him a noble savage, Banks would undertake responsibility for the man. Perhaps there was also a reward for Furneaux. Omai's proposal was quickly acceded to and, despite the warnings of his friends that he was sure to die on board, Omai took up the offered accommodation. There is no mention of this arrangement in Furneaux's journal but the ship's log is explicit. Omai had also been given the guarantee of a safe return. The warnings, however, continued to prey on his mind. On the second day after leaving Raiatea, when divine worship was being conducted in the captain's cabin, he suspected the close assembly of men to be plotting his death. He excused himself, went up on deck and tucked his valuables around his waist lest an urgent departure overboard be necessary.

When the time came to depart Huahine and make for Omai's birthplace, Raiatea, Cook misunderstood what Oree was saying to him. Cook thought that Oree was complaining that a number of his people had been taken on board the *Adventure* against their will and without his approval. Cook sent his compliments to Furneaux, desiring that he send all natives on board forthwith to the *Resolution*. When the cutter came alongside it carried but one native – Omai.

When Cook examined Omai he saw before him a slim young man, twenty-two years of age, 5 feet 10 inches tall and with small tattooed hands, who was evidently intent upon reaching England. With both ships now moving ahead, Cook agreed that Omai could remain aboard the *Resolution* until Raiatea when he would be able to transfer back to the *Adventure*. Cook did not believe Omai to be the best of specimens but since Furneaux, skipper of the *Adventure*, had given Omai his word that he could make passage on the *Adventure*, the die had effectively been cast. Cook was senior to Furneaux by one day and therefore not in a strong position to intervene. Omai's motive for wanting to go to *Pretane* was tied up with his fixation for revenge and righting the wrong against his family. He was clearly a man who cherished status, determined to climb back to the *raatira* rank from which he had fallen. He nurtured an idea that in England he would learn the skills of modern warfare, and return with weapons to recover that which was rightfully his. He told Furneaux whom he recognised from his *Dolphin* days that he was an assistant priest when what he had been in fact was an assistant to Tupia the priest in much the same way that the younger Tayeto had been.

Johann Forster wrote of his disappointment in the appearance and status of Omai but he had also been disappointed by Cook's refusal to permit him to bring his own hand-picked noble savage home: 'I was at first astonished that he should take on this particular Indian who was distinguished neither by birth or rank, nor do I consider his face and colour give a just idea of the inhabitants of these happy isles; for the natives of the first rank are much more beautiful and intelligent.' Admittedly, Omai was not a pretty picture. His nose, even by Tahitian standards, was broad and flat, so much so that he was teased by his friends over his untypical proboscis. William Hodges chose to paint Omai. A member of the expedition said of this painting that it was 'the only time I ever knew Hodges to flatter in drawing'. The notoriously plain-spoken Cook said of Omai that he was 'dark, ugly and a downright blackguard'.

Aside from the usual misunderstandings, Orio of Raiatea and his people proved to be perfect hosts. Socially, they specialised in dance and music which they performed in the evening for their honoured visitors. The majority of actors were men: some very good, so good that Jem Burney named one Garrick after his father's friend. The throbbing drumbeat and the flickering light from camp fires created the best of atmospheres for the star turn which featured Orio's beautiful, untouchable daughter, Poetua. The theme of the dance was successful theft and it could not be denied that this slender, graceful woman, her body glistening from the lightest glaze of perspiration, stole many a heart that night.

Burney observed how the fresh provisions available on the islands meant there was 'not one man down with scurvy now'. Jem Burney had been transferred from the *Resolution* to the *Adventure* at Cape Town. His private journal reveals that Omai could not resist going ashore at Raiatea to meet family friends. He explained to them that he had been accepted to go to England to procure guns with which he would return and use to evict the Bora Borans from Raiatea. It was not long before a number of Bora Borans heard of his intention and decided to nip that particular initiative in the bud. During the night, a friend warned him that if he did not leave immediately he would be killed where he slept. Without bothering to dress, he plunged naked into the sea, persuading fishermen out in a canoe to take him to the *Adventure*. Not once during the remaining week did he dare go ashore.

The Forsters were involved in their share of misunderstandings. They had a curious notion that on pleasant, bright days they should go off and kill something. There was little sport to be gained from shooting the albatross hovering above them. Returning from another shooting trip the pair encountered Cook, Orio and family to whom they showed several kingfishers they had bagged. The natives were horrified, Poetua running off screaming that they had killed her spirit. The kingfisher was a sacred creature in the South Pacific. Orio pleaded with Cook to make his men desist from killing kingfishers and herons. The Forsters, as ever obedient, next caused anxiety by peppering natives with buckshot. A rumour that natives had been killed and wounded by muskets sent the whole tribe inland until Cook could find the chief and persuade him that the rumours were unfounded. After eight days, the time had come to go.

Poreo, the young man Cook had brought from Tahiti having given the father appropriate gifts in lieu, had already absconded. It was down to love. 'I who knew he had found his female friend, took no notice', explained Cook, 'thinking he was only going to retire with her on some private business of their own, probably at the time he had no other intention. She however had prevailed upon him to remain with her for I saw him no more.' There were more than sufficient volunteers to take Poreo's place. From among them Cook selected the best of the bunch, from 'the better sort of people' – a young man, seventeen or eighteen years old, with class and presence, called Hitihiti, who would be known on board as Odiddy. Odiddy had a fair complexion in comparison with Omai to whom he was not only one of the despised Bora Borans but was also related to Opoony, conqueror of Raiatea. Strangely, Omai held Opoony in high regard. Oddidy's pedigree was undisputed, coming from the class of chiefs, a fact proven by his embarking on the *Resolution* accompanied by a servant.

Cook's intentions from the outset had been to return to the frozen south and then return to the Society Islands prior to making for home. He may have had in his mind's eye the repatriation of both Omai and Odiddy when he returned to the Society Islands. In the meantime, Odiddy served as the numerical replacement for Poreo as an interpreter, should the *Resolution* encounter any unexpected islands on its voyage westwards.

Bayly observed how, by 27 September, Omai was in high spirits having overcome seasickness and homesickness. He was known on board both as Omy and by an obligatory Christian name – Jack. Furneaux had little to do with Omai. The officers who took most notice of him were Jem Burney and the surgeon, Thomas Andrews, both keen during the homeward voyage to learn his language, at which they were more successful than he was in learning English. Burney recorded that their 'Indian' was intelligent, had a good memory and was extremely observant. His many qualities clearly overcame his less than perfect appearance, being 'strong, active, healthy and likely to weather the hardships of a long voyage as any of us'. Socially, Burney placed Omai in the chiefly class, the 'second son of an independent man'.

After leaving Raiatea, Cook set a south-westerly course knowing that he would encounter a number of islands in the Tongan archipelago. His intention was to maintain this westerly course until he reached Amsterdam Island, discovered in 1643 by Tasman, from where he intended to plunge southwards. For Cook, the prospect of discovery was his life's joy, particularly sailing in the path of his forbears, if only to verify their claims. Five days out they sighted land, followed on 1 October by a large island, Tasman's Middleburg, today's Eua and, on the 2nd, Amsterdam known today as Tongatapu.

Cook, Furneaux and Forster went ashore with the welcoming chief at Eua, passing through a great throng of happy, inquisitive natives without any form of weaponry in sight. Omai and Oddidy deeply disappointed Cook through their inability to penetrate and comprehend the local dialect. It was on an occasion such as this that he missed the intellect of Tupia. Forster wrote: 'when we explained to them the affinity of several words, they presently caught the peculiar modification of this dialect and conversed much better with the natives than we ever could have done after long intercourse with them.'

The visitors sat on a mat in a local house where they were regaled by music played on the nose flute and hollow logs used as drums. Burney believed the harmony so good that he jotted the tunes down. Three young women came in to sing a song which Cook enjoyed: 'their songs were musical and harmonious, in no way harsh or disagreeable.' By way of reciprocation he called the *Resolution's* Scottish marine bagpiper, Archibald McVicar, ashore. Socialising continued with the inevitable *kava*. The visitors watched the chief put the roots in his mouth, chew on them while salivating and progressively spitting the accumulating mixture into a small bowl which, once it contained a drinkable quantity diluted with water, he passed to Cook. Cook sipped the narcotic spittle and passed the cup back to the chief. The chief then offered the cup to a horrified Furneaux who declined, as did Forster. Food came in short commons in the form of fruit and stewed greens, for which the Europeans had little appetite, 'but Oediddee and Omiah, the man on board the *Adventure*, did honour to the feast'.

The visitors' good first impressions, formed over two days at Eua, were confirmed as being consistent on Amsterdam. The thievery, however, was as advanced as anywhere the visitors had been. The astronomer Wales took himself ashore but was obliged to wade from the boat to the beach where he sat down to put on his shoes. They had been on the ground a matter of seconds but when he turned to put them on they were no longer there. A 100-lb boat's grapnel was spirited away from the beach.

The Tongans were rated as more sophisticated than the Tahitians. Certainly the view was that their canoes were better constructed. The islands were also laid out in a more orderly fashion than was the case in Tahiti, with roads and paths running between blocks of cultivated land throughout which their homes were scattered. Cook waxes lyrical about the organisation and horticulture which had reached a remarkably high standard bearing in mind the water shortages which plagued Tongatapu. Cook wrote: 'Nature, assisted by a little art, no where appears in a more flourishing state than at this isle.'

Cook's concern for the health of the natives meant that women were forbidden from coming aboard and no man was permitted ashore without first being inspected by the ships' surgeons and declared free of venereal disease. Slow at first to come forward with provisions, the availability of nails, whose exchange was controlled by Cook, wore down the natives' diffidence to the extent that both sloops departed Tonga fully laden on 8 October for Van Diemen's Road.

On 21 October, New Zealand was sighted. The next day, around Cook Strait, the sloops were struck by constant gales which are a feature of these waters at this time of the year. The captains tried desperately to maintain contact in the mountainous seas while, one by one, the sails were shredded by high winds. At 11 a.m. on 25 October, Cook wrote how the gale 'came on in such fury as to oblige us to take in all our sails with the utmost expedition and to lay-to under our bare poles with our heads to the SW'. The situation was bad for the *Resolution*, worse for the *Adventure*. Bayly wrote of Omai's stoicism: 'Our Huaheine man was much terrified having never seen the like before but our ship being an excellent sea boat soon convinced him that he had little to fear as she rolled very easy with the sea.' The *Adventure* continued to beat about Cook Strait, dipping into troughs deeper than the height of the ship's masts and carried up to the shoulders of the troughs to fall away suddenly as on a roller coaster. With both sloops caught up in this involuntary game of nautical snakes and ladders they sighted each other through the driven spray only when each was riding the peak of a mountainous wave. Those occasions became fewer and fewer until, by the end of the month, they had lost visual contact permanently. In a case such as this, the plan was to resume contact in Queen Charlotte Sound.

The storm raged until 4 November, calming sufficiently for the *Adventure* to round Cape Palliser, but the storm had not finished, revisiting the ship with greater ferocity than before, blowing the *Adventure* back from where she had come. Furneaux's morale became visibly affected, and he wondered how he could possibly make Queen Charlotte Sound and rendezvous with the *Resolution*. There was sufficient food aboard but drinking water was in short supply. Bayly wrote of Furneaux being 'terrified' and that he 'knew not what to do'. That was an exaggeration for Furneaux took his ship northwards to seek out a sheltered anchorage from where he hoped to see the storm out and revictual. On 9 November he anchored in Tolaga Bay which provided protection from the westerly gales.

The Maoris were friendly and generous, but Omai made no headway with their language. The best use was made of the time allowed for the storm to blow out by collecting wood and filling water casks. While working among the natives, a sailor saw something in the bottom of a canoe which rocked him back on his heels in horror. He called over the nearby Captain Furneaux who remembered it 'had the appearance of being alive'. It was a severed, mummified, woman's head, assumed or very much hoped to be the 'relict of some deceased relation'. Explaining the head away as a relative reassured the sailors, for long had been the debate among them and their officers about whether or not the Maoris were cannibals. The visitors were reasonably certain that cannibals did not eat their own relatives so, on the cannibal question the jury was still out. But not for much longer.

Furneaux spent from 12 November to the end of the month attempting to reach Queen Charlotte Sound but twice the sea forced him back to take refuge in Tolaga Bay. On the third occasion, the sloop was able to pass through Cook Strait but then, the storm died as suddenly as it had arisen and the *Adventure* was unable to go anywhere. On the last day of the month, the ship passed into Queen Charlotte Sound, anchoring at Ship Cove. Of the *Resolution* there was no sign. Sailors who went ashore to refill water casks found an inscription carved on the root of a large tree: 'Look underneath.' There, inside a bottle, Cook had outlined his intentions as at 24 November:

> As Captain Cook has not the least hope of meeting with Captain Furneaux he will not take upon him to name any place for a rendezvous; he however thinks of returning to Easter Island . . . in about the latter end of March, it is even probable that he may go to Otaheite or one of the Society Isles but this will depend so much upon circumstances that nothing with any degree of certainty can be depended upon.

Omai was present when the letter was read and found it beyond his comprehension that the paper could talk, describing what had happened and what was going to happen. From that point, Omai decided to learn to write but became overwhelmed by an outpouring of goodwill that offered him paper, pens and writing tasks. Within a week he had abandoned the effort as one aspiration too far, an aspiration which was probably beyond his ability. According to Johann Forster, never slow to criticise, the simpler discipline of learning the spoken word, presented insurmountable difficulties.

Omai's language, which is destitute of every harsh consonant and in which every word ends in a vowel, had so little exercised his vocal cords that they were wholly unfit to pronounce the more complicated English sounds; and this physical, or rather habitual, defect has too often been misunderstood.

While at Ship Cove, a number of the *Resolution*'s officers had gone ashore to stretch their limbs prior to the ship's imminent departure, delayed again by high winds. They stumbled into the butchered remains of a cannibal feast. On the ground lay a shattered, severed head among the inedible bowels of the victim. 'They do not eat heads', explained Anderson, 'but keep them and fix the eyes in the same staring position as when they advance to fight and in that manner sometimes dry them, at other times throwing away both that and the entrails but of the penis of the man they commonly make a musical pipe.'

Lieutenant Pickersgill offered two nails for the head which he took on board as a souvenir. Some Maoris on board took an interest in it but apparently only as a source of food, thereby contradicting Anderson. Suspecting that to be the case, Lieutenant Clerke asked the natives if they would like something carved from the head. They replied enthusiastically in the affirmative, whereupon Clerke cut off a slice of flesh which was broiled in the galley and enthusiastically devoured. It was at that moment that Cook came on board accompanied by Wales, Forster and Odiddy. Cook was not quite certain that he believed what he was hearing, so Clerke proved that what was said to be so was so by repeating the process. The ship's company stood by, sickened, as the other Maori ate part of the head. The strongest reaction came from Odiddy who burst into tears, remonstrating with both Clerke and the Maoris in the strongest Tahitian words possible. Although they did not understand the words, they did understand the sentiment behind them. Here, therefore, on HMS *Resolution* we see being played out part of the great debate which surrounded the whole question of the noble savage as surely as it was being heatedly discussed in the drawing rooms of England.

Wales concluded that these people were cannibals by choice not by obligation – they had more than sufficient food and had no need to eat their enemy slain in battle. Many would conclude that conduct such as this was uncivilised but Cook pointed out that the Maoris were to some degree civilised:

> their behaviour to us has been manly and mild, showing always a readiness to oblige us; they have some arts among them which they execute with great judgement and unwearied patience; they are far less addicted to thieving than the other Islanders and are I believe strictly honest among themselves. This custom of eating their enemies slain in battle (for I firmly believe they eat the flesh of no others) has undoubtedly been handed down to them from the earliest times and we know that it is not an easy matter to break a nation of its ancient customs.

Cook's problem was that he had had only the shortest of exposures to the habits and traditions of the Maoris. What precisely was battle? Did it include encounter conflict? And the claim on behalf of the Maoris of their manly and mild behaviour proved horribly premature.

It was Furneaux's intention to repair his ship and follow Cook down to the Antarctic. It was a good though unrealistic plan. In the meantime, work continued in the pleasant December weather to get the sloop ready for sea. The natives of Queen Charlotte Sound were all but forgotten, taken for granted that is, until two raids were launched upon the encampment. There came a time in any visit when the tipping point had been reached and overstaying one's welcome was not recommended. By 17 December the *Adventure* was ready to sail but, aware that Cook had controlled scurvy aboard his ship far better than Furneaux had on his, the *Adventure's* captain decided to send out one last foraging party in the large cutter to Grass Cove. The cove lies in the eastern arm of the Sound where anti-scorbutic wild celery was known to grow. Wild celery is a genuine celery, *apium prostratum*, and was collected with scurvy grass which the Maoris called nau, *lepidium oleraceum*. Furneaux sent one of his natives off at dawn with nine men, expecting them to return by mid-afternoon with quantities of wild celery. Twenty-four hours passed and they had not returned. Furneaux assembled another party under Burney's command which included armed marines and sailors and sent them in the launch to Grass Cove to investigate. When Burney returned at midnight, his account of what he discovered sent the ship's company into a frenzy, demanding vengeance.

> We went ashore and searched a canoe, where we found one of the rollock ports of the cutter, and some shoes, one of which was known to belong to Mr Woodhouse one of our midshipmen. One of the people at the same time brought me a piece of meat, which he took to be some of the salt meat belonging to the cutter's crew. On examining this and smelling it I found it was fresh. Mr Fannin who was with me, supposed it was dog's flesh and I was of the same

opinion; for I still doubted their being cannibals. But we were soon convinced by most horrid and undeniable proof.

The reconnaissance party discovered approximately twenty baskets tied up which they proceeded to open.

Some were full of roasted flesh and some of fern root, which serves them for bread. On further search we found more shoes, and a hand, which we immediately knew to have belonged to Thomas Hill, one of our fore-castlemen, it being marked T.H. with an Otaheite tattoo instrument.

Henry Lightfoot watched the launch return to the ship; clearly, something was very wrong. Inside the launch were: 'some remains of they people which had been all murdered and the greatest part eaten by they natives, some remains were brought on board which had been roasted except one foot and hand'.

Burney then took his party into Grass Cove where:

we found no boat, but instead of her such a shocking scene of carnage and barbarity as can never be mentioned or thought of but with horror; for the heads, hearts and lungs of several of our people were seen lying on the beach, and, at a little distance, the dogs gnawing their entrails.

The meat inside the baskets was still hot from the fires. Among the decapitated heads was that of the captain's black steward. Cannibals considered their victims' soles of feet and palms of hands particular delicacies. One chief insisted the victims' fingers be reserved for him.

On his third voyage to the South Pacific Cook made a point of investigating this massacre. He, Omai and a strong protection party went into Grass Cove. Omai was instructed to ask out of curiosity why their men had been killed. There are some variations to this theme but it appears that while the men were having a meal late in the afternoon, several natives stole some bread and fish which led to a struggle during the course of which two natives were shot dead.

Before the available muskets could be recharged, the sailors were overwhelmed by a mass of bodies, knocked out and killed.

There was a temptation to get among the natives but in the previous engagement the *Adventure* had lost over 10 per cent of her complement. Furneaux decided that risks were not to be encouraged.

On 19 December the name of Tetuby Homy aged twenty-two from Huahine was added to the muster roll. It was an opportunity to make up numbers and also to ensure that Omai would be due pay when the ship reached England. The sum amounted to £15 15s 6d.

On 23 December, the *Adventure* sailed from Queen Charlotte Sound, not touching land again until 19 March. The crew were deflated by the loss of friends, and there was no prospect of regaining contact with Cook. Sickness, damage to food stocks, the need for a refit and rest and recuperation for the crew saw the *Adventure* anchor in Table Bay, Cape of Good Hope. She was going home

During the voyage from New Zealand to Cape Town via Cape Horn, a distance of 8333 miles (13,000 km), Omai kept a respectful distance from Tobias Furneaux even though the captain invited him to his cabin. Forster's constant reminder that Omai was a commoner may account for this apparent diffidence, for Omai sought out and found companionship on the lower deck. We see a repeat of this apparent preference for the company of those of humble origin when he eventually returned home. Among the 'common seamen' he befriended was the armourer and, in view of his ultimate intentions, there may well have been logic in cultivating that particular friendship. However, at Cape Town, which was reached on 19 March 1774, Furneaux called Omai to come and see him. Inside the cabin he was fitted up with one of Furneaux's velvet suits and taken ashore with Furneaux into the smart Dutch city of thatched and whitewashed houses. The Cape was controlled by the Dutch East India Company whose immediate territory lay to the north of the town, almost a mile in circumference. They had opened up the hinterland to the north-east by almost four hundred miles. According to Tobias Furneaux, the land to the north of the town was 'laid out in the most pleasant walks shaded with large oak trees, within the squares, which are enclosed with myrtle, bay and oak hedges, so close that the eye cannot penetrate through, produces the greatest variety of garden stuff, they are rendered not only pleasing but useful'.

The size of government buildings surprised Omai, leaving such a lasting impression that when he was taken to Greenwich to see Wren's masterpiece he was underwhelmed by the experience.

Furneaux introduced Omai to the Governor, Baron Plattenburg, as a priest and was pleasantly surprised by his decorum and confidence. According to the Forsters, Omai denied his low rank, claiming to be 'an attendant upon the king'. Inside the two enclosures which served as the zoo, he was amazed to see giraffes and ostriches, just a small sample of the animal treasures of the vast African continent. The Cape Town experience was a curtain-raiser for his celebrity status, a preliminary to the longer exposure to the curious public of London. While at the Cape, Furneaux wrote to the secretary of the Admiralty to explain how he had parted company with the *Resolution* and also to tell of the massacre. A letter was also left for Captain Cook, to await his arrival. There is no mention of Furneaux having written to Banks and Solander but it is probable that he did in order to reassure Banks that his noble savage had not only survived the voyage but would shortly be in England.

In April 1774, as the *Adventure* began the final leg home, Cook arrived for a three-week stopover at Tahiti to recalibrate instruments at Point Venus, to revictual, rest and to return Odiddy to his home. Cook was pleased to observe that Oberea had regained some of her original confidence and that food was again abundant on the island. During the course of his three years' absence, Cook had proved conclusively that the armchair experts who insisted that Terra Australis Incognita lay somewhere out in the southern hemisphere were wrong.

The *Adventure* reached Spithead on 14 July 1774 after an absence of two years, one year less than Cook, completing the first east–west circumnavigation of the globe. Furneaux thereby became the first person to sail round the world in both directions. He took Omai to

London to introduce him to the Earl of Sandwich. At this point, Furneaux drops out of the Omai story. He may have gained a reputation for lax discipline but he did claim Tahiti in the name of the Crown and played an important part in mapping the coast of Tasmania. Cook would have preferred that his curiosity had taken him further, to discover whether Tasmania was joined to the mainland. That information could easily have been gathered. Burney, observing from the masthead, wrote in his journal, 'it appears very likely to me, that there is a passage between that [the southern part of New Holland] and Van Diemen's land [Tasmania]'.

Furneaux died a young man aged forty-eight without issue. We have a striking portrait to remember him by. When a descendant recently visited the Furneaux Islands, she gave the farmer who runs the small local museum a copy. 'He surveyed the picture for a long time while I waited for some such observation as: "My God, they were brave to set out to the other side of the world." Instead of which, all he eventually said was: "I must say he had very kissable lips." '

CHAPTER 6

Omai's New World

Those who had the right to vote in Britain in the second half of the eighteenth century were male and privileged. There were arguably four divisions to Britain's political structure. First there was George III and his supporters. The King, *arii*, enjoyed more power than Parliament ever intended but in comparison with the king or principal chief of Tahiti, his actual authority was significantly less. Next there were the land-owning Whigs, the *raatira*, who were joined seamlessly to the third group, the Tories. English land-owners exercised considerable power relative to the small number of land-owners in Tahiti. The greatest similarity between the two systems lay outside Parliament in the fourth group, the rump of the people, the disfranchised masses who compared reasonably well to Tahiti's lower class, the *manahune*.

In the same way that the *manahune* were kept under control by *taboos* and *rahui*, so too were Britain's working classes controlled by uncompromising law and an unforgiving feudal system. The defacement of a bridge by scratching initials upon the structure could lead to gaol, and being found with one of the squire's pheasants could lead to the sack or the immediate termination of a tenancy. The conundrum is how was Omai able to pole-vault out of *hoi polloi*, where he belonged, into the centre of English society? The answer is in two parts. First, Omai appeared to be perfectly willing to be presented by his sponsors as having a higher status at home than he actually enjoyed and, second, those of the aristocracy and intelligentsia who received him, did so because he was to them a totem, a curiosity representing the subject of a hot debate raging in the drawing rooms of the thinking classes.

British politics in action can be illustrated by drawing upon a cast of characters, three of whom were active participants in Omai's story. The three characters were George III, the fourth Earl of Sandwich, Dr Samuel Johnson and an outsider called upon here to act as the catalyst, Mr John Wilkes.

Wilkes was a forthright, lively soul, a satirist and publisher of a provocative, entertaining journal, the *North Britain,* which he used as a device to criticise the Establishment. On many occasions, Wilkes, a Member of Parliament, sailed very close to the wind, but it was his issue no. 45 in particular which upset the government, the King and his supporters so much that they had him incarcerated in the Tower of London. His crimes had been to draw public attention to Lord Bute's relationship with the dowager princess, to attack the government and to suggest that one aspiration outlined in the King's speech to Parliament was bogus. On the face of it, criticism such as this from a Member of Parliament does not seem unreasonable. Wilkes's imprisonment stirred the disfranchised to exercise their political muscles. When the mob went on the rampage it was often as a spontaneous reaction to something people felt offended their interests or their sense of natural justice. The professional caricaturist James Gilray's sentiments – anti-French, anti-Whig and anti-Rome – were precisely the type of popular combustibility to start the mob on the move. Covent Garden was also a regular target of the mob. Clever politicians, however, could milk and inflame the mob as a device to be used in the pursuit of their own interests. The imprisonment of Wilkes infuriated the populace, with the result that Wilkes was released on the grounds that his imprisonment had been a breach of Parliamentary privilege.

Samuel Johnson's dislike of Wilkes went beyond the man's radicalism. Why, he had had the effrontery to criticise an entry in Johnson's famous dictionary. The rehabilitation of Wilkes in Johnson's eyes began when he used his undoubted influence to secure the release of Johnson's black servant from the Royal Navy. Boswell decided to use this suggestion of a thaw in their relationship to engineer an intellectual reconciliation by bringing both men together across the dinner table. Dinner proved to be a great success with Johnson capitulating before Wilkes's oozing charm. According to Johnson, he thought Wilkes a good man. Edward Gibbon was a friend of Wilkes but, in his book, goodness and Wilkes were incompatible. Wilkes was 'a thorough going profligate in principle as in practice, his life stained with every vice and his conversation full of blasphemy and indecency'.

Wilkes's scurrilous observations on the behaviour of the King's mother was as good an indication as any that he was not numbered among the many who thought George III could do no wrong. On one occasion, Wilkes declined to join a card game with the excuse that he could not differentiate between a king and a knave. Witticisms such as this had a fair wind through the coffee houses of London so it was inevitable that someone would come forward to defend the King's honour. That person had also been the subject of Wilkes's witticisms but was none the less thought to have been Wilkes's friend – the fourth Earl of Sandwich. The Earl had famously said to Wilkes that he, Wilkes, would die either of the pox or on the gallows, to which Wilkes nonchalantly replied: 'That depends, my Lord, upon whether I embrace your mistress or your principles.'

Wilkes's wicked humour extended to the writing of a parody on Pope's *Essay on Man* entitled *Essay on Woman*. To say that this contribution to English literature was anything other than downright rude would be an understatement. However, Wilkes had his essay printed by a small, private press for the intended titillation of close friends 'whose morals', according to Fanny Burney, 'were in no more danger of being corrupted by a loose book than a Negro being tanned by a warm sun'. Somehow an unauthorised copy was acquired and leaked to ministers and, unbeknown to Wilkes, put by Sandwich before the House of Lords on the first day of its session. Sandwich stood in the House, reading out to their Lordships the most saucy parts and injecting pious comments for good measure. But it was an exercise which did not reflect well upon the presenter. It was common knowledge that only two weeks before both men had been singing bawdy songs in one of London's most disreputable clubs. Lord Despenser criticised Sandwich, saying that his performance had resembled 'Satan preaching against sin', but the numbers were with Sandwich and the *Essay* judged to be libellous and a breach of privilege.

Satirists were the great levellers of their time, dealing in truth and untruth, in verse, essay or cartoon. They sometimes acted as a beneficial bridge between benign opposition and the unrepresented masses. When Parliament ruled issue no. 45 of the *North Britain* to be seditious libel to be seized and burned, the mob interceded and burnt as a *quid pro quo* a boot and a petticoat, symbolic of the third Earl of Bute and the King's mother. The *North Britain* was in reality the Earl of Bute. Mob activity made George III nervous, particularly since riots in one form or another had become a regular feature of the political scene. The Commons expelled Wilkes and declared him an outlaw.

Sandwich's treatment of Wilkes was exceptional, out of the ordinary for someone widely regarded as jovial, good-humoured and with a reputation for 'being careful not to offend public decorum'. He was fun-loving, an accomplished percussionist and sponsor of music appreciation, sufficiently intellectual to draw the intelligentsia as well as other friends to the many dinner parties he hosted at the Admiralty. The great sadness in Sandwich's life had been the break-down of his marriage to his eccentric wife. Divorce at this time was permissible only by private Act of Parliament, a route effectively closed for someone of Sandwich's status and reputation. His interest in music brought him by chance to a face-to-face meeting with Martha Ray, a seventeen-year-old milliner's apprentice, who became his mistress. He became besotted, and was devoted to this girl who had an exceptional voice. Sandwich paid for voice coaching and before long his protégée became the compulsory soloist at his country home, Hinchingbrooke, in the County of Huntingdon, to the north of London.

They lived together openly for seventeen years, having five surviving children. Their relationship became accepted by close friends but this was an age when relationships outside marriage were tolerated only when they remained covert. It was Sandwich's refusal, possibly because he did not have the funds, to make a financial settlement to give Martha peace of mind which led to the affair ending in tragedy.

Sandwich numbered among his good friends Dr Charles Burney whom he had come to know through a shared love of music. It was Charles Burney who introduced his friend Dr John Hawkesworth to Sandwich, who required 'a proper person to write the voyage' of the *Endeavour*. What Sandwich was looking for was an author he could commission to produce the official history not only of the voyage of the *Endeavour* but also of those that had preceded Cook into the Pacific and Polynesia – Byron, Carteret and Wallis – with support drawn from Banks's papers. Hawkesworth reassured Sandwich: 'I promise your Lordship that not an hour shall be bestowed upon any other object till the account is finished, either of business or pleasure.' Public interest had already been raised by an unofficial account of the voyage of the *Endeavour*. The Admiralty wanted the record put straight but that is not what Hawkesworth achieved. His *Account of the Voyages . . . For Making Discoveries in the Southern Hemisphere*, published in June 1773, stimulated the great debate of the relative values and merits of civilised and uncivilised lands but it was also panned for the liberties Hawkesworth took with the narrative. Horace Walpole thought *Voyages* 'might make one a good first mate, but tell one nothing at all'. Johnson dismissed *Voyages* even before having read it:

JOHNSON: Sir, if you talk of it as a subject of commerce, it will be gainful; if as a book that is to increase human knowledge, I believe there will be not much of that. Hawkesworth can tell only what the voyagers told him; and they have found very little, only one new animal, I think.

BOSWELL: But many insects, Sir.

JOHNSON: Why, Sir, as to insects, Ray reckons of British insects twenty thousand species. They might have stayed at home and discovered enough in that way.

What *Voyages* served to do was to raise heat rather than shed light. What John Hawkesworth was telling the British people fell beyond their comprehension and many became angered by what they read. A procession of satirical essays and pamphlets flowed from the pens of inflammatory authors who may have resented Hawkesworth's £7000 in fees for his three volumes going to him and not to them. A spoof *Epistle from Oberea, Queen of Tahiti, to Joseph Banks Esq* focused upon the erotic and an alleged affair between Oberea and Banks. Small wonder that she should have such a prominent role on the London stage. In *An Epistle From Mr Banks, Voyager, Monster-hunter, and Amoroso to Oberea, Queen of Tahiti*, Banks takes full responsibility for seducing Oberea:

> Carv'd is thy name upon the bread-tree's rind?
> Thy face, thy soul, are carv'd upon my mind;
> And, well I ween, blest produce of thy charms,
> My image lives and prattles in thy arms.

Another satirical ventriloquist even found cause in 1773 to resurrect Joseph Banks's jilted English rose, Miss Harriet Blosset, from the solitude of her Lincolnshire sanctuary, attributing to her *An Heroic Epistle from the Injured Harriet, Mistress to Mr Banks, to Oberea Queen of Tahiti*. He had the spurned Harriet, a lady of unquestionable pedigree, describing Queen Oberea in crude terms one of which was 'savage slut'. Joseph Banks had the good sense to remain above these commentaries.

Hawkesworth's sometimes lascivious *Voyages* therefore attracted considerable attention for the wrong reasons. The author used a certain amount of author's licence so that *Voyages* was not an entirely accurate account of the circumnavigators' voyages. It did, however, offend moralists and stimulate those enchanted by what they were led to believe Tahiti had to offer. The work divided in two those in society who had an opinion about it: the interventionists as exemplified by

Boswell and the non-interventionists as exemplified by Johnson. Interventionists based their arguments for wider exploration and presence in Polynesia upon commerce, prestige, evangelism and curiosity. Non-interventionists took the view that life in their sophisticated society was as good as it gets and nothing was to be either gained or learned by civilised people having harmful adventures in the territory of savages. This became a commission John Hawkesworth wished he had never undertaken. His premature death in November 1773 was attributed to an attack of fever but, according to Fanny Burney, he had been crushed by criticism.

The *Endeavour* debate interested George III. Cook and Banks both had audiences with him. Few of Britain's monarchs are as under-appreciated as the country's longest-serving king who, over a sixty-year period, lowered the barriers established by the Hanoverians between them and their subjects. George III is best remembered in England for the 'madness' which kept him hidden from the public for the last nine years of his life; and in both England and America as the reigning king when British colonials in America fought for self-determination and independence. Technically, the King was not insane but bore all the symptoms of insanity. In all probability he suffered the terrible consequences of porphyria, a physical and hereditary disease. The loss of America cut him to the quick. The accusation in the Declaration of Independence that he was 'unfit to be the ruler of a free people' hurt. The protocol whereby his subjects spoke only when spoken to ensured that this was not a subject discussed at Court. However, it cannot be said that his own subjects were a free people since they too were shackled, restrained from achieving complete freedom. One reason why Britain was not visited by the same form of revolution as convulsed France was due to George III's openness and the consequent warm regard in which he was held by the majority of his subjects, a veritable Father of the People.

Leaving aside the manner in which the King established a personal government and manipulated politics, he had a high sense of morality, respect for learning and a particular interest in agriculture. His was an active patronage of the Royal Society and the Royal Academy of Arts. He founded the Royal Agricultural College at Cirencester. His personal interest in farming earned him the sobriquet 'Farmer George'. His great interest in people and events, his common touch and his decision often taken on the spur of the moment to 'go walkabout' caused concern among those responsible for his security, particularly since he had suffered two attempts on his life. He lived through the Age of Enlightenment, a fertile period for the arts and sciences due principally to his interest and leadership. Music played an important part in the lives of King and Queen, both of whom loved the harpsichord, but this was not their only shared interest. The fecund Queen, formerly Princess Charlotte of Mecklenburg-Strelitz, produced fifteen children.

At the time when George III came to give an audience to Omai he had not completely overcome his shyness of meeting people and few could have been stranger than Omai. During audiences, the King did not stand still. He moved around the centre of the room, ending each question with 'what, what?' He also had a disconcerting habit, after greeting a foreigner, of enquiring of the visitor when he or she intended to leave the country – almost certainly an affectation caused by his shyness and his search for polite conversation. The association of arrival with departure is significant because it meant that in the King's mind there would have been the anticipation of Omai's eventual return to Tahiti. This fact could have been laden with consequences because the King was interested in colonisation and the benefits thereby that were likely to accrue to Britain. Tahiti would have been of particular interest to him since the island bore his name. If the requests made by Tahiti's monarch between 1822 and 1841 for Tahiti to become a British protectorate had been made during any but the last years of the reign of George III, which ended in 1820, today's inhabitants would in all probability be speaking English, not French. The possibility of Omai becoming a friend of Britain in the Tahitian Court would have occurred to the King. There is some clue here as to how Omai had been introduced to the

King, whether in the persona of a priest or prince. Circumstances suggest the latter, thereby underlining a very unfortunate misunderstanding, since the King is unlikely to have presented a sword to a priest or peasant. The King would have been quite relaxed about and thought unexceptional the eventual return of a prince to his own people and way of life.

Streatham Park, today deep in the suburbs of South London, home of Mrs Hester Thrale, the most successful literary hostess of the day, is one of the places where the noble savage debate would have had a full airing. Regular visitors included Oliver Goldsmith, Edmund Burke, Boswell, Johnson, Joshua Reynolds and Fanny Burney. When the latter joined the circle aged twenty-six she was thought to have missed the opportunity to be married. There could be no higher social accolade than to receive an invitation to join this exclusive circle, among whom were the so-called Blue Stockings, ladies of distinguished pedigree, wealth and influence. This was the chattering class of the eighteenth century. It is unlikely that Mrs Thrale would have been such a successful hostess were it not for the support and presence of Dr Samuel Johnson. Their purely platonic friendship was so firmly established that Johnson had his own room permanently available at Streatham Park. Johnson cannot be described as handsome, but as somewhat large and misshapen, an unlikely lover. He was also thirty-five years older than Hester Thrale. Theirs was an intimate friendship. Boswell scorned her modest literary efforts because he resented her friendship with Johnson and felt he was in literary competition with her. Boswell's friendship with Johnson was the most important thing in his life. When Mr Thrale died, the middle-aged Hester chose a younger man, an Italian singer and musician, becoming Mrs Thrale Piozzi. Johnson was unimpressed; some would say devastated.

Samuel Johnson was one of the most influential men of his time, seemingly presiding over the events of the day like some latter-day Nero at the Colosseum, giving a thumbs-up or thumbs-down after due consideration of situations put to him. His friendship with the

Burneys, Banks and Solander kept him *au fait* with events in the Pacific. He would speak well of Omai, despite having reservations about the man's virtues, and he became positively critical of Cook's voyages to the Pacific, 'lands of unprovided wretchedness'. People were beginning to ask in what kind of Arcadia was there nobility in infanticide and human sacrifice and precisely what benefit were the savages deriving from civilised contact? 'Much knowledge has been acquired', said Johnson, 'and much cruelty has been committed; the belief of religion has been very little propagated, and its laws have been outrageously and enormously violated.' Boswell came to enthuse over Omai and what he represented, cautiously dismissing Johnson's lack of enthusiasm as a reaction to the popularity of the contemporary cult of primitivism.

The very different perceptions and opinions of these two friends summarised the prevailing cultural uncertainties and the new unanswered questions as to the nature of mankind. Their conflicting views were a fair representation of the polarisation of opinion. Europe's Age of Enlightenment rose to its zenith in the 1780s. It was not a phenomenon to which all were persuaded, being essentially identified with radical intellectualism, but that too is not a precise categorisation. All light casts shadow and for every radical intellectual there was at least one detractor. Progressives absorbed the weight of seemingly endless new information and scientific discovery to reflect their changing attitude to a changing world. They positively enthused over the prospect of examining the Tahitian way of life in anticipation that they might learn and adapt their own way of life should it prove necessary and beneficial to do so. Conservatives saw the wind of change as an undesirable, irrelevant phenomenon, a challenge to Christianity even. Many attempted to ignore the multiplicity of information being brought home on the increasingly frequent voyages of discovery. They closed their collective minds to the possibility that anything gainful might be learned to challenge the European conviction of pre-eminence and superiority. These people could also be very unpleasant and uncompromising.

De Bougainville's introduction to *A Voyage Round the World* began: 'I am a voyager and a seaman; that is a liar and a stupid fellow, in the eyes of that class of indolent, haughty writers, who in their closets reason ad infinitum on the world and its inhabitants, and with an air of superiority confine nature within the limits of their own invention.'

As we have seen, armchair theoreticians took the popular view that the land mass of the northern hemisphere *must* be balanced by an equivalent hemisphere in the south and the proof, or otherwise, became the principal purpose of Cook's second voyage. Endemic cynicism was partly the reason why the activities of the voyagers were refereed by a team of on-board geographers and scientists. Nevertheless, people believed what they wanted to believe. A Scots academic writing to Banks said how much he was looking forward to Hawkesworth's narrative of the South Sea voyages: 'If you knew how many foolish and lying books of travel I have read, you would not wonder at my impatience.' How Banks's friend would have known Hawkesworth's work to be the embodiment of truth is not known. The truth would have disappointed him.

Neither the progressive nor the conservative sides of the argument were ever well founded. There simply was insufficient information. This was not a factor that would have prevented Boswell and Johnson from arguing the relative merits of breadfruit as compared to their own bread when neither had any experience of the former. These diametrically opposed perceptions meant that Omai was likely to face hostility from those inclined to the view that there was nothing to be learned from either him or his people.

Boswell attempted to argue for the superiority of savage life. Johnson would have none of it.

Sir, there can be nothing more false. The savages have no bodily advantages beyond those of civilised men. They have not better health; and as to care and mental uneasiness, they are not above it, but below it, like bears. No, Sir, you are not to talk such paradox: let me have no more of it. It cannot entertain, far less instruct.

William Cowper could be counted on the side of Johnson. In his poem *The Task* he asks of Omai, 'gentle savage', whether he has observed:

With what superior skill we can abuse
The gifts of providence and squander life.

Johnson's argument had left Boswell unconvinced and in returning to the subject, Boswell expressed his personal aspiration to go to Tahiti or New Zealand for three years. 'What could you learn, Sir?' retorted Johnson.

What can savages tell, but what they themselves have seen? Of the past, or the invisible, they can tell you nothing. The inhabitants of Tahiti and New Zealand are not in a state of pure nature; for it is plain they broke off from some other people. Had they grown out of ground, you might have judged a state of nature.

Boswell pressed on.

BOSWELL: I am well assured that the people of Tahiti who have the bread tree, the fruit which serves them for bread, laughed heartily when they were informed of the tedious process necessary with us to have bread – ploughing, sowing, harrowing, reaping, threshing, baking.

Johnson: Why, Sir, all ignorant savages will laugh when they are told the advantages of civilised life. Were you to tell men who live without houses how we pile brick upon brick and rafter upon rafter, and that after a house is raised to a certain height, a man tumbles off and breaks his neck; they would laugh heartily at our folly in building; but it does not follow that men are better without houses. No, Sir, (holding up a slice of good loaf), this is better than the bread tree.

BOSWELL: I do not think the people of Tahiti can be reckoned savages.

JOHNSON: Don't cant in defence of savages.

BOSWELL: They have the art of navigation.
JOHNSON: A dog or cat can swim.
BOSWELL: They carve very ingeniously.
JOHNSON: A cat can scratch and a child with a nail can scratch.

Omai's arrival in England provided a unique opportunity to observe the noble savage at close hand and to test related theories, both spoken and written. Native specimens had been brought to England from the time of Henry VIII but more recently it had been the lot of unsuspecting Red Indians and Eskimos.

One group of Eskimos which came to England in December 1772 in the care of the naturalist George Cartwright was relevant to the Omai experience by virtue not only of propinquity but also because of lessons identified. The party was led by a man named Attuiock, described, perhaps improbably, as a priest. He was accompanied by his wife and child and his brother with his wife. Compared with Omai's relatively low-key introduction, their arrival in London came in the full glare of publicity. They were sought after by society, dined at the Royal Society, fêted with a specially commissioned performance at Covent Garden and introduced at Court. Interest in them was not confined to fashionable circles but applied equally to the man in the street. When they arrived at Westminster Bridge they were mobbed by a pressing, curious crowd. It was strange that Londoners' curiosity about them was not reciprocated by the visitors. Such a complete lack of interest would have been a disappointment to those who placed so much store by contemporary achievements.

They were shown London Bridge but assumed it to be a natural phenomenon in the same way that they saw nothing out of the ordinary in Wren's still pristine white Portland stone St Paul's Cathedral. Inventive to the last, Cartwright decided to dress Attuiock in English attire and take him in disguise on a tour of the sights of interest of the world's largest city, showing him the Tower of London and Hyde Park Corner. Back at his lodgings, the Eskimo was asked if he had ever seen anything quite like it. Attuiock regretted that the

2 Playbill for the first performance of 'Omai, or, A trip around the World', 20 December 1785 (*British Library*)

3 William Hodges (1744–97): 'A General View of the Island of Otaheite' (*National Maritime Museum, London*)

4 G.T. Boult: 'View of Matavai Bay in Otaheite, taken from One Tree Hill'
(*National Library of Australia*)

5 John Webber (1752–93): 'A View inland of Matavai, Otaheite'
(*National Library of Australia*)

6 Philippe Jacques de Loutherbourg
(1740–1812): 'Obereyau
[i.e. Oberea] Enchantress'
(*National Library of Australia*)

obereyau Enchantress

7 M.A. Rooker (1746–1801):
'Oberea's Great Marae, Papara'

8 Francesco Bartolozzi (1727–1815): 'A view of the inside of a house in the island of Ulietea [Raiatea], with the representation of a dance to the music of the country' (*National Library of Australia*)

9 William Hodges (1744–97): 'Review of the War Galleys at Tahiti' (*National Maritime Museum, London*)

10 Nathaniel Dance (1735–1811): 'Captain James Cook, 1728–79'
    (*National Maritime Museum, London*)

11 Samuel William Reynolds (1773–1835) after Sir Joshua Reynolds (1723–92): 'Sir Joseph Banks, Bart.' (*National Library of Australia*)

12 Valentine Green (1739–1813) after Johann Zoffany (1733–1810): 'John Montagu, Earl of Sandwich, Viscount Hinchingbrook [*sic*], First Lord Commissioner of the Admiralty' (*National Library of Australia*)

13 John Hamilton Mortimer (1741–79): 'Captain James Cook, Sir Joseph Banks, Lord Sandwich and Two Others' (*National Library of Australia*)

14 William Hodges (1744–97): 'HMS 'Resolution' and 'Adventure' with Fishing Craft in Matavai Bay' (*National Maritime Museum, London*)

15 William Hodges (1744–97):
'Otoo [Tu], King of Otaheite'
(*National Library of Australia*)

16 James Caldwall (1739–1820)
after William Hodges
(1744–97): 'Omai'
(*National Library of Australia*)

17 John Cleveley (*c.* 1745–86): 'A View of Matavai Bay' (*National Library of Australia*)

18 John Webber (1752–93): 'View in Queen Charlotte's Sound [Ship Cove], New Zealand' (*National Library of Australia*)

19 John Webber (1752–93):
'A Portrait of Poedua'
(*National Library of Australia*)

20 James Northcote (1746–1831):
'Captain Tobias Furneaux'
(*Private collection*)

21 'Omaih the Indian from
   Otaheite presented to
   their Majesties at Kew
   by Mr Banks and
   Dr Solander' (*National
   Library of Australia*)

22 Whipcord: 'The Fly
   Catching Macaroni'
   [Joseph Banks] (*National
   Library of Australia*)

23 Sir Joshua Reynolds (1723–92):
'Omai of the Friendly Isles'
(*National Library of Australia*)

24 Francesco Bartolozzi (1727–1815)
after Nathaniel Dance (1735–1811):
'Omai, a Native of Ulaietea,
Brought into England in the Year
1774 by Tobias Furneaux'
(*National Library of Australia*)

An account of the Bills for Omai

	£	s	D
Taylor's Bill	66	10	0
Linnen Draper's Do	20	0	6
Hosier's	9	16	0
Shoemaker's	7	17	0
Hatter's	3	5	6
A Box for his Clothes	0	6	6
Two Drums	4	0	0
Two Prints King & Queen	2	12	6
Tin Ware &c	19	8	4
Ironmonger's Bill	20	7	7
Wine Merchant's Bill	12	4	0
For Toys	3	17	6
Beads	10	2	4
	182	8	3
Odiddee's Bill	46	16	3
	229	4	0
Two Suits of Ladies Clothes compleat			

25 William Parry (1742–91): 'Omai, Sir Joseph Banks and Daniel Charles Solander' (*National Portrait Gallery, London*)

26 Sir Joseph Banks (1743–1820), Papers: An account of the bills for Omai (*National Library of Australia*)

27 William Hodges (1744–97): 'Vaitepiha Bay' (*National Maritime Museum, London*)

28 'Omai's Public Entry on His First Landing at Otaheite' (*National Library of Australia*)

29 William Woollett (1735–85): 'A human sacrifice in a morai in Otaheite' [James Cook and Omai in attendance] (*National Library of Australia*)

30 Francis Jukes (1746–1812) after John Cleveley (*c.* 1745–86): 'View of Huaheine, One of the Society Islands in the South Seas' [The square building under construction, left of centre, is Omai's home] (*National Library of Australia*)

experience had not been one of his life's pivotal moments. He thought there were too many houses; he did not appreciate the smoke or the crush of people. Essentially he was missing his Labrador home where there was space to breathe and where seals were plentiful. Cartwright thereupon decided to take his Eskimos off to his father's country home in Nottinghamshire, which was more to their liking. The local hunt invited them out and foxhunting soon became a favourite activity.

The presence of the Eskimos in England proved to be of irresistible interest to Banks and Solander. Banks had seen none of these natives during his anticlimactic visit to the land of ice and snow. They called at the group's lodgings bearing the standard collection of beads and baubles associated with people of primitive origin. The by now obligatory portraits were commissioned, to leave for posterity a memento of the Eskimos' visit to English shores. Thereafter, Banks and Solander became regular visitors. It had always been Cartwright's intention to take Attuiock and his family home after their exposure to England. By May, it was clear that the time had come to fulfil their wish to see their homeland again. Prior to boarding at Plymouth, Attuiock's young sister-in-law complained of feeling unwell. She had contracted an extremely contagious viral disease, the symptoms of which were a high fever and the appearance of a rash on her face and extremities. It was not long before her relatives were similarly affected, thereby obliging Cartwright to terminate the voyage and return to Plymouth. Although the young woman survived, all her accompanying relatives died, killed by the same disease as had accounted for Aoutourou – smallpox.

Smallpox was endemic in England at this time but these noble savages with no defensive immunity were particularly vulnerable to it. Much medical research was dedicated to finding a cure for smallpox in the same way that today priority research is devoted to finding cures for cancer and Aids. Those able to pay for treatment in late eighteenth-century England thought it worth taking the risk of placing themselves in the hands of a man named Dr Thomas Dimsdale who had an

Inoculation Institute at Hertford, thirty miles from London. Dimsdale developed a system which had originated in Turkey and involved the inoculation of his patients with smallpox, a very risky business lest the process run out of control. It was not until 1796 that Edward Jenner developed a less dangerous vaccine extracted from the infectious scabs of the milder but related cowpox.

Banks had been immunised against smallpox at the age of seventeen. The existence of the Dimsdale treatment was well known in scientific circles for Dimsdale published his definitive work in 1767. His paper caught the attention of the Empress Catherine of Russia who invited him to St Petersburg in 1768 to inoculate her and her son. Concern lest the treatment should kill the Empress resulted in a planned relay system of fast horses to carry the doctor beyond the Russian border and the hands of those who might wish him ill. This contingency plan was not needed. Both inoculations proved successful and the grateful Empress paid Dimsdale £12,000, an annuity of £500 for life, an hereditary Russian barony and other valuable rewards.

Omai was different in so far as he was the living representative of Rousseau's 'natural man', thereby attracting an instant claim to topicality. Polynesia excited the public's imagination and Omai was its first representative to visit England. He was a curiosity but it was not so curious that this man of few intelligible words should be so readily received by aristocrats and into Mrs Thrale's literary circle. He undoubtedly had novelty value but his welcoming reception cannot be attributed entirely to that fact. What the literati and aristocracy found appealing were his manners, his courtesy and a vanity no less intense than their own. However, this was not a society that he was familiar with and it is from this point that he became disorientated and detached from reality. His expectations were unreasonably high but he could not be assimilated as he would have wished back at his place of birth. He became the foremost casualty of a social experiment that paid scant regard to its consequences. His presence in England for two short years had a profound impact upon romantic literature and inspired writers long after his repatriation and premature death. His fame was not limited to Britain but also spread into and through France whose people found in his record proof either for or against the philosophy of Rousseau. He may have been an obscure, insignificant individual who allowed himself to be drawn into a new world to which he neither belonged nor comprehended, but in making the journey, he left behind a lasting impression.

CHAPTER 7

Curiouser and Curiouser

Omai, who had originally embarked aboard the *Adventure* as a person of little consequence, disembarked at Spithead described by some as a Tahitian priest and now, by others, as a Tahitian prince. In his letter to a friend, Solander wrote of how he imagined Omai's departure from Raiatea to have been: 'He had four servants who all endeavoured to persuade [him] from going, so did also the king of Ulaietea [Raiatea], but Omai was resolute.'

Meanwhile there had been changes of circumstance and new influences upon the life of Joseph Banks, scientist and extrovert. The first was Rousseau's distancing of himself from his earlier association with primitive man and the establishing of a new, related concept awaiting empirical appraisal. Rousseau's new thinking had in effect prepared the ground for the arrival of Omai:

> but that living in the whirl of social life it is enough that he should not let himself be carried away by passions and prejudices of men; let him see with his eyes and feel with his own heart, let him own no sway but that of reason. The same man who would remain stupid in forests should become wise and reasonable in towns, if he were merely a spectator in them.

Here, therefore, was the challenge of a new anthropological experiment for which Omai was the first and only suitable test candidate.

If we link to this Banks's own circumstances, it can be understood why he and Solander should now attach so much importance to spending time with Omai. During the course of Cook's second voyage, Banks had visited Iceland and the Netherlands where he had made some interesting discoveries but these locations had none of the attractions of the South Seas. Arrangements with Furneaux ensured that a number of South Pacific artefacts did come back with the *Adventure* but these in themselves were insufficient to rekindle the waning interest in Banks and his tired collection from Cook's first voyage. Horace Walpole underlined this fact in a letter written the previous week, his pen dipped in *schadenfreude*, to Sir Horace Mann: 'Africa is, indeed coming into fashion. There is just returned a Mr Bruce, who has lived three years in the Court of Abyssinia, and breakfasted every morning with the Maids of Honour on live oxen. Otaheite and Mr Banks are quite forgotten.'

In Omai lay the promise of a change in fortune, the perfect foil with which to investigate the nature of man. Banks had repaired his relationship with Sandwich, which was just as well because the latter established himself as Omai's agent in so far as Omai was the Royal Navy's man. Access was through Sandwich.

Furneaux arrived in London with Omai on the night of 14 July. Next morning the pair reported to the First Lord at the Admiralty. Sandwich immediately sent a message to Banks's house at New Burlington Street recommending that he should make haste and come to Sandwich's office in the Admiralty building. Banks, accompanied by Solander and his servant, quickly responded. They encountered Furneaux in an adjoining office and soon became engaged in animated conversation. Omai, waiting in an outer office, heard voices which he recognised, and went through to investigate. Solander described the individual before them as 'not above 21 or 22 years old . . . He is very brown, almost as brown as a mulatto'. Tahitian nobility had pale skin.

Not at all handsome but well made. His nose is a little broadish, and I believe we have to thank his wide nostrils for the visit he has paid us – for he says that the people of his own country laughed at him upon the account of his flatish nose and dark hue, but he hopes when he returns and has so many fine things to talk of, that he shall be much respected.

It is apparent from this meeting not just how much Omai had positioned himself in the centre of events during Cook's first visit to Tahiti but also how he had been overshadowed by the older, more presentable, Tupia. 'He still was a boy', explained Solander, 'and not so remarkable as to make us remember him, but he perfectly well remembered all of us who had been there.' Omai recognised Banks immediately despite his having no powder in his hair and their meeting having been three years ago. 'I hear Tolano's [Solander's] voice', said Omai, but he did not recognise the scientist who, previously having been on short commons, had now returned to his usual, fuller figure. He walked round Solander, eyeing him suspiciously but thinking himself to be mistaken. Then he had the idea of asking Furneaux to invite Solander to say a few words. No sooner had Solander spoken than Omai was certain he was Tolano and before long all four were conversing in Tahitian of sorts. Omai bade Furneaux farewell and with Sandwich's agreement accepted accommodation in Banks's house.

Another person to have witnessed the reunion was Dr Charles Burney who had called on Sandwich for news of his son Jem. He told daughter Fanny what he had seen and heard and she in turn told her sister Susan. Burney reported having seen Omai still dressed in native attire, a very good-looking man with 'an interesting countenance'. He spoke little English and it appears that Banks and Solander had forgotten most of the Tahitian they had learnt. Dr Burney was delighted to hear that Jem had been rated the most fluent of the *Adventure*'s crew. After being introduced as Jem's father, Omai shook hands and repeated the name, 'Bunny! Bunny!' Furneaux explained how fond Omai was of Burney 'who spent a great part of his time in studying the language with him'.

Within three days of his arrival, an audience had been arranged for Omai to be presented to the King and Queen at Kew. A tailor was called immediately to make a maroon velvet coat, a white silk waistcoat and grey satin knee breeches. This was one of a number of bills submitted by tailors for kitting out a native who very quickly became intensely fashion-conscious, an improbable dandy. Over this short period, Omai rehearsed his bowing and practised a speech sufficiently short to be learnt by heart.

On 17 July, Banks and Solander escorted Omai to the modest palace at Kew which had become home to the King and Queen. Banks had been responsible for finding many of the exotic plants in the royal garden. (In the same way that bougainvillea is named after de Bougainville, banksia is named after Banks.)

By all accounts the King was pleased to meet this, the first representative from an island bearing his name, and he perhaps saw Omai as a useful foil to counter the expansionist desires of his enemies in the Pacific. It was Solander who admitted that it was not the intention of the English to force themselves upon the people of Tahiti but to treat Omai well and send him home and in that manner 'will we suppose make them our friends in a much more humane and agreeable manner'. The conclusion to be drawn from such an assumption is that Solander was unaware of Omai's actual social position for he would otherwise have known that such an aspiration would be untenable within Tahiti's own formal aristocracy.

Omai's audience with the King pre-dated by nine months the skirmish on Lexington Common when a colonial in Captain John Parker's company fired the 'shot heard round the world' at Major John Pitcairn's British advance guard. Meanwhile at Kew a more convivial meeting was taking place. One version of this meeting described Omai as being exceedingly nervous as he was led before the King, fearful that he might be eaten. His practised, elegantly executed, low bow passed off as intended, whereupon he took the King's proffered hand, forgot his rehearsed speech, saying simply 'Howdo! King Tosh!' He had no 'G' and therefore 'Tosh' was the best rendition he could manage of George. It sounds plausible but despite its popular appeal was probably untrue. Another account ascribes to Omai a fluency in

English which he did not possess. 'He was much struck at first, and soon made a speech to His Majesty to the following effect: "Sir, you are King of England, Tahiti, Raiatea and Bora Bora: I am your subject and am come here for gunpowder to destroy the inhabitants of Bora Bora, who are your enemies." '

George III gave Omai a warm welcome, presenting a sword which Omai adeptly fixed to his belt as though he had long been used to such practice. Obviously concerned for Omai's health and being well acquainted with the loss of Aoutourou and Cartwright's Eskimos to smallpox, the King recommended Omai's inoculation, for which he would pay the requisite fee. He granted Omai an allowance for the duration of his visit and gave a promise of a homeward voyage. Banks undertook all Omai's travel and subsistence costs when they travelled together though the tailoring bills, which were many, were the responsibility of the Admiralty. No sooner had the audience concluded than Banks began to make arrangements to take Omai to Hertford for his consultation with Dr Thomas Dimsdale.

The newspapers, at first slow to record the arrival of one of the South Pacific's 'savages', made up for this in sheer volume of print. The detail was at times found wanting: the *Adventure* was described in some newspapers as the *Endeavour*, captained by Captain Fonnereau. Within a week, though, the press contacted insiders who were more or less *au fait* with the passage of events. Omai's audience was widely reported, particularly his lack of inhibition before the King, and already at this early juncture invitations flowed in 'from many people of the first rank'.

As soon as editors realised the opportunities offered by the Omai story, little imagination was required to exploit the various angles. The association with Banks was guaranteed to sell copy. The caricaturist Mathew Darly found Banks an irresistible source for ridicule. His caricature, '*The Fly-Catching Macaroni*', established a standard for the day – Macaroni being a pejorative word to describe social dandies who had been on the Grand Tour of Italy. The more famous James Gillray took over the baiting of Banks, and throughout his life Banks was reminded in print of his association with Oberea. The public were now told that Oberea was in decline, having 'retired to the country'. For her part, Oberea would have been surprised but none the less flattered that she was well nigh universally known in the homes of educated Britons.

Political journalists on the *London Chronicle* used the Omai story to attack the social wrongs in the country. A ploy frequently used was to write a story or letter as though it had come from the individual in the news, in this case the 'savage' Omai, alias *Otaheite*. 'You had better have said, that all those who are not conversant with European manners are savages; for your definition, sir, is as injurious as it is unjust.' Gossip columnists followed Omai's progress, reporting where he had been and those people with whom he had been associated. Banks wrote to his sister, Sarah Sophia, an intelligent, religious spinster, apologising for not having replied to her letters. He said that she would have seen from the newspapers that the *Adventure* 'is arrived and has brought an Indian from the South Sea Islands. He has been put by the Admiralty under my care as I received so many marks of friendship from his countrymen.' Sarah Banks thereafter caught the same infectious enthusiasm for Omai and what he represented as her brother. For several months she wrote a series of memoranda on the 'South Sea Islander'.

For Banks, therefore, the opportunity to take Omai away to a place of isolation where he and Solander could enjoy exclusive access to him proved serendipitous. The Duke and Duchess of Gloucester were of such rank that Banks was unable to decline their royal summons to Omai for dinner on Thursday, 21 July. The Duke was a younger brother of George III. The Duchess, daughter of Sir Edward Walpole, was said to have been an outstanding beauty – so much so that Reynolds is believed to have painted her seven times. Also present was the competing social *lyon* (or lion), Mr Bruce, who had recently returned to England from Abyssinia. The lions were more or less elected by *les bas bleus* and their peeresses and were distinguished men of exceptional interest, a curiosity not so much for who they were as for what they had done. Eighteenth-century noble ladies adored 'lion hunting', as is evident from the comment of Hannah Moore: 'Mrs Garrick and I were invited to a fine assembly at Mrs Thrale's. There was to be a fine concert, and all the fine people were to be there; but the chief attraction was to meet the Brahmin and the two Parsees . . . but just as my hair was dressed came a servant to forbid our coming, for that Mr Thrale was dead.' Mr Thrale, a brewer, had been Mrs Thrale's senior by thirteen years.

There were at the time three principal social lions doing the rounds and highly sought after as guests in the most genteel company. One, a bejewelled Russian, never became more than an outsider. 'The present Lyon of the times', wrote Fanny Burney, 'is Omai, the native of Otaheite; and next to him, the present object is Mr Bruce, a gentleman who has been abroad twelve years.' Fanny had met David Bruce who had travelled in Africa. He had called at Queen Square, accompanied by a friend of the Burney family, Miss Strange. Her opinion of the man was mixed, not to say confused. 'His adventures are very marvellous . . . he is the tallest man I ever saw (six feet four inches) and exceedingly well made . . . he is a very manly character and looks so dauntless and intrepid, so that I believe he could never in his life know what fear meant.' This would appear to be a vote of approval but such an assumption would be misleading: 'I cannot say I was charmed with him; for he seems rather arrogant, and to have so large a share of good opinion of himself, as to have nothing left for the rest of the world but contempt.' Johnson debunked Bruce's claim to have found the source of the Nile, pointing out that that distinction had gone to a Jesuit priest many years previously.

In the meantime, on 23 July, Omai was in the exclusive care of Banks and Solander en route to meet Hertford's Member of Parliament and famed doctor, Baron Dimsdale. Dimsdale approached his task formally and professionally. His relationship with his patient was proper and uneffusive, behaviour which mystified Banks. Banks's and Solander's recall of the Tahitian language, with which they had become familiar three years previously, assisted in explaining some of the more complicated detail. They had also been joined by Thomas Andrews the *Adventure*'s doctor, a friend of Omai and a competent linguist. To them fell the difficult problem of explaining to Omai that he had to catch smallpox in order to be protected. This in itself was a dangerous process, particularly for one with absolutely no inbuilt immunity to any disease. Understandably, Omai was unable to fathom the logic of what they intended to do to him but put his faith instead in the probability that Banks and Solander would not support any measure which would not, on balance, prove to be beneficial.

In his letter to Sandwich giving news of Omai's inoculation, Banks explained how Dimsdale had been acutely conscious of the need to allay Omai's fears. He therefore delayed the process of infection, partly to allow Omai more time to prepare mentally and partly because it was not until now that he had had the 'matter to his satisfaction for communicating the disease'. Dimsdale introduced the supplier to Omai, which could not have been a reassuring experience. She had 'several large pustules on her face'. The doctor had also 'contrived to have several children inoculated at the same time'. Banks was now happy to conclude that, as a result of these careful preparations, Omai 'understood thoroughly the disease he was to expect and we were certain that he did understand it'.

There is an important variation of emphasis between what Banks told Omai's patron, John Montagu, and what his sister committed to paper.

> Omai who was very tractable and willing to be inoculated mis-understood what was told him upon the subject for he thought by these precautions instead of having the expectation of the illness in a favourable way thought he was never to have it at all in consequence of which, when it came out, he was very low spirited and said he would die but was soon comforted by those about him.

How, precisely, those around him were effective in comforting Omai is not clear, particularly when their idea of an interesting diversion was to take Omai to an English funeral. He reacted strongly, perhaps overreacted, to the funeral service and showed signs of being discomfited: 'He wept plentifully with them that wept at the grave, and at length he went away from the mournful scene.' Surveying the endless line of tombstones in the cemetery, he enquired whether these had also been Dr Dimsdale's patients. Omai's sensitivity is difficult to reconcile with his past experience in Tahiti where infanticide, human sacrifice and blood-letting were all common practice. Perhaps he felt a display of grief was expected of him. If so, he most certainly played to the gallery.

Walking beside the river at Hertford he observed individuals engaged in an activity with which he was familiar: fishing. Drawing near, he saw one of the anglers thread a live worm on to the hook. Turning away in horror, he declared he 'would never again taste fish caught with so much cruelty'. Sarah Banks thought that she could account for such behaviour: 'He will never eat fish if he knows they are caught with a live worm owing to a religious superstition which prevails in the Society Islands in favour of worms.'

The disease ran its course but, fortunately for Omai, he contracted only a mild form. Banks wrote to his close friend Charles Blagden, to his sister and to Sandwich, advising that Omai was now considered to be out of danger. A number of pustules remained on his throat, which had a detrimental effect upon his morale, but otherwise he was aware that he was on the path towards assured recovery. Sister Sarah filed this information away with other memoranda. In the meantime she had discovered from one of her brother's servants that, far from being a Tahitian dignitary, Omai was 'quite a common man', a fact which if generally known would have added a far wider dimension to the anthropological examination of a savage's compatibility with European society. Sandwich responded to Banks's letter on 14 August: 'You have made me particularly happy in the account you have troubled yourself to give me of our friend Omai's being out of danger.'

The relationship between Charles Blagden, Banks and Omai and the overall milieu in which the Omai story is set are of particular relevance. Blagden, born in Gloucestershire, received his MD at Edinburgh in 1768. He found Omai's inoculation of particular interest, persistently asking his friend Banks for details. Blagden became Secretary of the Royal Society in 1784 at a time when the Society was uncertain as to the efficacy of its president, Joseph Banks. Not only was Blagden a man of medicine but he was also a linguist and scientist. Evidence that he spent a considerable amount of time with Omai is to be found in his draft English–Tahitian dictionary. His experiments on the effects of dissolved substances on the freezing point of water led to 'Blagden's Laws', in which he concluded that salt lowers the freezing point of water in the simple inverse ratio of the proportion the water bears to its solution, something Richard Watson had discovered earlier in 1771.

It was never intended that Omai should remain indefinitely as a house guest of Banks but that in due course he would be found lodgings nearby. In his letter, Sandwich proposed making Omai and his friend Dr Andrews a grant of £160 a year as a board-and-lodging allowance. The fee he proposed paying Dimsdale – twenty guineas – fell substantially short of that paid by Catherine the Great, but to Sandwich's mind this represented 'a proper fee'. Sandwich then concluded his letter by expressing his pleasure that Omai, Banks and Solander would visit him at Hinchingbrooke. All he asked was that he be told when, so that he might come to London to accompany his guests.

In a long letter of 19 August to a Scottish friend, Solander indicated that Omai was

> now quite recovered, and tomorrow we propose to go up for good to town. Mr Banks and myself have almost constantly been with him here at Hertford, and Mr Banks' servant James Roberts and the surgeon of the ship he came home in [Mr Andrews] have lived in the Inoculation house with him during the whole time. Omai is [a] sensible communicative man, so he is a valuable acquisition. He has pleased every body, and is quite contented and pleased with his reception here.

Solander counted himself lucky that the Blue Horse Guards had been quartered at Hertford for otherwise the Omai party would have tired of the place. The officers of the Blues had been good company, among them an old acquaintance of Solander's, Captain Archibald Stewart, whose brother John had also taken the trouble to call. On another occasion, Lord Elibank, Governor George Johnstone and Captain Blair spent a day at the inoculation house. At the time, Omai was at a low point in his treatment, 'so they did not see him to great advantage'.

The now recurring problem for Omai was his inability to speak at length. He could manage standard phrases such as 'How do you do?' but beyond that he was severely disadvantaged. An island vocabulary of what was reputed to be a thousand words was inadequate when set against the depth and breadth of the European experience. The islands had but three quadrupeds – dog, hog and rat. How therefore was Omai to describe a horse or a cow? The answer is that he gamely extemporised. He described a horse as 'a great hog that carries people' and a cow became 'a great hog that gives milk'. 'No climb tree for coconut', he said enthusiastically, 'only put hand under and squeeze'. The Swede Solander summed up Omai's situation: 'Omai don't yet speak any English.' But he remained optimistic that he would eventually succeed. Although he was unable to pronounce K he was able 'to pronounce S tolerably well'.

Solander spoke highly of Omai's behaviour and manners and then made the telling observation that he was 'remarkably complaisant to the ladies'. As evidence of Omai's good breeding, Solander described an event after dinner at the Duke and Duchess of Gloucester's home. The Duchess, wishing to present some memento to Omai, gave him her pocket handkerchief upon which her coronet had been embroidered. 'He took an opportunity when she looked at him to kiss it.' It was his being *complaisant* to the ladies which arguably became a contributory factor in the King's decision to send Omai home.

Meanwhile, Jem Burney had returned to the family home at Queen Square, Bloomsbury. 'My brother is returned in health, spirits and credit', observed sister Fanny Burney. 'He has made what he calls a very fine voyage; but it must have been very dangerous. Indeed, he has had several personal dangers; and in these voyages of hazard and enterprise, so, I imagine must every individual of the ship.' Fanny would surely have been curious to hear her brother's opinion of Omai.

The Earl of Sandwich busied himself with planning an extravaganza of entertainment with which to engage Omai. Meanwhile Omai's movements were widely reported in the press; he was hardly likely to pass unnoticed in London. On the 24th he dined with Sir John Pringle in Pall Mall, on the 25th he was seen at the first of ten Royal Society official dinners at the Mitre Tavern and on the 27th there followed a report that he accompanied Sandwich, Banks and Solander to Hinchingbrooke.

An entry in Fanny Burney's diary of 1 September tells of her father having received an invitation from Lord Sandwich to meet Omai and Lord Orford at Hinchingbrooke and to spend the week there. Moreover, Sandwich further invited Dr Burney to bring with him his son, the lieutenant. 'This has filled us with hope for some future good to my sailor-brother, who is the capital friend of Omai, or Omiah, or Omy, or Jack, for my brother says he is called by all these names on board, but chiefly by the last appellation, *Jack*!' Fanny, the loyal sister, was always on the look-out for the advancement of her beloved brother. While serving on the Queen's personal staff she sought a favour in the interest of her brother, but to no avail.

Huntingdon buzzed with expectation at the imminent arrival of Omai. Instructions had been sent in advance to local musicians to practise the designated oratorio to be presented at Hinchingbrooke during the week. The local nobility indicated their wish also to be involved and 'vied with each other in varying his diversions, in order to raise his idea of the splendour and gaiety of this country'. Sandwich led the way with sailing on local waters on Monday. The Duke of Manchester, Lord Ludlow, Sir Robert Bickerton and lesser members of the county set also took part as invited guests. On Wednesday the musicians gave their rendering of the oratorio. Miss Ray, confined to her bed in London, had been unable to take part.

Lord Manchester hosted the entertainment on Thursday, one aspect of which left Omai decidedly unamused. Manchester had a scientific machine comprising vertical discs. When the handle was turned, so too did the discs, generating a low-voltage current which gave a mild shock to anyone grasping the electrodes at the top of the device. Someone thought it a good idea to shock Omai. He did not respond with good humour as expected but ran from the room, refusing to return until Jem Burney promised there would be no more tricks. Lord Ludlow, master of the local hunt, arranged a fox-hunt for Friday. At the weekend they were in the university city of Cambridge. They went their separate ways on Monday, Lord Sandwich escorting his important guests to Leicester.

Leicester promised two events about which Sandwich was greatly enthused. One, a day at the races, was, for Omai, something different and although another oratorio was not, the difference between the Leicester and Hinchingbrooke oratorios lay in their difference in scale. Rain fell heavily as they journeyed to Leicester, to the extent that the race meeting, although it went ahead, did not live up to expectations, the course being sodden and the going soft to impossible. That evening the parish church of St Martin's put on one of two performances of Handel's *Jephtha*, something which might have seemed overly ambitious, yet Sandwich had pulled strings to ensure the attendance of a gifted leader, Mr Giardini, virtuosi from the Opera House, and a noted choir from Lancashire bolstered by local singers. The musical arrangements had been left to Sandwich's friend Joseph Cradock, who combined his knowledge of music with keeping a diary that became part of his literary memoirs. Sandwich had a personal interest in this concert for it provided him with a prominent role attacking the kettledrums. The Earl's performance left a favourable impression on many members of the audience, including a four-year-old who, sixty years on, recalled how he had been 'so captivated with his Lordship's performance, that for a time I heard but little else'. Many were the eyes focused upon Omai to measure his reaction to this enormous volume of sound. They saw him standing for most of the concert 'in wild amazement', for this surpassed anything the *arioi* were capable of achieving.

Cradock observed Omai at the reception smiling happily and handing cake and bread and butter to the ladies. In the evening a civic dinner was held in the Town Hall for which men and women, who sat opposite each other at long trestle tables, had made a real effort to dress up in their finery. Cradock sat next to Omai who complained petulantly that 'the clothes prepared for him were not so good as those of the gentleman he sat next, although of the same fashion; the one was English velvet, the other from Genoa'. After dinner, the tables were collapsed and removed to allow room for dancing. The guests danced very well, executing enormously difficult moves in circles and columns, changing direction without the slightest indication or warning. The waltz, in comparison, was pedestrian, more novice-friendly, and this is the dance Omai was more likely to have attempted. Cradock, as usual, saw all: 'Had he stayed at Leicester and practised a week or two, he would dance gracefully and with little embarrassment.' They danced on into the early morning when the locals returned home and visitors sought out their rooms in local inns.

We have Cradock to thank for reminding us how closely Omai was being chaperoned by Banks and Solander. Cradock had been told by a waiter that Omai had absconded. He dressed hurriedly and went off in search of the 'stranger gentleman'. Leicester had barely stirred from the slumber of the night but another man was out and about, enjoying his morning constitutional. Cradock asked after Omai. The stranger had seen him but reassured Cradock that the person he sought was strolling and could be overtaken in next to no time. This they did; Omai returned to the inn with Cradock. 'This was the first time he seemed to have obtained his liberty and he made the most of it.' After Leicester, it was back to Hinchingbrooke and new experiences.

Omai continued to test the bounds of language to compensate for the imbalance between his and his host's vocabularies. He described Lord Sandwich's butler as the king of bottles, Captain Furneaux as the king of the ship, but to Sandwich he said, 'You are the king of all ships'. Cradock provides a further definition which Solander believed a naturalist could not improve upon. Omai entered the dining room during breakfast, his hand swollen and obviously in pain. 'He made us understand that he had been wounded by a soldier bird', which those present correctly interpreted as a wasp. On another occasion, while visiting Cambridge, he observed Lord Townshend taking snuff. When his Lordship offered Omai a pinch, he replied, 'No tank you, sir, the nose be no hungry'. His public display of improbable sensitivity continued. Cradock tells of an occasion when Omai and his circle had gone to Woolwich to see the launch of the frigate *Acteon*. Not greatly interested, Omai excused himself and went to the pub where they were to have lunch. He helped prepare the salad. This association with food reminded Cradock of an earlier occasion when stewed morello cherries had been presented for dessert. 'He instantly jumped up and quitted the room. Several followed him; but he gave them to understand that he was no more accustomed to partake of human blood than they were.'

Omai may not have been the first to introduce the barbecue to England but he did bring the end-product to such a high standard of excellence as to be fondly remembered long after his departure. The ubiquitous Mr Cradock's description of how Omai responded to Sandwich's invitation to cook 'a shoulder of mutton in his own manner' describes precisely the *ahimaa*, the *methode Tahitienne*, common practice throughout the South Pacific, New Zealand and Hawaii:

> Having dug a deep hole in the ground, he placed fuel at the bottom of it, and then covered it with clean pebbles; when properly heated, he laid the mutton, neatly enveloped in leaves, at the top, and having closed the hole, walked constantly around it, very deliberately observing the sun. The meat was afterwards brought to table, was much commended, and all the company partook of it.

Among those impressed by Omai's culinary skills was Banks who reported back to his sister who duly filed the information away.

'Omai dressed three dishes for dinner yesterday and so well was his cookery liked that he is desired to cook again today not out of curiosity but for the real desire of eating meat so dressed.'

The return to London saw Omai ensconced in Banks's home at New Burlington Street. This was a temporary arrangement until Omai and his companion, Dr Andrews, could find suitable lodgings nearby. Banks too was preoccupied with finding a new home elsewhere in London. Omai could not have been in better hands in New Burlington Street. One of Banks's servants had accompanied Banks to Tahiti and spoke the language passably well. Mrs Hawley, the housekeeper, fussed around Omai but she was a dreadful gossip whom Sarah Banks used unashamedly to maintain her record of Omai anecdotes. Omai confided in Mrs Hawley how he intended to return home in a ship with men and weapons to drive the Bora Borans from his property and, after establishing his brothers on the family land, he would 'return himself to England where he proposed having a wife, a young handsome English woman 15 years old'. The 1785 pantomime was therefore not overly fanciful.

They went off on their delayed visit to Cambridge. Omai, dressed in British uniform with his hair tied back, impressed the academics by his appearance. Back in London, Banks introduced Omai to the theatre. So much did he enjoy ballet at Sadler's Wells that he asked that he might go again the next day. Did Lord Sandwich go to the ballet, asked Omai? Banks thought not. Did any of the nobility go? Sometimes, but infrequently, replied Banks. Since ballet clearly did not appeal to the very best, Omai declared that he would go no more. Banks thereupon promised to take Omai to see the play *Isabella* at Drury Lane: 'I will carry you tomorrow to the play where great people frequently amuse themselves.' Omai found the play uninteresting but, as was often the case, the second feature of the evening, a pantomime, saved the outing from being a flop.

As each piece of intelligence regarding Omai passed from brother to sister, Sarah Banks reassessed earlier opinions. She was now convinced that Omai was indeed 'a priest in his own country' and, contrary to Mrs Hawley's information, did not care at all for English ladies and was not therefore looking for an English wife. Sarah was wrong on the first count and wrong to say that Omai was indifferent to English ladies. There was a thought that he fancied Lady Carew; 'Very nice', he said.

It was simply a matter of time before satirists would draw Omai into their salacious writing. The author of the latest Tahiti epistle called him Otaipairoo, bearing another letter from the 'voluptuous court' of Tahiti from Oberea for the long-suffering Joseph Banks. The secondary theme reported Omai as having had a relationship at the Cape of Good Hope with a Dutch lady. The author ascribed his apparent lack of interest in English women to the complications inherent in their *outré* dresses as compared to the simplicity of clothing in Tahiti. This did not mean that Omai was indifferent to English women, for the latest satire associated him with 'a lady on the first line of nobility'. Ladies did seem to be fascinated by Omai and he liked particularly 'those of a ruddy complexion who are not fat'. Tahitian men were said to be very forward in their approach to women. (In Paris, Autouhourou had to be prised away from an unsuspecting female he encountered in the street and began to ravish.) At a party given by the Duchess of Gloucester, Omai had worn the white *tapa* robes made from material given to Banks in Tahiti and which featured in the Reynolds painting. Sarah observed 'a great concourse of people about him'. Whether by design or accident, Banks had gone to his country home in Lincolnshire while Omai was once again a guest at Hinchingbrooke.

The Burneys had recently moved from Queen Square to a house in St Martin's Street, once the home of Sir Isaac Newton. While the location may have been less attractive, its positive points included the close proximity of Sir Joshua Reynolds and Robert Strange, the engraver. From here, on Thursday, 1 December 1774, Fanny Burney wrote to her old friend Samuel Crisp, 'I will tell you that I have seen Omai', and spared no words in providing a full account, beginning with the Monday performance of *Isabella* at Drury Lane.

Jem Burney had attended that same performance, sitting in one of the upper boxes. From here he observed Banks with Omai. Crossing over to Banks's box he gave Omai a hearty shake of the hand and joined the pair. Burney invited Banks to dinner – meaning lunch in the eighteenth century and taken at no precise time – but the latter regretted that his diary was full until Christmas when he would travel to Hinchingbrooke.

Late the next evening, Tuesday, a note arrived at the Burney residence addressed to Jem. It had come from Omai who did not have a full diary and suggested that if it was agreeable and convenient to him, he, Omai, would have the honour of having dinner with Burney the next day, Wednesday. Omai asked for a reply and, if possible, begged Burney to fetch him. Early on Wednesday morning Jem Burney, bearing his father's compliments, invited Banks and Solander also to join them, but both had a prior engagement at a Royal Society dinner. They agreed to drop Omai off early and spend some time in discussion with Dr Burney.

Apart from the family, the only other dinner guests were family friends Robert Strange and John Hayes. Omai had spent the morning at the House of Lords from where he had seen and heard the King make his speech from the throne. Although dinner was not scheduled until 4 p.m., Omai, Banks and Solander arrived at 2, the latter pair having allowed time to discuss business with Dr Burney. Fanny remained upstairs, having been confined to her room for three days due to a heavy cold. That did not mean that she would not come down to meet 'this lyon of lyons, for such he now is of this town', but rather that she would wait until Banks and Solander had gone.

I found Omai seated on the great chair, and my brother next to him, and talking Otaheite as fast as possible. You cannot suppose how fluently and easily Jem speaks it. Mama, Susy and Charlotte were opposite. As soon as there was a cessation of talk, Jem introduced me, and told him I was another sister. He rose, and made a very fine bow, and then seated himself again. But when

Jem went on, and told him I was not well, he again directly rose, and muttering something of the fire, in a very polite manner without speech insisting upon my taking his seat – and he would not be refused.

Fanny now surveyed the man about whom she had heard so much. Having come directly from Court, he still wore his suit of Manchester velvet, lined with white satin, a bag, lace ruffles and the sword given him by the King. 'He is tall, swarthy, and young, extremely well made, and a fine figure and though by no means handsome, he has a good and pleasing countenance', she confided to her diary. The 'remarkable good' bows were impressive, for this man 'who seemed to shame education for his manners are so extremely graceful, and is so polite, attentive and easy that, you would have thought he came from some foreign Court'.

They sat together at dinner, the assumption being that both would benefit from being close to the fire. Omai's ease and confidence at the table surprised and pleased Fanny. He took the underdone beef in his stride – 'very dood, very dood', he reassured his hostess. 'It is very odd, but true', wrote Fanny, 'that he can pronounce the th as in thank you, and the w as in well, and yet cannot say g which he used a d for. But I now recollect, that in the beginning of a word, as in George, he can pronounce it.' Beer and wines were served with the meal.

Omai explained to Jem that at six o'clock he had an appointment to meet twelve ladies. Jem translated this interesting piece of news to the other guests. Omai understood what Jem was saying and by way of reinforcement began to count with his fingers, '1, 2, 3, 4, 5, 6, 7, 8, 9, 10 – twelve woman!'

The coach arrived shortly before six. The butler came in to announce 'Mr Omai's servant', to which Omai said, 'Very well'. He remained at the table for a further five minutes before collecting hat and sword. He paused for a further few minutes while Dr Burney finished his conversation and, after extravagant bows to everyone present, Jem escorted him outside to the coach.

Omai's visit had a considerable impact upon the Burney household. Comparisons were drawn with Lord Chesterfield's son, Philip Stanhope. Chesterfield owed his fame, or notoriety, to having committed to paper his views as to the proper way to behave or, as he would have it, to be familiar with the Graces. 'No scrambling at your meals, no awkward overturn of glasses, plates and salt cellars; no horse play. On the contrary, a gentleman of manners, a graceful carriage, and an insinuating address, must take their place. I repeat and never shall cease repeating to you, the Graces, the Graces!'

Fanny Burney developed the comparative theme in her letter to Crisp, as to how Stanhope, first,

> with all the advantage of Lord Chesterfield's instruction, brought up at a great school, introduced at fifteen to a Court, taught all possible accomplishments from an infant, and having all the care, expense, labour, and benefit of the best education that any man can receive, – proved after it all a meer pedantic booby; – the second with no tutor but nature, changes, after he is grown up, his dress, his way of life, his diet, his country and his friends; – and appears in a new world like a man who had all his life studied the Graces, and attended with unremitting application and diligence to form his manners, and to render his appearance and behaviour politely easy, and thoroughly well bred! I think this shows how much nature can do without art, than art with all her refinement unassisted by nature.

There could be no doubt that there would come a point when Banks's concern for Omai would have to be subordinated to the conflicting demands being made upon his time. It is reasonable to suggest that the tilt point was reached over Christmas 1774. Banks had not, as he informed Burney he would, gone to Hinchingbrooke for the Christmas and New Year celebrations. Claims on his time leading up to the Christmas season included laying out in his home for viewing a recently acquired herbarium and the continuing demands being made by the Royal Society following his re-election to the council. In a letter to Banks of the 29th, Sandwich sent a mild rebuke at Banks's failure to honour his commitment. He sent the letter to London with Omai.

> I own I am grown so used to him, and have so sincere a friendship for him, from his very good temper, sense and general good behaviour, that I am quite distressed at his leaving me; and, knowing the dangers of a London life to an European of twenty one years old, am full of anxiety on account of the winter he is to pass in town in a lodging, without the sort of society he has been used to, which has kept him out of dissipation.

Omai's saving graces included his good nature and the fawning obsequiousness shown to his highborn social acquaintances, something which came naturally to one not highborn. He saw instinctively that the gods of his hosts and hostesses were 'wealth, vanity and convention', and that 'a man was respected by his fellow in proportion to the fineness of his dress and manner'. Sandwich's concerns would have been considerably alleviated had Omai made appreciable progress in learning English. Educationalists who examined him spoke despairingly of his lack of both drive and curiosity. The Reverend Michael Tyson, Fellow of Benedict, or Bene't, College, which is now Corpus Christi, Cambridge, observed Omai and recorded his impressions, the most telling of which records the impossibility of teaching Omai to form words and, by implication, Omai's inability therefore to teach his own countrymen English. Another intellectual to have assessed Omai was the Reverend Sir John Cullum who wrote of his disappointment not to have found 'that any steps have been taken towards giving him any useful knowledge, Mr Banks seeing to keep him, as an object of curiosity, to observe the workings of an untutored unenlightened mind'.

There were those, however, mostly of a religious disposition, who recognised Omai's plight. Their concern to teach him English had less to do with the amelioration of his situation as a single man in lodgings in London than with the perception that he should be baptised as a preliminary to spreading 'Christian light over a new race of men'.

Foremost among those who held such a view was the proselytising anti-slavery advocate Granville Sharp, working at the Ordnance Office. Using the old boy network, he applied for access to Omai through his friend Joah Bates who happened to be Lord Sandwich's secretary. Sandwich agreed, but Sharp had no experience in teaching foreign languages. He co-opted friends to the task, one of whom warned him that he would 'have more difficulty than that of language to encounter'.

Sharp's attitude to Omai was different from that of Banks. To Sharp, Omai was a subject for enlightenment and for education rather than an interesting native to observe. He met both Banks and Omai on 13 February and agreed a timetable of work which failed to live up to expectation. By March, daily lessons intended to have taken two or three hours had become pointless:

> 11th and 13th, Omai for two hours.
> 26th, Omai called but had no time for a lesson.
> 28th and 4th April, Omai for a very short time.
> 6th, Omai was so taken up with engagements that I could have no more opportunity of giving him lessons, which were but fifteen in all. However, in that time I taught him the use of English letters and made him sound every combination of vowels and consonants that letters are capable of.

There are no surviving examples of Omai's written work and although Sharp rewrote for his benefit a pamphlet on English pronunciation, his biographer felt 'the course of education was probably a failure'.

The time Sharp and Omai were together was not always spent upon formal language training. During discussions they would express their own views of the world and one such debate was recorded by Sharp:

> When sitting with him at table one day after dinner, I thought it a good opportunity to explain to him the Ten Commandments. I proceeded with tolerable success in reciting the first six Commandments. He had nothing to object against any of them,

though many explanations were required before he understood all the terms; and he freely nodded his assent. But when I recited the seventh Commandment, 'Thou shalt not commit adultery', he said: 'Adultery! What that? What that?'

'Not to commit adultery', I said, 'is that, if a man has got one wife, he must not take another wife, or any other woman'. 'Oh', says he, 'two wives – very good; three wives – very, very good'. 'No, Mr Omai', I said, 'not so; that would be contrary to the first principle of the law of nature'. 'First principle of the law of nature', said he, 'what that? What that?' 'The first principle of the law of nature', I said, 'is, that no man must do to another person anything that he would not like to be done to himself. And, for example, Mr Omai', said I, 'suppose you have got a wife that you love very much; you would not like that another man should come to love your wife'. This raised his indignation: he put on a furious countenance, and a threatening posture, signifying that he would kill any man that should meddle with his wife. 'Well, Mr Omai', said I, 'suppose then, that your wife loves you very much, she would not like that you should love another woman: for the women have the same passions and feelings, and love toward the men, that we have toward the women; and we ought, therefore, to regulate our behaviour toward them by our own feelings of what we should like and expect of faithful love and duty from them toward ourselves'.

This new state of the case produced a deep consideration and silence for some time, on the part of Mr Omai. But he soon afterwards gave me ample proof that he thoroughly comprehended the due influence of the law of liberty, when it is applied to regulate, by our own feelings, the proper conduct and behaviour which we owe to other persons. There was an ink-stand on the table with several pens in it. He took one pen, and laid it on the table, saying, 'There lies Lord S . . . ' (a nobleman with whom he was well acquainted, and in whose family he had spent some time); and then he took another pen, and laid it close by the side of the former pen, saying 'and there lies Miss W . . . ' (who was an accomplished young woman in many respects, but, unhappily for herself, she lived in a state of adultery with that nobleman); and he then took a third pen, and placing it on the table at a considerable distance from the other two pens, as far as his right arm could extend, and at the same time leaning his head upon his left hand, supported by his elbow on the table, in a pensive posture, he said, 'and there lie Lady S, and cry!'

Thus it is plain that he thoroughly understood the force of the argument from the law of liberty, respecting the gross injury done to the married lady by her husband in taking another woman to his bed. There was no need to explain the rights of women any further to Mr Omai on that occasion.

Omai's celebrity, his place in history, can be measured by those who came forward to paint him. Chronologically, the next painting of Omai to follow the flattering oil by Hodges had been a 1774 portrait by Nathaniel Dance, said to be a faithful representation of the real Omai. He poses as a prince, clad in the same style of *tapa* robe or toga as painted by Reynolds, a feather chaplet and plaited bag in his right hand and in his left hand a wooden headrest or stool. (Omai gave this stool to Tobias Furneaux in whose family it remained until 1986 before coming up for sale at Christie's. Assisted by Lord McAlpine and a Mr George Ortiz, the Tahiti museum purchased Omai's stool for £80,000.) Francesco Bartolozzi made an engraving of the Dance portrait, not a precise engraving because the face is too thin, the nose over-pronounced and there is an excess of hair. Nevertheless, given the interest in Omai, the prints sold well.

Conventional wisdom has it that Omai went along with this harmless masquerade as prince, chief or priest rather than playing an active part in the deception. While the pretence did provide him with rather obvious benefits, the real beneficiary was Joseph Banks. The Omai phenomenon provided a timely rehabilitation for his reputation, the memory of his participation in Cook's first voyage having passed into recent history. There is, however, one small clue left behind for posterity to suggest the part Omai played in the masquerade. It can be seen in the Bartolozzi engraving of Dance's portrait of Omai in which the headrest is rather more than an ethnographic prop. To carry a headrest in that manner is a symbol of aristocracy in Tahitian society, in the same way the coronet symbolises the British aristocracy. The origins of this particular headrest are unknown. We do know that when Omai fled would-be assassins for the sanctuary of HMS *Adventure*, he had nothing, and as a commoner, would not have had access to a restricted symbol of status. It is also unlikely, given the availability of Cook and Furneaux, that one of the chiefs would have handed to a commoner a gift intended to be placed in the hands of Banks or even George III. In the perpetual exchange of gifts, it is possible that the headrest may have been presented to Cook or Banks in recognition of their authority. What seems most likely is that, at the time Omai left Huahine, the headrest was already in England among the collection of Joseph Banks.

It was not accidental that Dance, Reynolds and, later, Parry all painted Omai dressed in white *tapa*, the cloth of Tahitian chiefs. Omai expressed a wish to be so represented, wearing a kind of uniform to which he had no entitlement. The headrest epitomised the way Omai lived out his private fantasy, portrayed not as he was but as how he wanted to be. Few of his English hosts would have been aware of the significance of the white *tapa* or of the headrest. Clearly, Omai felt confident in wearing these symbols of refinement which an unofficial ambassador to the Court of St James's would quite naturally wear. He acted out the role of ambassador, flattered by reciprocal words of respect, so much so that it would be virtually impossible for him to return home and pick up the threads of his former life.

During the time Omai spent in England, the two leading portrait painters were Sir Joshua Reynolds and Thomas Gainsborough. Reynolds founded the Royal Academy of Arts in 1768 and became its first president. He set the standard for fashionable portraits, initially formal but, over a period of time, in the 1780s, he developed a more relaxed, naturalistic style which other artists followed. He lived at 47 Leicester Fields, near the Burneys, and it was to his painting rooms there that Omai went, at the beginning of Reynolds's 'natural' period. It is not known for certain when Reynolds painted his masterpiece of Omai. His diaries for 1774–76 were lost. The portrait seems not to have been commissioned, but was perhaps painted because it was a subject that interested Reynolds. Certainly he rated the portrait as among his best. It underlined the reality of Omai's social acceptability – in modern parlance, he had arrived.

A number of Reynolds's 1775 preliminary works of Omai still survive and are treasured; he did not often make preliminary drawings of his subjects. One such, a pencil drawing of Omai's face, can be found in Australia's National Library, Canberra. It is particularly important, showing him as undoubtedly Polynesian despite the largish flat nose and unseeing eyes. There is also an oil portrait of Omai's face, again by Reynolds, in the Yale University Art Gallery. The existence of two preliminary portraits is thought to be unusual. One suggestion as to why this occurred is the idea that the Yale portrait came first, painted straight upon canvas, and was not accurate, the nose being less flat than it should have been. This might account for Reynolds picking up his pencil to draw a difficult head to his satisfaction before addressing the life-size canvas with oil paint.

Reynolds's principal portrait of Omai sees him wearing both a toga and a form of turban. Dance omitted the latter. In both portraits he is barefoot. Reynolds has him with his hands free, the tattoos on one hand being plainly visible. The painting was shown in the Royal Academy in 1776 to great acclaim.

Another significant painting is William Parry's 1776 composition of *Sir Joseph Banks with Omai, the Otaheitian Chief and Doctor Daniel Solander*. Parry, a Welshman, had been one of Reynolds's students and again appears content to have stayed with the exotic, painting Omai in his white toga. The significance of the Parry composition lies in the three subjects, all of whom made important contributions to the knowledge and history of the South Pacific. By coincidence, at the same time as Tate Britain found itself in negotiations to buy Reynolds's *Omai* for £12.5 million, the National Portrait Gallery, which had Parry's painting on loan, could not afford the £1.8 million to buy it and the buyer who applied for the licence failed to pay. Parry's portrait remained in the National Portrait Gallery until the owner decided what to do with it. Its price was subsequently reduced to £950,000 – a not inconsiderable sum for a painting by an artist described by Beaglehole, Cook's biographer, as 'fourth rate'. A consortium of interested parties – the National Portrait Gallery, the Captain Cook Memorial Museum, Whitby, and the National Museums and Galleries of Wales – jointly acquired Parry's group portrait following a successful fundraising campaign.

For its time, the Parry painting is heavy in symbolism, showing an Englishman, a Swede and a Raiatean in a rigidly posed group where none appears subordinate to the other. To those who despised Rousseau and his philosophy, this painting became a source of annoyance. Speaking of Rousseau to Boswell, Johnson deplored Britain's action in giving him asylum: 'Rousseau, Sir, is a very bad man. I would sooner sign a sentence for his transportation, than of any felon who has gone from the Old Bailey these many years.' Although Johnson had a valued black servant, Francis Barber, he could not conceive the circumstances in which a 'native' could have as much merit or value as a European. Such an attitude can account for the logic which dismissed Cook's voyages of discovery and their description in books as irrelevant. 'There is little entertainment in such books', said Johnson airily. 'One set of savages is much like another.' He had an ally in Horace Walpole: 'Captain Cook's voyages, I have never read or intend to read. I have seen the prints – a parcel of ugly faces, with lubber lips and flat noses, dressed unbecomingly as if both sexes were ladies of the highest fashion; and rows of savages with backgrounds of palm trees.'

It was inevitable that the overlapping of social circles would ensure that Johnson would eventually meet Omai and, given his stated views, it was a meeting which attracted some interest at Streatham. What transpired, reminiscent of Johnson's change of opinion vis-à-vis John Wilkes, was that he left with a favourable impression of Omai, a turn of events for which he produced what was, to his mind, a plausible reason:

> Sir, he had passed his time, while in England, only in the best company; so that all he had acquired of our manners was genteel. As proof of this, Sir, Lord Mulgrave and he dined one day at Streatham; they sat with their backs to the light fronting me, so that I could not see distinctly [his eyesight was badly impaired] and there was so little of the savage in Omai, that I was afraid to speak to either lest I should mistake one for the other.

It was impossible that Omai could have duped the cream of the British intelligentsia. He must have had qualities that they recognised and valued beyond good manners. Winning over Johnson had been a qualified success, but there was one event that questions how precisely Omai could have done quite so well in English society. The curious story of Omai and Johnson's friend Guiseppe Baretti, translator of Shakespeare and language tutor to Mrs Thrale's eldest daughter. Where precisely Omai learnt to play chess and back-gammon is unknown, possibly aboard the *Adventure*. That he could defeat such eminent people as Baretti, who rated himself an accomplished chess player, is a mystery.

Mrs Thrale, who watched games unfold between the relaxed Omai and the tense, prone to be volatile, Italian Baretti, said: 'When Omai played at chess and backgammon with Baretti, everybody admired at the savage's good breeding and at the European's impatient spirit.' Baretti could never own up to Johnson to having been beaten twice by Omai at Reynolds's home, and found it expedient to lie to him. Many years later, in the autumn of 1784, Baretti visited Johnson who, though seeming well and in good spirits, was close to death, but still enjoyed baiting his excitable friend. On this occasion, Johnson asked Baretti directly whether or not it was true that Omai had twice beaten him at chess at Sir Joshua's house. 'Do you think I should be conquered at chess by a savage?' 'I know you were,' replied the doctor.

Baretti's continual denials evoked a flash of temper in Johnson who could abide nothing less than complete truth. He rose from his seat in a violent rage, shouting, 'I'll hear no more.' Baretti, taking up his hat and stick, fled the room in what one observer described as 'a choleric mood'. Baretti took a while to calm down. Just before he intended to visit his old friend to apologise, he learnt of Johnson's death.

The hanging together of two of Reynolds's life-size portraits, of Omai and the Duchess of Devonshire, at the Royal Academy in 1776 would on the face of it seem to represent two social extremes, but it was Omai who criticised the Duchess for her slovenliness. The Duchess, painted by Reynolds and Gainsborough, mistress of Chatsworth in Derbyshire, who used her beauty to buy votes with kisses, was upbraided by the noble savage. Fanny Burney provided the corroboration.

Fanny was in the park one Sunday morning with friends when they encountered Georgiana, Duchess of Devonshire, 'walking in such an undressed and slatternly manner'. Two of her curls had become unpinned and had fallen lank upon her shoulders, one shoe was in need of repair, the trimming of her jacket and coat had come adrift, her cap was awry, her cloak, said to be 'rusty and powdered', hung half on and half off. Behind her followed a servant in a superb livery. 'Every creature turned back to stare at her. Indeed, I think her very handsome and she has a look of innocence and alertness that made me quite sorry she should be so negligent of her person.' She was accompanied by the Duke, her husband William, 'who is the very reverse of herself, for he is ugly, tidy and grave. He looks like a mean shop keeper's journeyman.' They were an odd couple, having married when Georgina was seventeen. It was once said of him that 'constitutional apathy formed his distinguishing characteristic'. Omai, also in the park that day, confronted the Duchess and asked her why her hair was so dishevelled. 'Don't you laugh at her having a lesson of attention from an Otaheitian?' wrote Fanny Burney.

CHAPTER 8

Preparations

The drift towards armed conflict with the North American colonies can be monitored through the movements of Fanny's brother Jem. In London there was talk of a return voyage to Tahiti and a number of scientists had already begun to jockey for attention. Jem, however, clearly wanted to return to Tahiti, undoubtedly for old times' sake, but there is also an interesting reference in a letter of 22 August 1774 from Crisp to Fanny, 'as he does but once more visit Otaheite and his dear piece that he left behind there'. Can there be any other meaning of 'his dear piece'? Whatever his reasons, he was at that moment an officer aboard Captain John Simmons's *Cerberus* with orders to sail for the colonies.

When Fanny called on her friend Mrs Strange on 13 March 1775, she found her taking tea with her two daughters and the ubiquitous Mr Bruce. The assembled company became curious as to the contents of a letter she had brought with her from Jem for Mrs Strange. It was no more than a thank you letter. When Bruce heard that Jem was under orders to sail for America, he said he was sorry and he mentioned the intention to assemble another South Seas expedition which 'would have been much more desirable'. In theory, time was on Jem's side because Sandwich had said there would be no new expedition until after Cook's return.

'And much more agreeable to him; for he wishes it of all things. He says that he should now make a much better figure at Otaheite, than when there before, as he learnt the language of Omai in his passage home,' said Fanny.

'Ah weel, honest lad,' said Mrs Strange, a Scots lady. 'I suppose he would get a wife or something pretty there.'

'Perhaps Oberea,' added Mr Bruce.

'Poor Oberea', said Fanny, 'he says is dethroned.'

'But,' said he archly, 'if Mr Banks goes he will reinstate her! But this poor fellow Omai, has lost all his time; they have taught him nothing; he will only pass for a consummate liar when he returns; for how can he make them believe half the things he will tell them? He can give them no idea of our houses, carriages, or anything that will appear probable.'

'Troth, then,' said Mrs Strange, 'they should give him a set of dolls' things and a baby's house, to show them; he should have everything in miniature, by way of models; dressed babies, cradles, lying-in women, and a' sort of pratty things.'

The idea was not immediately dismissed as idiotic. 'There is humorous ingenuity in this', thought Fanny, 'that I really believe would be well worth being tried.' And try it the authorities did.

At the end of March, the *Cerberus* sailed for America. In addition to officers and crew, the warship carried three generals and their staff. 'Their stay is quite uncertain,' wrote Fanny. 'Jem prays for his return in time to go to the South Seas.'

Omai did not entirely enjoy his time spent in lodgings in Warwick Street, rented from his landlord Mr Vignolles for £80 a year. He found the city's winter cold and forbidding. He discovered the mysteries of the coal fire and its ineffectiveness in heating a room. As winter gave way to spring, he made visits to the Royal Navy, Mulgrave Castle in Yorkshire and to Hinchingbrooke where he was a regular, welcome visitor.

By Easter, thoughts turned to the *Resolution*, now on the last leg of a voyage which, at its conclusion, would have lasted three years and eighteen days. At the Cape, Cook saw Hawkesworth's *Voyages* for the first time. What he read 'mortified' him. Claims had been made that he had read the draft yet the work was replete with nautical errors, and he barely recognised himself because much of what was attributed to him should have been attributed to Banks.

Reasons for interest in the movement of the *Resolution* varied according to the individual concerned. Sandwich wanted detailed news of Terra Australis Incognita. On 19 March 1775, despatches sent ahead by Cook from Cape Town to the Admiralty, included: 'If I have failed in discovering a continent it is because it does not exist in a navigable sea.' Banks and Solander wondered about the nature of new botanical specimens aboard and Omai simply worried about the extrovert Odiddy and his likely impact in a world in which Omai had enjoyed exclusive sway. Cook's despatches were entirely silent on the subject of Odiddy. Sarah Banks learnt from her brother that Omai was not greatly enthused about this development, apparently not because he sensed a rival but because Odiddy was a loathsome Bora Bora man.

It is interesting that, up to this point, Omai had taken no positive steps to acquire weapons with which to defeat the Bora Bora enemy. Cook would have been unwilling to allow him any access to weapons which could not be justified solely on the basis of his own personal protection. Omai then surprised everybody by saying that Odiddy would be welcome to stay at his lodgings. The issue, however, was academic, for Odiddy was not aboard the *Resolution.*

It may be recalled that Cook returned Odiddy to his home during his short return visit to the islands. Despite there having been much wailing and gnashing of teeth, Cook believed this to have been the right decision: 'He was a youth of good parts and like most of his countrymen, of a docile, gentle and humane disposition, but in a manner wholly ignorant of their religion, government, manners, customs and traditions, consequently no material knowledge could have been gathered from him, had I brought him away.'

This is curious, for Cook rated Odiddy superior to Omai, the 'downright blackguard', though when Cook spoke of a 'blackguard', he did not associate the word with villainy but used it to describe a person of low social standing. After Cook had been acquainted with Omai's progress in England, he wrote:

since my arrival in England [I have] been convinced of my error;

for excepting his complexion (which is undoubtedly of a deeper hue than that of the chiefs or gentry, who, as in other countries, live a most luxurious life and are less exposed to the sun), I much doubt whether any other of the natives would have given more general satisfaction by his behaviour among us. Omai has most certainly a good understanding, quick parts and honest principles.

The newspapers renewed their interest, telling their readers what the *Otaheitan* was doing, although the reports were founded more upon imagination than fact. Apparently, Omai could now read and write sufficient English to be able to hold a conversation. This was not the experience of a social climber who had met him in the British Museum and described his English as being 'far from intelligible'. Then there was the recurring theme that he was to marry a twenty-two-year-old English lady whom he would take back to the South Pacific. His name was now automatically associated with the anticipated voyage to Polynesia, due to commence at some date after Cook's return home.

It was at about this time that an understandable assumption made by a number of London's social elite caused Omai acute embarrassment. There was an expectation, indeed it was taken for granted, that members of society could ride horses – it formed part of their upbringing – so it was reasonable to assume that a Tahitian prince could also ride. No one had stopped to consider whether the islands had horses, which of course they did not. Someone who until recently had never seen a horse could be excused for thinking that riding a horse through London's streets was a straightforward business. The journey on this particular day appeared unambitious – from Carlisle Street, Soho, to a country house at Acton. Horses are shrewd creatures and can tell whether or not their rider is confident and capable. In this case, as the journey progressed, Omai grew increasingly nervous and tense, a fact which he of course conveyed to the horse, which was by now also becoming worried. Halfway up Oxford Road the horse decided it would go no further and stopped, rejecting all encouragement to continue. The whips came out, which for the horse proved to be the last straw. It turned around and trotted back whence it had come, with Omai hanging on for dear life. At the stables the hosts selected a less challenging horse and the journey was completed without further ado.

On 2 June 1775, Omai and Banks accepted Sandwich's invitation to accompany him on his annual tour of southern and south coast naval establishments aboard the Admiralty yacht *Augusta*. Fellow guests included the Earl of Seaforth, who had raised a regiment of Highlanders, and two of Sandwich's senior staff including Joah Bates. Solander remained behind as a precaution lest the *Resolution* should appear off Spithead. He was the diplomatic choice, thought to be the more acceptable face of the two. Banks had no clear idea as to Cook's disposition towards him following his fit of pique and the fiasco which had surrounded the ship's departure from England. He preferred that Solander should test the waters to the extent that he made a journey which took him away from London. They made their first call at the Royal Hospital, Greenwich, where they had the same lunch as the pensioners – pease pudding and beer – before travelling the short distance to the Observatory where they examined the *camera obscura*. Returning to the *Augusta*, they were joined by guests who would stay for dinner, leaving at 9 p.m. Dinner guests included Martha Ray and Sandwich who made little effort to hide their attachment. After fond *adieux*, the *Augusta* made for Chatham.

At Chatham, Omai observed the exchange of gun salutes at the beginning of the inspection. He also saw a massive, 100-gun, three-decker, laid down during the Seven Years' War. (This famous ship, HMS *Victory*, Nelson's flagship at Trafalgar in 1805, can now be seen at Portsmouth.) The voyage of the *Augusta* may have been described as an inspection but in reality it had rather more to do with socialising and enjoyment. While Sandwich attended to the formal programme, Banks went his own way and botanised as well as keeping a diary of events.

When work caught up with Sandwich and detained him on the Isle of Wight, his guests went off shooting on horseback. There are no reports of Omai's competence on this his second outing on a horse (although at a later date he hired what may have been an armchair of a horse, riding to Hertford to make a courtesy call on Baron Dimsdale). On two evenings, Omai took the ship's guests to the theatre. He had not forgotten that the theatre was the favoured entertainment of the aristocracy and the discerning. By all accounts the acting in one of the plays was dreadful.

Solander sent a letter to Banks asking for his guidance as to how to handle Odiddy whom he had every reason to believe was aboard the *Resolution*: 'It does not appear from any thing Capt Cook has wrote if *Oridi* is on board or not. I should rather think that he is; as they mustered the day they came into the Cape of Good Hope as many men as when they left the Cape – and I think one man fell overboard off New Zealand.'

He also relayed a summary of flora and fauna on board the *Resolution* as catalogued by Forster. The guests dallied for over a week at Plymouth enjoying an extravaganza of entertainment, eating and drinking, which continued on board until the inspection came to an end in the Thames on 13 July. There was no further news of the *Resolution*.

After making a reassuring report to the King on the condition of his navy, Sandwich returned to the *Augusta* and cruising, inviting on board Martha Ray, Omai, Banks and the explorer Constantine Phipps, son of the late Lord Mulgrave. It was Phipps who sat with Omai at the Thrale house in Streatham in front of Dr Johnson, whom Johnson could not differentiate from Omai and whom Mrs Thrale described as 'fond of coarse merriment'. As before, Solander remained in London, his ear to the ground to intercept the earliest information of the *Resolution*'s arrival. At the end of the second cruise, Sandwich's guests journeyed to Hinchingbrooke.

Often seen in the company of Sandwich throughout the country, Martha Ray's favourite destination happened to be Hinchingbrooke. It was not unusual for her to be there unaccompanied, Sandwich being in London, the war in America requiring more and more of his attention. During the seventeen years they had lived together openly as man and wife there had been wobbles in their relationship. Sandwich's heir, Lord Hinchingbrooke, opposed the relationship and the Earl had to be eternally vigilant to ensure that they never met. There was the 1771 settlement problem, when Sandwich confided to a friend that the loss of Martha Ray would be a calamity but 'giving way to a woman in unreasonable points never does any good'. His friend endeavoured to persuade Sandwich to give his mistress an allowance: 'she is a fine woman whom you debauched very young, whom you tell me has lived with you eleven years. I see she still possesses your fondest wishes.' Sandwich would not listen. Martha craved respectability and during this difficult period she met a young army recruiting officer in Huntingdon by the name of Captain James Hackman. Here was someone nearer her own age, thirty, who loved her and would marry her, and this may have been the principal reason for her visit to Hinchingbrooke.

Martha encouraged Hackman but worried that marriage to him might involve the loss of her five children. The army officer persevered, joining the clergy with a view eventually to finding a living with Martha beside him as his wife. Why he thought his bishop would allow him to oversee a parish married to the cast-off mistress of a well known public figure is not clear. There are indications that he was not right in his mind in so far as on two occasions he told Martha the story of men who murdered their lovers.

At two o'clock on 31 July, Solander wrote to Banks from the Admiralty, 'this moment Captain Cook is arrived'. The *Resolution* anchored off Spithead on 30 July 1775. After arriving at the Admiralty, Cook went directly into the Board Room to report on the voyage. Solander thought he looked well, rather better than when he left. After the passage of some time and after having spoken to Cook, Solander sent to Banks the best possible news: 'Captain Cook desires his best compliments to you, he expressed himself in the most friendly manner towards you, that could be, he said: nothing could be added to the satisfaction he has had, in making this tour, but having had your company.' Solander examined the art of William Hodges, 'a very well behaved young man', whose work is only now attracting the attention it deserves. Solander closely examined Hodges's portrait of Odiddy and pondered what this handsome man would be like as a person. A number of officers contacted Solander with souvenirs they hoped to pass to Banks – for a suitable reward. Among those to have returned with 'curiosities' was Charles Clerke, friend of Banks and, having participated in Cook's two previous voyages, the officer widely tipped to lead the return to the South Seas at the year's end.

The news caused Sandwich and Martha Ray to return to London but Banks, despite understandable curiosity, continued with his planned trip to Yorkshire with Omai. The *Cerberus* also arrived back in England at this time to take on new supplies for the North American garrison. Two weeks represented the turnaround time, ample for Jem Burney to persuade his father to represent his strong interest in the next South Seas expedition. Sandwich reassured his old friend that he was aware of the lieutenant's interest and that there would still be time after his return to England in November.

Ordered from Spithead to Galleons Reach, the *Resolution* arrived with the intention of going on to Deptford to be paid off and laid up. Cook had gone home to Mile End for a family reunion. Of his five children, only his eldest and youngest boys were still alive. They, like their father, would both predecease their mother Elizabeth. Cook left his house on 9 August for an audience with the King at St James's Palace. He took his leave of George III promoted to post-captain and in command of a 74-gun ship, the *Kent*. Within twenty-four hours that plan had been consigned to the wastebasket. The death of Captain Michael Clements in the Royal Hospital, Greenwich, left a vacancy for a pensionable captain. The mark of Sandwich was left on a posting which Cook described as 'a fine retreat and a pretty income (£230 p.a., free quarters, fire and light and 1*s.* 2*d.* per diem table money) but whether I can bring myself to like ease and retirement, time will show'. Cook accepted the appointment subject to one condition, that their lordships would allow him 'to quit it when either the call of my country for more active service, or that my endeavours in any shape can be essential to the public'. This therefore was Cook's death-wish, for without that caveat he could have lived a peaceful, long life in an exceptional environment.

Another change of plan was to repair and refurbish the battered *Resolution*. Solander witnessed the 'welcome home' ceremony which he described in a letter to Banks. Sandwich was there, accompanied by Miss Ray. Those so recommended were promoted accordingly and Clerke was promised the ship, whose duties would include the return of Omai to his island. The visitors showed considerable interest in the curiosities on board which included three Tahitian dogs, a springbok, drawings of birds for Banks, live birds for Queen Charlotte, and the surgeon's mate had taken the time and interest to assemble a botanical collection. All this was found to be very interesting until Pickersgill revealed the pickled New Zealand head from which two slices of meat had been cut, which sickened the ladies. Solander made a mental note to acquire the head in the morning. That night, Sandwich entertained all the officers to dinner at Woolwich.

Banks and Omai did not accompany Sandwich to London but went in the opposite direction up the Great North Road in a leviathan of a coach belonging to Banks. The summer of 1775, which for Omai would be the best summer of his short life, has been well documented by George Colman Jr who wrote his account of this memorable period in his own life half a century later. Colman tells us that Banks's extraordinarily heavy-duty coach took six passengers inside and provided so much storage space, fully taken up with 'books, maps, charts, quadrants, telescopes etc' in support of Banks's studies, that the coach resembled a ship victualled for a long voyage. Banks's coach may have been unusual but it was not unique. Lord Peterborough had something similar which could sleep four in a 'stupendous vehicle (which) was a moving house, having in and about it every convenience appertaining to a mansion'. Peterborough's intention 'was to ensure for himself every common comfort when travelling upon the Continent, especially through Italy'. Banks' lumbering coach, designed neither for speed nor comfort, did have, unsurprisingly, an element of the Heath Robinson about it. Inside there was an odometer called a hippopedometer to inform passengers the speed at which the coach was travelling. Unfortunately the device broke down after 10 miles. Another interesting device was a heavy dragchain, a new idea for braking this heavy vehicle, particularly in the descent of steep hills. On the first occasion the driver put the chain to the test, the carriage ran over the postboy, coming very close to crushing him to death.

The destination of coach and passengers was the York races to rendezvous with the explorer Constantine Phipps who was associated with the nugatory attempt to discover the North-East Passage. After the races, Banks planned to accept Phipps's invitation to visit the stately but ramshackle family home near Whitby, close to Cook territory. The house party also included Phipps's younger brother, the thirteen-year-old Augustus, the impresario George Colman who had kindly put *Cymbeline* on at the Covent Garden Opera House for the benefit of Cartwright's unfortunate Eskimos, and his twelve-year-old son also by the name of George, to whom we owe a vote of thanks for registering the events in great detail. There are two points regarding this extended journey relating to Banks. First, this was not the behaviour of someone accused of neglecting Omai, but, second, it was also not the behaviour of someone who was intensely interested in what the *Resolution* had to tell and show. It could be argued that Banks was still too embarrassed to meet Cook and Omai presented a convenient diversion, a good reason to postpone the meeting between these two men.

A slow coach to Whitby was bad enough but its progress could also be interrupted by the hawk-eyed Banks spotting some botanical specimen of interest en route: 'a halt was immediately order'd, out jump'd Sir Joseph; out jump'd Omai, after us all. Many articles which seem'd to me no better than thistles, and which would not have sold for a farthing at Covent Garden Market, were pull'd up by the roots, and stow'd carefully in the coach as rarities.'

In addition to flora there were also fauna, as evidenced by Banks's close examination of a frog which he held in his hand. To the great amusement of those present, the frog leapt into Banks's open mouth, proving, as young Colman insisted, that to describe the frog as poisonous was obviously an old wives' tale.

On leaving the port town of Whitby, the travellers descended a hill which the designers of the chain braking system would have considered a supreme test. The hill 'up-gang', like all very steep two-way roads, also had its down-gang and that was their direction of travel. After surviving the descent, the coach negotiated a narrow 3-mile route between the sea and the cliffs. By now the wind was on the increase and the sun had recently dipped below the horizon. The roar of crashing waves startled the four horses who plunged into the sea carrying the coach with them. After their eventful journey they arrived at Mulgrave, an uninspiring pile later destroyed by fire, allowing architects to design a more magisterial building appropriate for a lordly domain.

In 1775 the sea off Scarborough was known as the German Sea but it seems that when the Germans got too big for their boots it was no longer considered appropriate to concede this stretch of water to them and so it became the North Sea. The water temperature in 1775 was colder than it is today and even now it tempts only the most hardy. It seemed a most inhospitable stretch of water for a Polynesian used to swimming in a sea as warm as bath water. Imagine the surprise, therefore, of the pre-teen Colman, about to launch himself upon his maiden ducking into the cold brine from the bathing machine, to see Omai wading out in front of the steps leading down from the box on wheels. What the representatives of the northern tribes of Yorkshire out on the beach that morning might have thought of the apparition that was Omai is not recorded. But to a dour, phlegmatic people who acknowledge 'folk' to be queer (meaning strange), Omai would have been of only passing interest.

His was not an entirely unblemished body but it was a body

beyond the run of the mill. He had holes through his earlobes, a scar on his arm, possibly caused by a spear and a scar on his leg where he had been hit by debris from the *Dolphin*'s cannonade upon One Tree Hill. His shoulders, broad and muscular, framed a solid chest which tapered down to a narrow waist and flat stomach. He was tall, had long, perfect legs with calf and thigh muscles a rugby prop forward would have envied. His life and activity to this date had produced a specimen absolutely to type with what Jan Prince described as the 'dexterity of an amphibious animal in the water'. The junior Colman was not from these parts, and his impressionable mind took on board an image that remained undeveloped for half a century.

> The coast of Scarborough having an eastern aspect, the early sunbeams shot their lustre upon the tawny Priest, and heighten'd the cutaneous gloss which he had already received from the water: he look'd like a specimen of pale moving mahogany, highly varnish'd; not only varnish'd, indeed, but curiously veneer'd; for, from his hips and the small of his back, downwards, he was tattow'd with striped arches, broad and black, by means of a sharp shell or a fish's tooth, imbued with an indelible dye, according to the fashion of his country.

Omai called out to his young friend, 'Tosh', to gain his attention. Then came a burst of words, reinforced by mime to convey to the boy his meaning – 'back, swim, I, me, carry, you'. The invitation to swim out to sea with Omai, a stranger, 'and that stranger a savage', was not something to embark upon without due, not to say rapid, consideration. George Colman had never seen the sea until the day before, 'nothing more than a very great puddle', and the month before had come close to drowning in the Thames. Nevertheless, he leapt from the machine on to Omai's back, signifying his 'immediate acceptance of his offer'.

Scarborough beach, like George III's much-loved Weymouth beach, is not a place recommended for spontaneous skinny-dipping for it is extremely shallow, extending 'with a gentle declivity, very far into the sea'. A long way from the shore, when the water eventually came up to Omai's chin, he struck out, the boy astride his back. 'I found myself on board the Omai, decidedly not as commander of the vessel, but as a passive passenger, who must submit without effort, to the very worst that could happen', a risk that appeared minimal for 'my wild friend appear'd as much at home upon the waves as a rope-dancer upon a cord'. At first Tosh was afraid but his fears subsided. They spoke of words, of language, and the boy had no problems on those occasions when, still swimming, Omai used the comb he carried in one hand to sweep back the black locks falling over his shoulders. After swimming for three-quarters of an hour, Omai and passenger arrived back at the beach to be met by a concerned father. Banks and Phipps laughed, calling Tosh, 'a tough little fellow; and Omai and I were, henceforth, constant companions'. Tosh did his very best to improve Omai's English in exchange for being taught a number of phrases in Tahitian.

Here, finally, at Mulgrave, Omai paid serious attention to musketry and skill at arms. He knew that time was running out and that he would be obliged to return home to take revenge. It soon became evident that Omai would not have objected if he had been unable to return home. Frequently he would ask Banks, as a man with a fatal illness interrogating his doctor, 'How long do I have?' He never learnt the difference between game birds and domestic animals, the latter becoming unfortunate substitutes to be shot down as Bora Borans: 'he popp'd at all the feather'd creation which came in his way; and which happen'd for the most part, to be dunghill cocks, barndoor geese, and ducks in the pond. His slaughter of domestic birds was by no means inconsiderable.' He was also capable of accounting for animals by stealth alone as the young Colman explained:

I was out with him in a stubble field, (at the beginning of September) when he pointed to some object at a distance, which I could not distinguish; his eyes sparkled; he laid down his gun mighty mysteriously, and put his finger on my mouth, to enjoin silence; he then stole onwards, crouching along the ground for several yards; till, on a sudden, he darted forward like a cat, and sprang upon a covey of partridges, one of which he caught, and took home alive.

What precisely Omai would do next attracted the curiosity of the two boys (Tosh and Augustus Phipps) who stayed close by him. For his part, Omai appeared to prefer the company of the boys to that of the adults, a strange choice to be replicated later in Polynesia where he preferred the company of the ordinary folk rather than making an effort to ingratiate himself with a leadership which coveted the artefacts he had brought with him. At Mulgrave, the boys watched in amazement at Omai's impulse to go horse riding:

He seized a grazing horse by the tail; the astounded animal galloped off, wincing and plunging, and dragging his tenacious assailant after him, till he slipped from his grasp, and left him in the mire; how Omai contrived to dodge the horse's heels, and escape with his brains in his head, I cannot explain. He was not always so intrepid; there was a huge bull in the grounds which kept him at a respectable distance, and of which he always spoke reverentially, as the man-cow.

The group often left Mulgrave to make excursions to nearby estates, to go on picnics or indulge in archaeology. On one such day they visited the fox-hunting Sir Charles Turner who had a hard, uncompromising, no-nonsense attitude to the bringing up of children. His son dashed into the drawing room holding in his hand a live mouset. His Father said, 'Bite off his head, Charles', which is what the boy did in front of his father and guests.

The picnics were comprised of more than Sandwich's sandwiches. Banks rated himself a master chef of the outdoors, a position to which Omai did not aspire but was capable of achieving. Ambition tempted Banks to over-reach himself in competition with Omai. His stews, which he cooked in a 'tin machine', were palatable but not overly challenging. His determination to barbecue a hog took him beyond the boundary of his capabilities. No finesse was exercised in dealing with the hog, almost casually set down on a blazing fire in the field where he was 'burn'd, scorch'd, blacken'd, till he looked like a fat Protestant at the stake, in the days of Bishop Bonner: we all had a flap at him, with a rag dipp'd in vinegar, at the end of a stick, by way of a basting ladle, otherwise he would have done to a cinder'.

Omai chose to cook chickens in the traditional Tahitian manner in a hole in the ground. He improvised, using English substitutes for unavailable Tahitian items: 'He cook'd fowls in stead of dogs, which last he would have preferred . . . for plantain leaves to wrap up the animal food, he was supplied with writing paper smeared with butter; for yams, he had potatoes; for the breadfruit, bread itself, the best home-made in Yorkshire'.

Colman minor found Banks's hog 'very nasty' but heaped praise upon Omai's food which 'in the eating, nothing could be better dress'd, or more savoury: the smouldering pebble-stones and embers of the Otaheitan oven had given a certain flavour to the fowls, a *soupçon* of smokiness, which made them taste as if a ham accompanied them'.

Following his summer excursion into Yorkshire, Omai returned to Hinchingbrooke from where he commuted to London until February 1776, an impediment to Hackman's uninterrupted wooing of Martha. There are Ray–Hackman love letters and related papers within the literature but these appear to have been subjected to editorial embellishment after the sub-plot came to its conclusion in April 1779. Stripped of that embellishment, however, there is a sound academic argument in support of the spirit of the love letters being genuine. There is no reason to doubt that Omai became aware of Martha's relationship with Hackman. 'Omiah's simplicity is certainly very diverting, but I should like him better, and take more pains with him, if I did not think he suspected something', wrote Martha. 'The other day I am sure he came to spy the nakedness of the land.'

The *dénouement* occurred outside Covent Garden's Opera House as Martha Ray stepped into Sandwich's coach; he was working late in the Admiralty. She had told Hackman that their relationship was over, but the spurned lover appeared, a pistol in each hand. With one, he killed her instantly with a shot to the head. He turned the other upon himself, fired, missed and was arrested, condemned and hanged. They took the news to Sandwich at a time when he was already under considerable pressure. 'His Lordship stood, as it were, petrified; till suddenly seizing a candle, he ran up the stairs, and threw himself on the bed, and in an agony exclaimed, "Leave me for a while to myself – I could have borne anything but this".' In the morning he sent a note to his friend Captain Walsingham to come and give him support. His duty was unavoidable, a case of *noblesse oblige*, but Sandwich rejected all entertainment and socialising.

Eventually, as part of his rehabilitation, Walsingham invited Sandwich to dinner. Guests included his secretary Joah Bates and his wife who shared Sandwich's love of music. All went well until after coffee a guest asked Mrs Bates if she would sing 'Shepherds, I Have Lost My Love'. She readily agreed – too readily for her husband to intervene and stop her. Bates's obvious anxiety merely fuelled the distress of the occasion. Once Mrs Bates had begun it was impossible to prevent her from finishing. 'Shepherds, I Have Lost My Love' was the first air sung by Martha at Hinchingbrooke and every time she was there it was requested by Sandwich.

Lord Sandwich for a while struggled to overcome his feelings, but they were so apparent that at last he went up to Mrs Walsingham, and in a very confused manner said he hoped she would excuse him from staying longer at that time, but that he had just recollected some pressing business that required his return to the Admiralty.

Colman senior seems to have told Garrick of Omai's grand repast at Mulgrave. In his response, Garrick advised his friend that he expected to see Colman 'as brown and as hearty as a Devonshire ploughboy who faces the sun without shelter and knows not the luxury of small beer and porter'. As one professional of the theatre writing to another, Garrick floated past Colman his idea to make a farce upon the follies and fashions of the times and your friend Omai was to be my Arlequin Sauvage – a fine character to give our fine folks a genteel dressing – I must lick my fingers with you at the Otaheite fowl and potatoes – but don't you spoil the dish and substitute a fowl for a young puppy?

The French first staged the pantomime *Arlequin Sauvage* in Paris in 1721. In it, Harlequin calls to account the conduct and behaviour of a civilised state. The connection with John O'Keefe's 1785 performance therefore is minimal since the latter is a fictitious, costume love story involving Omai and a voluptuous English girl, Londina, in which there is a heavy ladling of homage to James Cook. What in fact was made of Garrick's idea was not a farce but the famous pantomime to which Garrick, who died in 1779 aged sixty-two, predeceasing both Omai and Cook, made no contribution.

The idea of a pantomime – a theatrical medium not intellectually challenging, essentially a simple, entertaining, often far-fetched story involving colourful characters, extravagant scenery accompanied by rousing, even jingoistic music and strident songs – went into abeyance. Its reawakening was undoubtedly due to the 1784 publication of Cook's posthumous, three-volume account of his third voyage, *A Voyage to the Pacific Ocean*, completed by Captain James King, edited by Canon John Douglas and illustrated by John Webber. There is a widely accepted view that the catalyst had been Webber's extensive collection of pictures of places and personalities, verified to a large extent by the Theatre Royal's employment of Webber as an artistic consultant. William Hodges's 1773 drawing of Tu, principal Chief of Tahiti, father of Omai in the pantomime, is faithfully re-created in Philippe Jacques de Loutherbourg's authentic drawings of the stage characters. Joshua Reynolds, who attended the first night of *Omai, or a Trip Round the World*, expressed 'the utmost satisfaction at all landscape scenes'.

On 23 November 1775, a number of Cook's new associates successfully proposed his admission to membership of the Royal

Society in London. The first five signatures on the resolution are those of Banks, Solander, Mulgrave, Forster and Seaforth.

Captain James Cook of Mile End, a gentleman skilful in astronomy and the successful conductor of two important voyages for the discovery of unknown countries, by which geography and natural history have been greatly advantaged and improved, being desirous of the honour of becoming a member of this Society, we whose names are underwritten, do from our personal knowledge testify, that we believe him deserving of such honour, and that he will become a worthy and useful member.

Great was the number of welcome visitors to pass through the Burneys' London home, Newton House. In November 1775, Fanny happily welcomed Prince Alexsei Grigorevich Orlov, said to have been the leader of the band of officers who assassinated the husband of Catherine the Great. Although one of the popular *lyons*, Fanny Burney could equally have been describing a Fabergé Christmas tree: 'Besides a Blue Garter, he had a star of diamonds, of prodigious brilliance; he had likewise a shoulder knot of the same precious jewels and a picture of the Empress hung from his neck, which was set round with diamonds of such magnitude and lustre that, when near the candle, they were too dazzling for the eye.' The Burney girls were too short to see the Empress's portrait properly. 'Take it off that we might see,' they pleaded. 'The ladies might undress me completely if they wish,' came his risqué reply.

Fanny's diary entry for 14 December reveals the visit of someone, a more senior *lyon*, no less exotic but rather less well decorated and flamboyant: 'To our great surprise, who should enter late in the evening, but Omiah.' To Fanny it was a mystery how he had found the house since his only previous visit had been a year ago. His language had obviously not improved greatly and she was careful to pen the diverse reasons why that should have been so. If truth be known, Fanny found Omai less intimidating than either Bruce or Orlov, both giants of men, she being 'dwarfish'. 'He is lively and intelligent, and seems so open and frank hearted, that he looks everyone in the face as his friend and well wisher.' The conversation opened on the subject of Jem Burney.

'Lord Sandwich wrote one, two, three (counting on his fingers) months ago, – Mr Burney – come home.' (Sandwich had said as much to Mrs Burney: 'I have heard of your son madam; and expect him home daily.')

'He will be very happy to see you,' cried Fanny.

Omai bowed and said, 'Mr Burney very dood man!'

Had he seen the King lately? they asked. Indeed he had, dressed in the favoured white cloth he had met the King, Queen and three of their pretty daughters.

'Yes; King George bid me – "Omy, you go home". Oh very dood man, King George.'

With some assistance, Omai was able to say how pleased he was at the prospect of going home but at the same time expressed his sadness at having to leave his friends in England. 'Lord Sandwich', he added, 'bid me, – "Mr Omy, you two ships, – you go home". I say (making a fine bow), "Very much oblige, my Lord".'

Changing the subject, the Burneys asked if he had been to the Opera. 'He immediately began a squeak, by way of imitation, which was very ridiculous; however, he told us he thought the music was very fine, which when he first heard it, he thought detestable.' How then did he like the theatres? He could not be made to understand, a fact which he conveyed to them 'by his bows and smiles'. The conversation then switched to horse riding, a subject which fell within his comprehension. He sought to explain riding pillion: 'First goes man so (making a motion of whipping a horse), then *here* (pointing behind him), *here* goes woman. Ha! Ha! Ha!' A guest of the Burneys that afternoon was a Miss Lidderdale of Lynn, dressed in a riding habit, who told him in no uncertain manner that she was prepared to go on horseback. Quick to spot the possibility that he may have offended the good Miss Lidderdale, Omai began with 'a very civil bow' and said, 'Oh you, you dood woman, you no man; dirty woman, beggar woman ride so; – not you.'

Fanny mentioned to Omai her half-brother Dick, now at Harrow School. He did remember him and associated school with reading from books. He told of the indelible impression made by a master hitting a boy a violent blow upon his shoulder with a book. Miss Lidderdale asked him whether he had seen Lady Townshend lately.

'Very pretty woman, Lady Townshend!', cried he. 'I drink tea with Lady Townshend in one, two, *tree* days: Lord Townshend my friend, Lady Townshend my friend. Very pretty woman, Lady Townshend! Very pretty woman, Mrs Crewe! Very pretty woman, Mrs Bouverie! Very pretty woman, Lady Craven!' The assembled gathering approved his taste. He went on to amplify that when any of his acquaintances wished to see him, 'they write and bid me, Mr Omy, you come, – dinner, tea or supper, then I go'. When Fanny asked Omai if he would like to go back to Tahiti, he replied in the affirmative: 'Yes, Miss, no mutton there, no coach, no dish of tea, no pretty Miss Horneck [Reynolds's beautiful model]: good air, good sea and very good dog. I happy at Otaheite.'

The truth of whether Omai had liaisons can never be known. The regular diarists would not have been present, decorum may well have prevented the lady in question passing comment and as for Omai, there being no written Tahitian language, he was denied the possibility of writing a Casanova's diary. But Omai had changed. The early universal impression that he was an ugly person had given way to reappraisal. His complexion, it was now said, 'much resembles that of an European used to hot climates', which meant that his skin colour had lightened. 'He is lusty and strong made, though not in the least heavy.' One reason for Omai's increasing popularity among the wives of the gentry was his closeness to their age as opposed to their husbands'. In comparison, he was truly exotic; his long, shining, dark black hair falling down over his shoulders was undoubtedly capable of raising the pulse of frustrated aristocratic wives. His were deep brown, 'come hither' eyes, soft and twinkling with the light of fire, framed by long, dark, curling lashes. There was one particularly notorious woman, Lady Carew, so notorious that other ladies avoided being seen with her, even abroad. 'Since she is mentioned more than once as an admirer of the savage, it may be that rumours of her immorality and her association with the popular Omai combined to start a scandal which enveloped all the ladies of the native's acquaintance.'

The social scene became Omai's scene. He was not given the benefit of any useful instruction to prepare him for his return home. George III would have been in a position to direct him towards instruction in modern farming techniques, and he would have had the chance to learn wood- or leatherworking. These were the skills which the London Missionary Society exported to Tahiti in 1796. The mission placed emphasis on manual rather than intellectual skills, so the *mechanic* missionaries to a man found on their arrival that they could not begin to communicate with the natives. Religious observers, including Sir John Cullum, Michael Tyson and Thomas Haweis, blamed Banks and Sandwich for a missed opportunity. Haweis, a founder member of the London Missionary Society, complained:

> The foolish Omai was an expense more than would have maintained a mission to the island. Not so much as an attempt was made to give him any knowledge tending to the saving of his soul. He was led away to stare, and be stared at, at our public places, and be as abandoned as those who frequent them.

Omai's association with society ladies did not pass without comment. Here, after all, was a dimension to Rousseau's philosophy that the philosopher had not considered. The problem was not so much that Omai *was* a stud on the rampage but that gossips and lampooners could lead others to such a conclusion. An anonymous 1776 poem, *Omiah's Farewell; Inscribed to the Ladies of London,* begins with an open-ended introduction:

> The novelty of his figure drew much upon him, more particularly from the women of quality, for with many of them he was intimate

and familiar – I have a higher opinion of my fair country women, than to think they would be so condescending; and yet, philosophy cannot reconcile the depravity of female inclinations.

The long poem then proceeds, in these extracts, to point fingers at identifiable ladies:

> This, on thy rosy pinions, Cupid, Bear,
> To the soft hands of Lady C— fair;
> To her white hands these plaintive strains I send,
> To beauteous Christian, and the Indian's friend:
> To her chaste bosom I confide my flame,
> And with an E— leave Omiah's fame.
> Oft' Lady C— hast thou promise made,
> To sleep with me beneath the Bread-tree's shade,
> For brighter suns, to leave this clouded sky,
> And with Omiah share Eternity.
> O hear a poor untutor'd Indian's vow,
> And make her stoop to one thou'st made so low;
> Or else abate more than am'rous fires,
> Which rise in tumult as this Saint inspires.
> To ev'ry angel of the British coast,
> Omiah drinks, and makes their charms his toast.
> To Lady— first the glass he quaffs,
> While o'er the rosy wine her Cupid laughs;
> To her pledges constancy and truth,
> Not with the coldness of the Gallick Youth.
> To beauteous B—, and the courteous C—,
> His warmest, chastest, fairest thanks are due;
> Be yours gay days of ease, and nights of pleasure,
> And joys Elysian, flowing without measure.
> Ah beauteous B— how shall I define,
> Thy many virtues o'er the rosy wine;
> How in two lives can I such merits hit,
> The charms of beauty and the fire of wit.

To thee my lovely T— I devote,
Each wish that may inspire a virtuous thought.
What purest love can feel, with thee shall live,
And all that sensibility can give.

Although George III did give chase to Fanny Burney on one of his difficult days, he was essentially a moral, family man. There can be no doubt that the prevailing gossip and rumour surrounding Omai contributed to the King's decision to say, 'Omai, you go home'. Whereas in England Banks had the status and position to be able to shrug off sexual innuendo and tittle-tattle, Omai did not. Moreover, he was not even close to being considered indispensable. It is more than probable that it was Banks, using his access to the King, who persuaded George III to tell Omai to go home, thus exonerating Banks from any further obligation towards him. Omai had served his purpose in raising Banks's reputation at a time when it was low. Now that Banks had a buoyant career involving much strategic thinking, Omai had become expendable. George III would have considered Banks's recommendation carefully. Based upon the truth as he knew it, there were sound reasons for sending Omai home. The cost of Omai's upkeep was not cheap, a factor which would have resonated with a cost-conscious King who believed Omai could serve George and his country better in the Society Islands than in London. Omai's most profound discovery on arrival in England would have been that there was no prospect of living off the land. For his two years in London he was entirely dependent upon the generosity of others. The unwelcome satire did not help but, essentially, George III would not have seen a problem in a prince or chief returning to his own people, for that is what he believed Omai to be. For the evidence, we need only remember the initial presentation of a sword and now, finally, the gifts being assembled to accompany a friend of high rank home.

To return to Newton House, Dr Burney asked Omai to sing a song of his own country – a song he had heard him sing at

Hinchingbrooke. By the time he had finished, the ladies may well have wondered why the good doctor wanted to hear the song again, forewarned being forearmed. The storyline can be described as quaint, involving an old woman, a young man and a young woman. The latter two are flirting when the old woman enters and tries to entice the young man away. Short on beauty and youth, she attempts to make him 'observe her taste and fancy'. All this Omai acted out as though in pantomime. Unimpressed, the youth avows his interest in the younger woman, whereupon the elder of the two women sends the younger away. She approaches the young man, offering herself. 'Come! Marry me!' Horrified, the young man bows, asks to be excused and runs off.

It was some act to sing to a noted musical family such as the Burneys. Fanny described his singing voice which took two or three attempts to get going:

> Nothing can be more curious or less pleasing than his singing voice; he seems to have none; and tune or air hardly seem to be aimed at; so queer, wild, strange a rumbling of sounds never did I before hear; and very contentedly can I go to the grave, if I never do again. His song is the only thing that is *savage* belonging to him . . . Though the singing of Omy is so barbarous, his actions, the expression he gives to each character, are so original and so diverting, that they did not fail to afford us very great entertainment of the visible kind.

Lord Sandwich promised Mrs Burney that Jem Burney would soon be home from America, an event recorded with 'great joy' in Fanny's diary entry of 30 December. 'He is now in very good time for his favourite voyage to the South Seas, which we believe will take place in February.' There had been another visit by Omai accompanied by Dr Andrews, formerly of the *Adventure*. Andrews' command of the Tahitian language was so advanced that Omai had no need to struggle through his limited vocabulary bolstered by mime, thereby rendering him 'far less entertaining than on his former visit'.

Unlike Johnson, the Rousseau-phile Boswell never met Omai. He had not completely abandoned his hope of taking passage with Cook to either New Zealand or Tahiti and to that extent sought him out. Cook's experience of the senior Forster left him disinclined to take non-essential civilians ('botanists and designers') on the third voyage with which his name was now being associated. If the newspapers were to be believed, beyond acting as a taxi service for Omai, the mission was for exploration and not science: 'Captain Cook in the new voyage which he is going to make (Captain Clerke the commander of the second ship) is to take Omiah to Otaheite; and from thence to proceed upon the discovery of the North-West Passage to the northward of California.' Conventional wisdom had it that an attempted landing was to be made on California 'whose inhabitants were originally of Japan and are supposed to have travelled into the remote and western parts'. A prize of £20,000 had been offered for the discovery of a northern route between the Pacific and the Atlantic with the bonus of a further £5000 for the first ship to come within a degree of the North Pole. Having taken considerable time and at considerable risk, Cook had scotched the idea of Terra Australis Incognita. Now he was being sent out to probe the second great illusion that there *must* be a way through the North-West Passage because, as many scientists were prepared to say, sea-water cannot freeze.

To what extent the prospect of a substantial reward acted as an incentive to draw Cook from the confines of the Royal Hospital to offer his services is not clear, although it was undoubtedly a contributory factor. The Commissioners of the Admiralty had already consulted him with regard to which ships to commission for the next voyage of discovery. The *Resolution* was available and self-selecting, and the principle of safety in numbers meant that a second ship was required. Again, a former collier, the Whitby-built *Diligence*, 298 tons, entered naval service as the *Discovery*. On 10 February Cook succumbed to pressure that he should lead the expedition, subject to the condition that 'on my return (they will) either restore me to my appointment in the Hospital, or procure for me such other mark of the Royal Favour as their Lordships upon the review of my past services shall think me deserving of'. In the meantime, Omai attempted to make the most of a winter more intense than the previous year's. He taught himself to ice skate, undoubtedly a first for any Tahitian, cutting a fine figure on the Serpentine in Hyde Park. In Parliament Street, close to the Admiralty, he had a chance meeting with an old friend, Joseph Cradock. 'I was informed that he was not at all concerned at the thoughts of leaving us; and indeed I felt rather vexed that we should have wasted so much anxiety about him.' Cradock discovered the contrary to be true: 'He was miserable and I was very much affected.'

Boswell had his first meeting with Cook and Mrs Cook, 'a decent plump Englishwoman', on 2 April 1776 in the home of Sir John Pringle, author of a famous paper on the health of seamen. Boswell agreed with Pringle's description of Cook: 'a plain, sensible man with an uncommon attention to veracity'. The emphasis Cook placed upon truth was borne out by reference to the Scottish judge and intellectual Lord Monboddo's attempt 'to establish an unbroken "chain" of existence between man and beings of a lower order'. Monboddo, formerly James Burnett, wrote two six-volume works on language and metaphysics yet attracted ridicule for claiming the orang-utan as part of mankind. Some have suggested he was the predecessor of Charles Darwin. The judge assumed from something which arose in the account of the second voyage that Cook had said 'that he had seen a nation of men like monkeys'. On being told this by Pringle, Cook protested: 'No, I did not say they were like monkeys. I said their faces put me in mind of monkeys.'

Boswell tells how Cook had said that, in his opinion, Omai would attempt to return to England shortly after his arrival in Tahiti and so, accordingly, Cook intended to leave before Omai had time to become entirely dissatisfied with his lot. There is no doubt that this was the official policy while that which Fanny Burney espoused – 'they are to carry Omai back and to give him a month for liking, at the end of which, if he does not again relish his old home, or finds himself not well treated, he is to have it in his power to return hither again' – was fanciful. The establishment did not desire Omai's return. According to Cook, he thought Omai would enjoy something of a honeymoon period feeding off the tales he had to tell the islanders, the assumption being that the islanders would be prepared to listen. Already, Omai had indicated some of those goods with which he would wish to return home. One was port wine, his favourite drink, and another, gunpowder, which Cook refused to concede due to Omai having 'some ambitious design', a refusal which did not prevail.

Boswell and Cook had two further meetings. At the first, again in the Mitre with Pringle, Boswell made a point of sitting next to Cook. The meal had been indifferent, for which Sir John apologised. Boswell replied to the contrary: 'I have had a feast (pointing to Cook), I have had a good dinner, for I have had a good Cook.' Boswell and Cook discussed the possibility of establishing ambassadors in Tahiti, New Zealand and New Caledonia for three year periods with the purpose of the individuals learning the language and, on their return, reporting on their discoveries. Boswell believed himself to be a suitable ambassador, felt himself willing to volunteer if so encouraged by a government prepared to pay 'a handsome pension for life'. Johnson provided absolutely no encouragement, nor did Cook, and the idea evaporated.

Cook's wish to sail by the end of April did not come to fruition even though the loading of ships and the taking-on of crew had begun in February. The *Resolution*'s complement remained at one hundred and twelve while seventy were to man the *Discovery*. The unwanted delays meant that both ships suffered persistent desertions by sailors desperate to avoid a voyage of up to three or four years' duration. Cook had been directly involved in the production of the written account of the second voyage; the lessons of Hawkesworth had been learnt. There was to be no ghost writer nor any writer other than Cook, a decision which led to a long-drawn-out and hostile battle with Forster who had hoped to co-author the work. Right up to the time of sailing, Cook was writing to Banks seeking botanical descriptions. This distraction meant that he was not entirely free to monitor the six-month refit of the *Resolution* at the naval yard in Deptford. That is something of an reason but not an excuse for neglecting to maintain an overview of the refit. Previously he had meticulously supervised the work because the Royal Dockyards had a reputation for corruption. That he did not do so on this occasion meant that when the *Resolution* set out on her voyage proper, she was found to leak like a sieve.

There was also the matter of a time-consuming portrait. Cook had been painted by both Reynolds and Hodges but it is generally believed that the mood of the man is best captured in Nathaniel Dance's portrait in the National Maritime Museum. This had not been a sitting long in the planning because the work was done in May, a month after the *Resolution* and the *Discovery* should have been at sea. Banks had been the driving force in encouraging Cook to sit. Perhaps Cook had a premonition that this was something that had to be done for posterity. He had suffered bouts of illness during his second voyage and his occasional, uncharacteristic, displays of impatience and heavy-handedness during the third have been attributed to his having been unwell. One piece of news to raise spirits had been the awarding to Cook, Fellow of the Royal Society, of the Copley Medal for his paper on the prevention of scurvy during extended ocean voyages. The citation for the medal, named after Sir Godfrey Copley, would not be presented until 30 November 1776 when Cook was well into his third voyage. Sir John Pringle said of Cook to the Society: '[he] not only discovered, but surveyed, vast tracts of new coast, *who hath dispelled the illusion of a terra Australis Incognita*, and fixed the bounds of the habitable earth, as well as the navigable ocean in the southern Hemisphere.'

Cook took command of the *Resolution*, the *Discovery* being put under the command of his friend, the expedition's second-in-command, the very experienced Captain Charles Clerke. There was, however, a problem with Clerke in so far as at some time after his return from the second voyage he acted as guarantor for a loan taken out by his brother Sir John Clerke. Sir John, a captain in the Royal Navy, sailed off to the East Indies leaving his brother high and dry as the inheritor of his debt. When it became public knowledge that

Charles, too, was to go to distant places, Sir John's creditors applied for their money. It is a mystery how Captain Charles Clerke, a key component in an extremely important operation supported by the King, the Admiralty and the Royal Society, could be allowed to be thrown into the King's Bench prison without the debt having been dealt with administratively. While the planning and preparation for the voyage went ahead, a vital supervisory figure was therefore languishing in gaol, picking up the deadly tuberculosis bacillus. In a dictated letter to his friend Banks on 10 August 1779, twelve days before his death aged thirty-eight, Clerke explained: 'The disorder I was attacked with in the King's Bench prison has proved consumptive, with which I have battled with various success, although without one single day's health since I took leave of you in Burlington Street.' While in gaol he remained optimistic that he would 'outsail the Israelites and get to sea'. With the attention of both captains held elsewhere, it might be thought surprising that the expedition set out in the relatively good order that it did. This is because the lieutenants in particular had to a large extent been associated with previous voyages to the South Pacific and there were familiar names among the veterans: the American John Gore, one of seven Americans in the two ships, James King, Jem Burney and surgeon and linguist William Anderson.

Among the new lieutenants was the prickly John Williamson and a new master for the *Resolution* aged twenty-two, about whom Cook had no reservations. He had been selected on the basis of his reputation as a skilful cartographer. The master was of warrant officer rank, responsible for the navigation of the ship. He would visit Tahiti twice after the conclusion of Cook's third voyage; his name, William Bligh. The Royal Marines officer Molesworth Phillips, formerly of the Royal Navy, twenty-one years old, came from Ireland and suffered all the advantages and disadvantages of that fact. Described as 'fine made, tall, stout, active, a manly looking young fellow', he had the charm and words to disarm Fanny's and Jem's sister Susan, becoming her unsatisfactory husband. The man selected to maintain the pictorial record, the twenty-four-year-old professional artist John Webber, was almost the last man to be appointed to the expedition. His was not the only portfolio of paintings to come from Cook's third voyage. A carpenter on that voyage, and keen amateur artist, James Cleveley, had a brother, John, who converted four of his sketches into representations of events which occurred during the course of the voyage. One would prove to be controversial because it challenges the official version of Cook's death. The competent astronomer William Bayly was again found a berth. Finally, David Nelson came aboard, in effect representing Banks as a botanical collector. As to pure scientists, none had been appointed to the voyage. Forster had left an indelible mark.

After the victuals had been stored, the time had come to shoe-horn personal effects into any available spaces. The animals had special pens on deck, a problem that the sailors themselves would have been gratefully rid of. During the course of his audience with George III, the King told Cook of his desire to establish English farming practices among the subject-natives of *his* island. The King had the 'benevolent view of conveying some permanent benefit to the inhabitants'. Delivered to the two ships for loading were two cows with calves, a bull, a mare, a stallion, a quantity of sows with several hogs, a small flock of sheep and some rabbits. The *pièce de resistance* happened to be the gift of a Lord of the Admiralty, the Earl of Bessborough, who included in the manifest of animals a peacock and a peahen.

An examination of Omai's effects indicated his intention to introduce English habits to the Society Islands, a risky prospect as likely to lead to resentment as admiration. The sailors loaded his bed, table and chairs, plates and cutlery, gallons of port wine, an organ, a globe, an electrical device of the kind which had shocked him, as well as a sprung-serpent compressed in a cylinder to shock in a different way, and fireworks to impress and entertain. Granville Sharp presented him with a large illustrated Bible and this went aboard but would never be put to the use intended. Omai had his way with muskets, ball and powder for his personal protection, in addition to which a suit of body armour from Lord Sandwich, ordered specially from the Tower of London, had been included in his baggage.

Banks took it upon himself to be involved in all aspects of the preparation of gifts. He produced a generous, even lavish amount of clothing and effects for Omai, both male and female, including the miniature toys – the idea for which had originated in Streatham. Included almost as an afterthought were pictures of the King and Queen, silver watches and 'medecines for the Venereal disease'. There was even provision for Odiddy – two suits of clothes and a sword, having a total value of £50. There was another list of presents from the King for the 'Chiefs only who have shown themselves best deserving of such honours'. Banks advised the King not to skimp on cost so that his presents did not appear ungenerous by comparison with that which the officers and crew would give. The King took Banks' advice, having delivered to the *Resolution* laced hats and feathers, loose gowns of fine materials, trousers of fine linen, broadswords, cut-glass bowls, cases of knives and forks, magnifying glasses, chess boards and telescopes. Among the haberdashery were handkerchiefs with 'Great Britain' printed on them.

If there was a moral dimension influencing the decision whether or not Omai should be returned home, then the question of whether George III was aware of Omai's antecedents becomes academic. Among the population at large, there were those who knew his true origins and others who believed him to be a priest or prince. A priest or prince could act as a friend of Britain in Tahiti's Court and thereby deny France one port of call in the South Pacific. To inveigle a low-class warrior into Tahiti's structured aristocratic society and expect him to be effective, to be heard, to have influence, would be extraordinarily difficult. Yet Cook knew precisely where Omai's origins lay. He knew Tu and he knew the environment, but whether he had a grand plan at this stage is not known. It sufficed that the King and the Admiralty were making a prodigious effort to honour an explicit obligation to return Omai home. What Cook thought therefore did not matter, for he was complying with the wishes of his monarch, his patron and his Service. The commissioners at the Admiralty required of Cook, 'upon your arrival at Otaheite, or the Society Islands, you are to land Omiah at such of them as he may choose and to leave him there'. There were no options. Cook would do the best he could for his country and for Omai the man. The focus of public attention on Omai proved serendipitous for it obscured the principal reason for the voyage, described by Clerke as 'our intended attack on the North Pole'. The *General Evening Post* advised its readership:

> Omiah who is now on board the Resolution, in order to return to Otaheite, has made such good use of his time while in England, that he was able to write his sentiments in our language: the following is a copy of the card he sent to several of his friends, which we give upon the best authority. 'Omiah to take leave of good friend. He never forget England. He go on Sunday. God bless King George. He tell his people how kind English to him.'

The newspaper proved both premature and inaccurate in its report. The fact of the matter was recorded by Cook on 24 June 1776: 'At 6 o'clock in the morning I set out from London in company with Omai, we got to Chatham between 10 and 11.'

CHAPTER 9

To Tahiti

That Cook and Omai travelled together that morning the 38 miles (61 km) to Chatham dockyard tells us something of the changed relationship between the two. It might be argued that Cook shared his carriage with Omai to safeguard the interests of his powerful senior sponsors. Yet it went further than that, inasmuch as Cook enjoyed Omai's company, treating him not so much as an equal as a valued staff officer. Cook recognised that his first impressions of Omai had been misconstrued and he took steps to expunge criticism of him from his earlier written work. Having Omai in such close proximity must have concentrated Cook's mind, not so much upon his principal operational task – to seek out either the North-West Passage or North-East Passage – but upon how on earth he was going to rehabilitate Omai as an honorary British consul among his own people. 'Every method had been employed', wrote Cook, 'both during his abode in England, and at his departure, to make him the instrument of conveying to the inhabitants of the islands of the Pacific Ocean, the most exalted opinion of the greatness and generosity of the British nation.'

The fact that Omai had been unable to achieve competence in the English language would not be a significant shortcoming because he would explain to the Tahitians what he had seen in his own tongue. But of skills other than the use of firearms with which to hold the attention of the islanders, he had none. 'He should', said Forster, 'have been presented with tools, not trinkets.' Omai's perambulations around the drawing rooms of the great and good and his ready acceptance – hospitality not extended to someone of Cook's humble origins – would prove to have been a nugatory experience. A knowledge of English social customs would hardly be useful in his homeland. Had Cook been more socially acceptable, he might well have been in a better position to see the warning signs – Omai's playing to the gallery, his tantrums, his flouncing off – all symptomatic of a spoilt child. Omai's social experience quite ruined him because it made a snob of him and gave him expectations that could never be realised. Provision would be made, through the accompanying floating menagerie and other attractive gifts, for Omai to demonstrate the generosity of the British nation, but for a commoner to tell his chiefs of the greatness of another kingdom required a level of tact and discretion which Omai did not possess. Furneaux brought an unsophisticated native as a crew member to England whereas Cook brought back a different person; someone of inflated status, aloof, inflexible and unable to compromise. None of this of course was apparent to Cook whose impression of Omai that morning was of an individual experiencing mixed emotions, of regret and joy. When Omai spoke of those who had been kind to him, his spirits sank and he came close to tears, but when he spoke of home 'his eyes would sparkle with joy'. Cook found his attitude 'truly natural; he was fully sensible of the good treatment he had met with in England and entertained the highest ideas of the country and people but the prospect he now had of returning home to his native isle loaded with what they esteem, got the better of every other consideration.'

Captain Charles Proby, the Navy Board's commissioner at Chatham, awaited the carriage of Cook and Omai. Proby had met Omai before, during the *Augusta*'s tour of inspection, and he was looking forward to meeting both visitors. Charles Proby had a distinguished naval career including having been among those to have survived Anson's circumnavigation of the globe. By all accounts he provided a good lunch before making his yacht available to take the pair to Sheerness from where Cook's boat carried them on to the *Resolution*.

The quasi-diplomatic role envisaged for Omai meant that he was not going to be let down lightly in preparation for his homecoming. His close proximity to Cook, even having an adjoining cabin, spoke of his status and optimism for his future. The ship's officers soon grew to appreciate Omai's ability to interrelate, skills which he had honed in grander environments than the *Resolution*'s wardroom. For him, that was no challenge. On 25 June, Cook's diary recorded: 'About noon, weighed and made sail for the Downs.' The next day they anchored by arrangement off Deal to take two boats on board, an event which caused a buzz of excitement throughout the small coastal town and brought many spectators to line the pebble beach. They had come for a sight of Omai but would return home disappointed. He may still have been suffering the effects of seasickness. Jem Burney took the *Discovery* to Plymouth where she awaited the arrival of the *Resolution* on 30 June – and her Captain, still in gaol for want of £4000 to clear his brother's debt. The authorities maintained absolute faith in Charles Clerke, accepting that the *Resolution* might have to sail unaccompanied to the Cape of Good Hope, via intermediate islands for the collection of wine and fodder, and wait there for the arrival of the *Discovery*.

Revictualling or the topping-up of supplies took very little time but as so often seems to have been the case, ships or convoys on England's southern coast spent an inordinate amount of time waiting for the right wind. Cook gave Omai three guineas for a run ashore, a very handsome gift for one 'caressed here by every person of note, and upon the whole, I think, he rejoices at the prospect of going home'. As events would show, there existed the strongest of possibilities that Omai may have been caressed by a lady of Plymouth not ranked among 'persons of note'.

The contrary winds drove a convoy of sixty-two transports into Plymouth Sound, 'the greater half being Dutch ships', wrote Bayly, and their escorts, the warships *Ambuscade, Diamond* and *Unicorn*. Cook needed no reminding that all was not proceeding well along North America's seaboard.

It could not but occur to us a singular and affecting circumstance that at the very instant of our departure upon a voyage, the object of which was to benefit Europe by making fresh discoveries in

North America, there should be the unhappy necessity of employing others of his Majesty's ships, and of conveying numerous bodies of land forces, to secure the obedience of those parts of that continent which had been discovered and settled by our countrymen in the last century.

This massive convoy carried a division of Hessian troops with their horses and equipment. Britain, a maritime nation, engaged mercenary troops, when necessary, to top up the British Army's slender order of battle.

Perhaps Cook was thankful he was well out of it. Not until 1780 did the expedition become aware that, in addition to America, France and Spain were also at war with Britain. In an unique development, the governments of all three enemy states provided the highly respected Cook with a free licence of passage subject to his not indulging in hostilities. Cook's neutrality had been negotiated by Benjamin Franklin in grateful recognition of which Sir Joseph Banks, President of the Royal Society, awarded him a Cook medal. Banks became President of the Royal Society in 1778 and was to remain so until his death in 1820. Franklin, the Minister Plenipotentiary from the Congress of the United States at the Court of France, issued a communiqué on 10 March 1779 to all American captains and commanders of armed ships, that 'in case the said ship, which is now expected to be soon in European seas on her return, should happen to fall in your hands, you would not consider her an enemy, nor suffer any plunder to be made of the effects contained in her, nor obstruct her immediate return to England.'

Taking advantage of what at first appeared to be a favourable wind, Cook sailed during the evening of 12 July, almost two years after Omai had arrived in England and precisely four years since Cook's departure from Plymouth on his second voyage. Cook left an order with Burney for Clerke that he was to follow as soon as he joined his ship. The *Resolution* had not been at sea long before the neglect of the Deptford yard became readily apparent, 'the rain pouring into the officers' cabins through the ship's sides to the destruction of everything therein', complained Lieutenant Williamson. Progressively the sea and rain-water damaged sails in the sail room and ruined fodder, the capacity for which was limited, and entailed an obligatory call at Tenerife.

Cook preferred Tenerife to Madeira because he judged that animal food would be more abundant and the wine cheaper. The wine was cheaper, principally because it was less good than the wine available in Madeira. The *Resolution* anchored on 2 August, providing the crew with a welcome three-day break. Anderson was among those officers not required for duty or for the making of duty calls. He and a number of friends hired mules for a hike up to the city of Laguna. Omai discerned little difference between the British and Spaniards except that the latter appeared 'not so friendly and in person they approached those of his own country'. Anderson's mate, Welsh Minister's son, David Samwell, took a typical low-church view of the Spanish Roman Catholics: 'a set of gloomy, bigoted, praying, priest ridden miscreants.' Cook had the good fortune to meet professional colleagues, the French Captain Jean-Charles Borda of the *Boussole* and the Spanish Captain Joseph Varela, in Tenerife to test chronometers and fix the island's longitude. After Tenerife, Cook made for the Cape Verde islands on the off-chance that the *Discovery* might be there. On 10 August, during his watch, Cook narrowly avoided driving the *Resolution* on to the rocks on the island of Bonavista. Was the world's most famous navigator beginning to lose his touch? The *Discovery* was not at St Jago so on the 16th Cook took the *Resolution* southwards.

Omai's skill at pulling large fish aboard only added to his reputation. Cook told how 'Omai first showed us the way and caught twice the number of anybody besides'. He taught the crew how to catch dolphin and shark which was not only a useful way of alleviating the monotony of routine through sport but also provided a very valuable supplement to their diet. They crossed the Line in early September and the traditionalist Cook allowed the ducking of those crossing the equator for the first time. On board the *Discovery*, following after the *Resolution*, Clerke allowed a double ration of rum in lieu of ducking.

Those aboard the *Resolution* not inclined to be ducked could claim exemption upon payment of a bottle of rum. Few did. The officers, however, were not greatly enamoured of the practice. 'We had the practice of ducking put in execution to afford some fun,' wrote Bligh. William Anderson thought the ceremony 'ridiculous'.

David Samwell, surgeon's mate to Anderson, kept an interested eye upon Omai and provided a useful account from the time Omai joined the ship to his farewell. Samwell, an educated man, described Omai as very 'hearty' and had no doubt that he would live to see his home again. His inoculation against smallpox represented a sound insurance policy which the unfortunate Aoutourou and Cartwright's Eskimos had not had.

He is not such a stupid fellow as he is generally looked upon in England. 'Tis true he learn'd nothing there but how to play at cards, at which he is very expert but I take it to be more owing to his want of instruction than want of his capacity to take it. He talks English so bad that a person who does not understand something of his language can hardly understand him or make himself understood by him. They have made him more of the fine gentleman than any thing else.

Fine gentleman he may have appeared to be but deep down he remained 'like all ignorant people very superstitious'. He pointed to a northward-heading meteor claiming it to be God going to England. The crew, to a man, said he was talking nonsense – a claim which offended him and made him angry that he should be contradicted by such blasphemy.

At about two in the afternoon on 17 October they sighted the distinctive Table Mountain and by the afternoon of the next day had anchored in Table Bay. One of the priorities here was to attend to caulking the ship. The officers and crew suffered from sea water breaking through the side seams so that 'few could sleep dry in their beds'. 'Negligence of those who caulked her had been the cause of this,' continued Anderson. With no way of knowing when he might see the *Discovery*, Cook established a more sophisticated, long-term encampment ashore than might be usual, including an observatory. But he had the urgent business of caulking the *Resolution* to attend to as well as putting the King's animals to grass so that they might recover from the hardships of the voyage. There is no doubt that the crew enjoyed the Cape but Cook, now on his fourth visit, found less to hold his interest: 'after as favourable a passage as I could wish, but nothing new or entertaining happened, and I am now at one of the worst places in the world to find either one or the other.' There was benefit to be derived from his knowing the merchants, the Port Commandant Christoffel Brand and not least the Governor, with whom Cook dined in state. This was Samwell's first impression of the Cape, the beautiful scenery and the 'dear girls'. Cook, he discovered, was 'as famous here and more noted perhaps than in England'.

While waiting for Clerke to appear, life went on at a leisurely pace. Cook found time on 23 October to write a short letter to Sandwich to catch a French Indiaman about to sail:

Before I sailed from England, your Lordship was pleased to allow me the honour of writing at all opportunities. I embrace the first to acquaint your Lordship with my safe arrival at this place with Omai and every animal intend for Otaheite in a fair way of living to arrive at their destination spot. Omai desires his most dutiful respects to your Lordship and I am well assured it is from the sincerity of his heart for no man can have a juster sense of your Lordship's favours.

It is uncertain precisely how Clerke got out of prison but he made all haste to Plymouth, spent a day completing essential adjustments on board the *Discovery*, dashed off letters to Banks and the Admiralty on 1 August 1776 before beginning his catch-up. He arrived safely at Cape Town on 10 November. On 23 November he wrote a letter to Banks which began: 'Here I am hard and fast moor'd alongside my old friend Capt Cook.' His arrival had worked wonders upon Cook and the others who had preceded him, all now turning their attention to getting the *Discovery* victualled, shipshape and away. On 26 November, Cook wrote similar letters to both Banks and Sandwich. He informed Banks that 'nothing is wanting but a few females of our own species to make the *Resolution* a complete ark for I have added considerably to the number of animals I took on board in England'. Cook had been obliged to replace a number of the original sheep, injured by a dog at the Cape. In support of the King's idea of taking all these animals 'with the benevolent view of conveying some permanent benefit to the inhabitants', there were embarked in addition to the original animals two young bulls, two heifers, two young stone horses (stallions), two mares, two rams, several ewes and goats, some rabbits and poultry. Cook told Banks that Omai was in a good state of health 'and great flow of spirits, and has never once given me the least reason to find fault with any part of his conduct'.

The account of what Omai did at the Cape is brief. There is no mention of the Dutch lady with whom he is said to have associated in 1774 but he did apparently make an impression on the Port Commandant's daughters. McCormick tells how 'towards the end of his stay explicit references to his actions became more frequent'. This may well have been a close-run thing, for setting aside the basic understanding of doctor–patient confidentiality, the surgeon Anderson revealed in a letter to Banks: 'He brought a pox with him but now is well.' Anderson, Omai and others had been on an expedition to the north-east of Cape Town, botanising and collecting animals on behalf of Banks. The two 'shooters' had been the American Gore and Omai. They bagged only a few small birds which were bottled in preservative.

In his letter to Sandwich of 26 November, Cook exercised his prerogative 'of writing at all opportunities' for the very last time. He told Sandwich of Clerke's arrival on the 10th and how the taking on board of a number of horses had pleased Omai who 'consented with raptures to give up his cabin to make room for them, his only concern [one shared by Cook] is that we shall not have food for all the stock we have got on board'. Writing of Sandwich's 'great kindness' to Omai, Cook went on to embellish the point:

I have the pleasure to assure your Lordship that they have not been lost upon him and that he has obtained during his stay in England a far greater knowledge of things than any one could expect or will perhaps believe. Since he has been with me I have not had the least reason to find fault with any part of his conduct and the people here are surprised at his genteel behaviour and deportment.

On 30 November 1776 Cook took a south-easterly course from the Cape, each ship's crew reassured by the presence of the other. They soon encountered bad weather and rough seas which, combined with the cold, took their toll of sheep and goats. In addition to his principal tasks, Cook undertook the location of two small islands discovered by Marion Dufresne and Kerguelen and marked upon a map given to him by Crozet at the Cape eighteen months previously. The position of Marion Island was confirmed and twelve days later the equally desolate-looking Kerguelen Islands were found through the fog. The principal island of the Kerguelen group is called *la Grande-Terre*. The birds and seals were unimaginably tame, their killing and collection to replenish food stocks a simple matter. A sailor found a quart bottle fastened with a piece of wire to a projecting rock, indicating that the French had been there in 1772, something which did not deter Cook from claiming the Kerguelens in the name of George III. The hoisting of the flag had left Anderson singularly unimpressed, 'a circumstance not only contrary to the law of nations but if seriously meant to the law of nature as being in itself not only unjust but truly ridiculous and perhaps fitter to excite laughter than indignation'. The Kerguelens had once been assumed to be the northern shore of a southern continent. Cook proved them to be islands – cold, inhospitable islands whose unwelcoming climate continued to take a toll on his animals. On 30 December Cook left sub-Antarctica for the kinder climate of New Zealand but, out of necessity, called en route on 26 January at Furneaux's Adventure Bay in Tasmania to replenish the animals' food stocks.

Furneaux had not encountered the inhabitants in 1773 but this time their camp fires were clearly in evidence from the shore. Working parties spread out tentatively from both ships in search of wood and fodder, of which there was much of the former and little of the latter. All the men felt apprehensive, ill-at-ease, wondering about the inhabitants who lived in the dark woods. On the 28th the first group of eight native men and a boy nonchalantly appeared before a working party. They were completely naked and the darkest of colours. The first man to see them was a marine engaged at that precise moment in cooking. He fled in terror towards the boats, crying out, 'Here they are, here they are!' Cook was very poorly served by the quality of his marines. A section of them stole the rum ration, became dead drunk and had to be hauled on board to face his wrath.

Cook went with Omai to meet the inhabitants, bearing gifts of food. It was all very amiable. One native had a pointed stick, a spear of sorts. Omai invited him to throw it, which he did without any accuracy, missing the designated target completely. Keen to show what he could do, Omai raised his musket and blasted the target. The noise of the discharge left them standing rigid, not knowing what to do next until slowly they realised they might be in danger, turned on their heels and fled into the woods, leaving behind them most of the gifts they had been given. Omai's behaviour in frightening the natives away left Cook seriously unamused but Samwell wrote in his partial defence: 'This impatience of Omai to show his new acquired tricks was certainly natural enough, but yet we could not help blaming him as we thought it would prevent our having further intercourse with these people.'

The next day a larger group of natives appeared from the woods, both male and female. The women were also naked except for kangaroo skins which they wore *au bandolier* as slings to support their children. These people lived in rough shelters and hollowed out trees, and they possessed an infectious sense of humour. When one laughed, they all caught the mood, joining in the collective merriment. Omai's attempts to engage them in conversation failed and they showed absolutely no acquisitiveness towards their visitors' possessions. What the civilised component found most disconcerting was the inhabitants' custom of not only relieving themselves either standing or sitting without making any attempt to direct the stream but also the male preoccupation of 'pulling or playing with the prepuce' – 'as a child would with any bauble or a man twirl about the key of his watch while conversing with you'. Few people, believed Burney, could be said to be living in such a state of nature. The women, dirty and louse-ridden, permitted the British sailors to fondle their genitals but to go no further. It would seem that the sailors of the day were prepared to mount almost anything, no matter how ghastly the prospect. Cook was never surprised at his men's capacity to disappoint: 'This conduct to Indian women is highly blameable, as it creates a jealousy in the men that may be attended with fatal consequences, without answering any one purpose whatever, not even that of the lover obtaining the object of his wishes.'

Cook made no attempt to investigate whether Tasmania was joined to mainland Australia. He saw little merit in leaving behind anything more than a boar and a sow which he took the precaution of taking deep into the forest in the hope that they might breed before being hunted and killed. A number of vegetables and fruit were planted out before the ships sailed on 30 January for Queen Charlotte Sound, and they arrived at Ship Cove on 12 February. Cook sailed to New Zealand rather than making directly for Tahiti because the Admiralty desired the collection of flax seeds and other New Zealand plants. Cook selected Queen Charlotte Sound because it had been the agreed point of rendezvous should the *Resolution* and the *Discovery* become separated. Cook therefore used Queen Charlotte Sound, an important Maori communication route, on each of his three voyages. He knew the place as an excellent anchorage, yet he must have been aware that there was the potential for trouble among his men who bore grudges against the indigenous people for the massacre of the *Adventure*'s foraging party.

Four Maori canoes followed the two ships into Ship Cove, at all times keeping their distance. Once anchored, the canoes drew forward tentatively, an occupant in one waving a white garment, not as a sign of surrender but of peace. The man must have been alarmed when he saw and recognised Omai, who told him Toote was on board, as Maoris would have expected Cook to exact retribution for the Grass Cove massacre. But when Cook appeared, he assured those in the canoes that he had come in peace so convincingly that one of them, someone they knew, the teenage son of a dead chief by the name of Tiarooa, came on board. Another, known by Cook from his previous visit as Pedro, was not so sure, preferring the safety of the canoe. Not for the first time did Omai annoy Cook by mentioning the Grass Cove business at the first opportunity, for in so doing he indicated to the natives Cook's familiarity with the event, but Cook did all that was possible 'to assure them of the continuance of my friendship, and that I should not disturb them on that account'. They heard what Cook said but they saw in Cook's apparent turning of the other cheek a sign of inherent weakness. They may have wondered whether he would even scores, drawing upon all the power available to him once they had relaxed their guard.

Almost immediately fatigue parties were sent ashore to cut timber, draw water and collect grass under the protection of a cordon of ten marines. Thus far, the ships had not been visited by scurvy and sensible precautions were taken including, here in Ship Cove, the immediate brewing of spruce beer. Had it not been for the air of uncertainty hanging over the British encampment, the sailors would have thoroughly enjoyed this visit to a part of the world they believed most closely resembled their own. There is a painting by Webber of Ship Cove depicting a European landscape. There is no reason to believe that this is not how the cove looked at that time. The sailors were sufficiently relaxed, however, to come ashore to sleep, which they much preferred to sleeping on board. During the first evening, native families arrived, setting up their own shelters, but they were kept at a respectable distance from the sailors. The intention of the natives was to trade and, according to Cook, they brought three items of commerce: curiosities, fish and women: 'The two first always came to a good market, which the latter did not: the seamen had taken a kind of dislike to these people and were either unwilling or afraid to associate with them; it had a good effect as I never knew a man quit his station to go to their habitation.'

The Maoris appear to have exercised a form of quality control, presenting for the sailors' gratification only the roughest of their available females, holding the 'fine girls' back at home.

Cook's report of his men's reticence towards the Maori women was not supported by Second Lieutenant John Rickman's observations nor by reference to the sailors' past behaviour. In exchange for nails and trinkets the sailors did satisfy their lust, but at a price which would become readily apparent once on the high seas. Rickman of the *Discovery* wrote not only of the loose conduct of the sailors but also of Omai. When not at Cook's side it appears Omai indulged 'his almost insatiable appetite with more than savage indecorum' and he 'set no bounds to his excess, and would drink till he wallowed like a swine in his own filth'. For his company he often chose the common sailors, for he had been 'by accident . . . raised to the highest pitch of human happiness, only to suffer the opposite extreme by being again reduced to the lowest order of rational beings'. There is a pattern to Omai's frequenting the lowest order of rational beings but it was rarely involuntary, being brought about either by choice or through irrational stupidity. Whether Rickman's report was true is not known. He, like so many others on this expedition, maintained a diary intended for future publication, the success of which would no doubt be assisted by a few choice words of controversy.

That these visitors were far from ordinary became apparent to the Maoris the next morning when, to their mild surprise, animals with which they were unfamiliar – horses, cattle, sheep, goats, peacocks, turkeys, geese and ducks – poured ashore to stretch their limbs and eat the succulent grass. The natives exhibited no great curiosity about anything. Omai was a great favourite among them and, exceptionally, they would gather round him to listen to his tales and experiences of 'when I was in *Pretane*', invariably heavy on the hyperbole, but, as Cook noted, although they listened with attention they were 'like people who neither understood nor wished to understand what they heard'.

In the space of twenty-four hours a veritable trading post had not only been established but had become fully operational. Close to the water's edge, great barrels sat over fires as the sailors rendered the blubber they had brought from Kerguelen. Throughout this hive of activity meandered Cook, with Omai as ever close at hand. Cook dispensed handfuls of beads from his deep pockets, for the possession of which young and old scrambled in open competition.

On 15 February, while Cook and Omai were ashore, a chief by the name of Kahura came aboard the *Resolution*. His boldness surprised even the Maoris on board who were quick to identify him as having led the action against the *Adventure*'s grass-cutting party. In the same way as did their compatriots ashore, the Maoris, in Cook's words, 'said he was a very bad man and importuned me to kill him, and I believe they were not a little surprised that I did not, for according to their ideas of equity this ought to have been done'. Kahura openly admitted that it was he who had killed Rowe with his own hands. The return of Cook and Omai coincided with Kahura's departure. Omai, chastened by the man's effrontery, urged Cook to kill him, threatening to do so himself if the man were to return. 'It seemed evident', wrote Burney, 'that many of them held us in great contempt and I believe chiefly on account of our not revenging the affair of Grass Cove, so contrary to the principles by which they would have been actuated in the like case.'

As for Omai, his status became enhanced by virtue of his being seen as Cook's right-hand man. Somehow, along the way, his sophistication had strengthened his linguistic skills, but some doubted that these skills were as advanced as Omai led people to believe. Cook wanted to hear the Maori account of what had happened to Furneaux's working party but he was prepared to wait for the right moment. That moment arrived after he had been out with a large working party in five boats which, once filled, he directed to Grass Cove where he encountered an extremely nervous Pedro, whom he had met during his second voyage, and another, both showing 'manifest signs of fear'. Pedro and friend fully believed that after Cook had heard their account he would go on the rampage and that they would be the first objects of his retribution. Cook listened to their story, interpreted by Omai, and it was very similar to what he had heard before. Sitting there in an informal position of judgement, Cook decided the killing had not been premeditated but initiated by Rowe's high-handedness. 'If these thefts had not, unfortunately, been too hastily resented no ill consequence had attended for Kahoura's [Kahura's] greatest enemies [had] . . . owned that he had no intention to quarrel much less kill.' He was well aware that the sailors' lunch would have been washed down by a liberal amount of liquor.

Cook's decision to take no action can be identified with sound Christian principles. Carved into the Cook Monument on the high Easby Moor overlooking his birthplace in north-east England are the words: 'While it shall be deemed the honour of a Christian nation to spread civilisation and the blessings of the Christian faith among the pagan and savage tribes, so long will the name of Capt Cook stand out among the most celebrated and most admired benefactors of the human race.'

The first of two contradictions lies in the fact that Cook rarely held Christian services or espoused Christian beliefs.

We debauch their morals already too prone to vice and we introduce among them wants and perhaps diseases which they never before knew and which serves only to disturb that happy tranquillity they and their forefathers had enjoyed. If anyone denies the truth of this assertion let him tell me what the natives of the whole extent of America have gained by the commerce they have had with the Europeans.

The second contradiction is to be found in the inconsistency of Cook's actions. At the outset, his approach to the natives had been fair and honourable, driven by a desire to succeed through a policy of influencing hearts and minds. The native propensity for theft, however, so exasperated, influenced and dominated his later actions that those actions could not be described as Christian behaviour. His reactions or over-reactions often became cruel and disproportionate.

How deep was the exasperation felt by Cook's men at his refusal to deal with Maoris prepared to admit openly that they had killed Hodges and his men is not fully known. After the interview with Pedro at Grass Cove there is a record of the quartermaster of the *Resolution* being flogged for insolence and contempt. Omai aboard the *Resolution* and Burney aboard the *Discovery* were both intimately involved at the time of the massacre. While Burney's respect for Cook prevented him from being openly critical, he did privately attribute the expedition's difficulties with the natives to Cook's passivity. The same measure of restraint is not true of Omai with his different upbringing. Cook sensed his men's disaffection and, there being nothing further to be gained, on 23 February he ordered camp to be struck as a preliminary to resuming the voyage towards Tahiti. Ultimately, he intended to be in the Arctic during the northern summer. Observing signs of imminent departure, Maori notables came on board to make their last bids on the available gifts. The chiefs coveted the animals, none of which Cook had originally intended to leave, but on receipt of guarantees of impeccable animal husbandry he left behind two breeding goats and two pigs.

During their stay in Ship Cove, Omai cultivated a friendship with the eighteen-year-old Tiarooa. Omai's intentions were transparent; indeed, he had discussed his idea with Cook. He had observed in England how people of the best quality had their retainers and therefore so too must he. Tiarooa, though, was the son of a dead chief and he had no means of knowing Omai's true status short of observing Omai's position relative to Cook. So conscious of his rank was Tiarooa that he refused Cook's invitation for him to act as a waiter in the wardroom.

Tiarooa came aboard the *Resolution* shortly after the ship's arrival,

Cook being relaxed because he assumed the youth would leave after he had extracted as many presents as possible from Omai. As sailing time drew near and with no sign of any intention of leaving, Cook made clear to Tiarooa that if he came away there was no prospect of his returning. Tiarooa accepted what Cook had to say. Moreover, as the son of a chief, he too was entitled to a retainer, recruiting a ten-year-old by the name of Koa. Cook interviewed the boy's father who, on taking leave, removed all the boy's clothing, leaving him naked on deck and with 'far less indifference than he would have parted with his dog'. Cook agreed to take both Maoris because he believed that in taking them away from a people described by Samwell as 'the most barbarous and vindictive race of men on the face of the globe', some good might flow from their relocation. Omai was allowed to have his way. Tiarooa's farewell to his mother more closely resembled what might have been expected of a mother and son bidding each other farewell, never to meet again. Tiarooa's mother wept, tearing at her head with a shark's tooth until streams of blood flowed down her face. She had come aboard for the last instalment of Omai's gifts to her. In effect, Omai paid in kind for both retainers. To his mind, Koa was no less his than was Tiarooa, both of whom were said to have cost him two hatchets and a few nails.

Cook took his two ships out of Ship Cove on 24 February but problems with the wind necessitated anchoring nearby at Motuara. The local people did not pass up the opportunity to come out to trade, among them Kahura. Omai, who in England had shrunk before a bowl of cherries, urged Cook to kill Kahura, a demand which Cook ignored. While in Cook's cabin, Kahura saw a drawing of one of his countrymen. Might he, he asked Cook, also be drawn? Cook agreed, called for the artist Webber and, in so doing, further stoked his men's incredulity. In believing there was nothing to be gained from killing Kahura, Cook had the support of Clerke. 'I must confess', wrote Cook, 'I admired his courage and was not a little pleased at the confidence he put in me.'

The next day, being fearless or stupid, or having confidence in

Cook's amnesty, Kahura, 'a stout active man and to appearance turbulent and mischievous', arrived at the anchored *Resolution* with twenty family members. Omai escorted the chief to Cook's cabin, again stressing to Cook the importance of disposing of Kahura. When the chief took his leave of Cook unharmed, Omai took Cook to task, demanding to know why he had not been killed. 'You tell me if a man kills another in England he is hanged for it, this man has killed ten and yet you will not kill him' – a speech to which a majority of Cook's officers and men would have said 'Amen'. Omai was more forthright with Cook than Cook's own people would have dared to be, not only because he was not one of Cook's people but also because he had become accustomed to dealing with people far senior to Cook.

On 25 February Cook, aboard the *Resolution,* led the *Discovery* out of Queen Charlotte Sound, no doubt thankful to be gone and in the expectation that emotions would now subside.

Cook's timetable, worked out in an Admiralty office, envisaged him being in latitude 65°N, off the American coast, in June 1777, or four months after he actually left Queen Charlotte Sound. There had been delays, but in the age of sail Cook could do little other than proceed according to his own discretion. After leaving Queen Charlotte Sound the ships made such good progress that he may have believed he could reach Tahiti in ten weeks, as he had done in 1773. On this occasion it was even more important that Tahiti should be reached without delay, otherwise the embarked animals would be dead. As luck would have it, the wind thereafter proved entirely contrary.

That was one frustration Cook had to contend with. Another was a bolshie crew, one of whom had stolen food. Unable to ascertain precisely who, Cook put the entire ship on three-quarters rations for a day unless the culprit owned up. The crew, letting it be known that they did not believe that the innocent should be punished alongside the guilty, refused their food. Cook described the protest as a 'very mutinous proceeding' and promised to continue with the rationing. Living cheek by jowl as they were on a small ship severely tested Cook's leadership skills at a time when his morale would already have been bruised. Then there was concern for the New Zealand boys, hit concurrently by severe bouts of seasickness and homesickness. Understandably the little boy, called Cocoa by the crew, was the most severely affected but his misery also upset Tiarooa. Omai tried to reassure them both and Cook gave them two suits made of the normally favoured red material, but all to no avail. Time had to be allowed to heal and that was as true of the New Zealanders as it was for Cook's crew.

Gradually, by talking to them, Omai managed to bring both boys out of their state of acute misery and restore their confidence. Confidence, though, remained a fragile commodity. When Charles Clerke was rowed from the *Discovery* for a meeting with Cook, both boys assumed the worst, thinking that they were to be disposed of. In their tradition, such an act could follow a meeting of chiefs. Omai was in a position to reassure them from his own experiences, referring to a similar occasion when he left aboard the *Adventure*. Coming out of their shells as they did, both boys became popular and were adopted by the crew. Cocoa became 'a favourite of all and every one of the Jacks took a delight in teaching him something either in speech or gesture . . . Tiarooa was a sedate sensible young fellow . . . they were very fond of two or three glasses of wine after dinner'.

The boys told of a visit to their people by a ship, *Tupia's* ship. A visit by the high priest Tupia would have been of significance to the Maoris, coming as he had done from the most sacred *marae* in all Polynesia, Taputapuatea at Opoa on Raiatea. Raiatea, known as the sacred island, is considered to be the cradle of Polynesian civilisation and the birthplace of the god Oro. People on Raiatea tell the story of their first king, Hiro, over thirty generations ago, having sailed away in a great canoe to Rarotonga and New Zealand. In religious terms, the visit of Tupia would have been equivalent to a visit from the pope. There are a number of sacred sites in New Zealand also known as Taputapuatea so Tupia's visit had been both momentous and significant. Tiarooa went on to say that the captain of Tupia's ship had fathered a son by a New Zealand woman and the crew of that same ship had introduced venereal disease to the country. Cook had been the captain of Tupia's ship, namely the *Endeavour*. The parenting allegation, if true, would seem to have been a case of mistaken identity; Joseph Banks had been on this voyage. 'But both Tiarooa and the other', wrote Cook, 'who seemed to be as well acquainted with the story though not born at the time, assured us there was no mistake in neither time nor place and it was well known to everybody about Queen Charlotte's Sound and Teerawitte.'

On 29 March, when still five degrees short of Tahiti, a lookout aboard the *Discovery* sighted the island of Mangaia, the southernmost island in the southern group of Cook Islands. The ship hoisted the Dutch ensign, the signal to indicate the sighting of land. Mangaia is the second largest of the Cook Islands, its central hills surrounded by an outer rim of stepped, fossilised coral reef known as *makatea*. The island's name was relatively new, having been assumed in 1775, and means 'temporal power'. Prior to that date there had been forty-two recorded battles between those living on the small island, until one leader became predominant and was thus able to exercise power over the island and bring peace. There may have been inward peace but, as Cook examined the three or four hundred natives on the shore, they appeared far from peaceful; indeed, they were decidedly unfriendly. Boats sent ahead to breach the *makatea* found no place to land and no suitable place to anchor. One of the natives made 'wry faces' at the sailors, 'intended most probably to divert us, as he seemed to exert his physiognomical abilities according as we testified our approbation by our laughter', wrote Cook. One native did come aboard where he was accosted by Omai determined to discover whether they were cannibals, a question which, according to Anderson, was met with an equal share 'of indignation and abhorrence'. The man's humour was not to be improved when he tumbled over the ship's goat. 'What kind of bird is that?' he cried. Omai found conversation easy; their language was little different from that of Tahiti. 'If Omai is a general character of that people', wrote King, 'these will have the advantage in colour and in shape, being much fairer, taller and infinitely better made.' Dallying here would not get the animals fed. Sailing in a northerly direction, the island of Atiu was sighted on Tuesday, 1 April.

Atiu has the same kind of *makatea* as Mangaia. Its population had a reputation as having been the region's warriors, persistently attacking smaller neighbouring islands. The visitors' reception among Atiu's warlike people proved initially friendly compared to the hostility found among the peaceful Mangaians. The wind dropped, becalming the two ships, and they were unable to advance to anchor. In the meantime, Cook sent Gore off with a protection party to identify an anchorage and a place to land. A number of canoes came out from the island, bringing presents for Cook and Clerke – plantains, a hog and some coconuts – the quid pro quo requested being a dog, now extinct on the island. Omai again displayed his lack of diplomacy when he called down to the canoes enquiring whether these people were cannibals. They took offence, responding indignantly in the negative. One of the young gentlemen had two domesticated dogs which Cook would have been pleased to see the back of but, being aware of their most likely fate, he declined with due apology to hand them over. Omai stepped forward and released one of his dogs. Gore reported his inability to breach the *makatea* but suggested that Omai might be able to persuade the natives to shuttle their requirements over the *makatea* to the boats waiting on the calm side of the surf.

Gore led the reconnaissance party comprising Omai and the linguists Anderson and Burney to negotiate for the foodstuff and water required by men and animals aboard the ships. Canoes took them up to the *makatea* and on to the island, where they were instantly mobbed by a crowd of people curious to know whether they were sons of the god Tetumu. Burney and Anderson in the first canoe found themselves ushered forward through an avenue of coconut palms to meet the chiefs. (Earlier in the century there had been seven *mataiapo* or chiefs. After a succession of battles, three of the *mataiapo* became promoted to the rank of *ariki* or high chief while the other four suffered relative demotion to priest.) Shortly, the rattling of spears and the arrival of three ranks of warriors signified the arrival of Gore and Omai. After each of the three *ariki* had been given the anticipated presents, Gore said he wanted to trade – an aspiration the chiefs declined. Gore would have to wait until the morning. Meanwhile the tightly-packed mob allowed the visitors no room, picking their pockets with the skill common throughout the islands.

It would seem that lives were never at risk but the close proximity of the natives proved disconcerting. After Omai and the senior chief had made their essential speeches, and area was cleared and dancing began. Omai made the mistake of taking out his ornamental dagger to cut a coconut which he handed to one of the pretty, dancing females – 'there are some very pretty lasses here I'll assure you', wrote John Gore. When Omai next felt for the weapon's reassuring hilt, it was no longer there. He complained to the chief who was not interested, merely saying they should not anticipate returning to their ships before nightfall. Any attempt to move was met by a club-wielding native blocking the exit. The natives had mixed feelings about their visitors. They were quite prepared to accept an association with Tetumu and that Gore and his people were of divine origin. They would also have been mindful of a heathen prophecy that one day, a god named Tanemei-tai would visit them, that he would speak a strange language, would introduce strange articles and customs and – here lies the rub – would ill-treat the natives. Thus the entertainment went ahead under an umbrella of pleasure and trepidation.

As the day wore on, the visitors became hungry. To Omai's horror, he saw an earth oven being heated and again, to his companions' annoyance, he asked the hosts if they were cannibals preparing the fire on which to cook their guests. The hosts appeared disconcerted at being asked such a question and wondered 'if that was a custom with us?' Omai did not relax until he caught sight of the hog being prepared for dinner. While the food was cooking, Omai made his own contribution to the entertainment, going through Tahitian weapon drills, though not without some tittering from among the two-thousand-strong audience. After sitting down, Omai then regaled the chiefs with his experiences in *Pretane* and answered their questions. The English, he told them plainly, had ships as large as their island (26.9 km²) carrying enormous guns which several people could sit inside, any one of which could destroy their entire island with one shot. Cook explained how this discussion developed:

> This led them to ask what sort of guns we had, he said they were but small, yet with them we could with great ease destroy the island and every soul in it: they then desired to know by what means this was done, accordingly fire was put to a little powder, the sudden blast and report produced by so small a quantity astonished them and gave them terrible ideas of the effects of a large quantity. Omai then confided in the chiefs that 'if he and his companions did not return on board the same day, I should fire upon the island'.

After eating, the visitors were informed that they were free to go.

While on Atiu, Omai was surprised to encounter four Tahitians. About twelve years previously, a crew of twenty had set out from Tahiti for Raiatea, which they missed, and eventually arrived at Atiu. There had been five survivors, found clinging to their canoes by Atiuans who brought them ashore. So well cared for and content were they that they declined Omai's offer of a passage home. The English decided that it was in this way that many of the islands had become populated. Steering a native canoe hundreds of miles from one speck in the Pacific to another was fraught with dangers. To miss invariably proved fatal. Not only did the canoeists have to contend with supply problems but the weather and problems with navigation, sometimes caused by the loss of the navigator overboard or his death on board, often doomed voyages to failure. Of the fourteen *waka* which originally left Rarotonga in search of New Zealand, one of the Pacific's larger targets, only seven survived the voyage.

The Atiuans resembled the Tahitians, except perhaps that they had larger holes in their ears because, unlike the Tahitians' earrings, they wore artificial roses made from red feathers. Their language was understood perfectly by Omai and the New Zealanders. Interesting as the experience may have been, the reconnaissance party returned with nothing of substance with which to replenish crew and animals. Cook decided therefore to head for the small sand cay of Takutea 10 miles to the north-west and visible from Atiu, to whom it belonged. Despite a heavy surf running, Gore managed to get ashore and bring back a quantity of scurvy grass, coconuts and pandanus branches which, chopped up, the cows ate without protest. A hatchet and a few nails were left in an empty hut on the uninhabited island.

Continuing the voyage, Cook came to the two tiny, unpopulated islets known today as the Manuae Atoll, formerly Hervey Island discovered by Cook on his previous voyage. Manuae then was not unpopulated, canoes from the islets coming out to meet the ships with no purpose other than to steal. They asked Omai the captain's name, where they had come from and the crew's strength. Omai saw this as a bad omen, for in this part of the world such questions were asked by people contemplating an attack. Omai said that the manners of the islanders and their method of treating strangers were much the same as on Tahiti and neighbouring islands. The natives had with them a small quantity of food to trade. Cocoa received a large fish for a piece of discarded brown paper he had picked up on deck – a case of stealing from thieves. Neither boy could understand the explorers' tolerance. They 'are much surprised that so many within the reach of our power we have neither killed or made prisoners of any', wrote Burney.

The natives had seen the *Resolution* and the *Adventure* pass by in 1773 but now the ships needed to anchor. A suitable anchorage could not be found and moreover the natives were hostile. The lie of the land did not favour collecting and carrying water over the reef and now Cook had to consider his position. Since leaving New Zealand it had taken him six weeks to reach this point, well short of his ultimate destination. He could not continue on the off-chance that he would consistently encounter small islands capable of offering up one or two days' supply of fodder. Nor could he waste his own ships' supplies that would be needed in the bleak, cold climes of the Arctic. If he did not find fodder in quantity, his animals would die before they could reach Tahiti. The obligation to take one man home became an enormous liability threatening the success of the entire mission. Little did Cook know that either of the nearby islands of Rarotonga or Aitutaki could have satisfied his needs.

> I therefore determined to bear away for the Friendly Islands (the Tongan Group) where I was sure of being supplied with every thing I wanted; and as it was necessary to run in the night as well as in the day, I ordered Captain Clerke to keep about a league ahead of the Resolution, as his ship could better claw of a lee shore than mine.

Before setting his new course, Cook imposed water rationing.

The gods, whoever's gods, smiled favourably upon the expedition now in dire straits, for on 13 April the ships fortuitously came upon an uninhabited atoll in the Palmerston group, discovered in 1774. Setting aside the absence of women, this place was possibly the closest to being idyllic of all the places where the ships had called. Its particular usefulness lay in the abundance of scurvy grass and plantains. Seabirds in their thousands nested there, so tame that they could be lifted uncomplaining from their nests, only to reappear on the ships' menu or in Omai's stone oven. Clerke recognised 'men of war, tropic birds, boobies, noddies and egg birds', so many that 'the trees and bows in many places seemed absolutely loaded with them; but we were a most unhappy interruption to their wonted security, for unfortunately for them we found them very palatable and well flavoured'. Omai and his two retainers waded into the shallow, crystal-clear water to catch brightly-coloured fish which had no hiding place against a background of coral outcrops and a floor of white sand. They taught the sailors the tricks of fishing so well that through 'dexterity and goodwill' there was enough fish for those who had gone ashore as well as those still on board. 'We had good luck to have Omai on shore', wrote Burney, 'who was a most useful companion for a party of this kind; being a keen sportsman and excellent cook and never idle.'

Omai was among those who preferred to spend his time ashore and, having no duties to perform, he could do as he wished. Samwell observed his delight 'with these islands and used often to say afterwards that he would come from Tahiti and settle on them'. He saw himself returning as king, but since he appeared to have no sense of direction 'we may rest well assured that Omai will not be so foolish as to make the attempt'. On the island, Omai demonstrated how water might be found by digging into the sand, but the quantity available was negligible: the islet was as good as dry. After the voyagers set off for Nomuka, bypassing Niue or the Savage Island, the skies opened to provide ample fresh water.

The explorers had their first sight of the Tonga Group on 28 April, taking until 1 May to reach an anchorage to the north of Nomuka used by Cook three years previously. There is no clearer indication that Cook had time on his hands, for he remained within the Group for eleven weeks. During those eleven weeks it is possible to observe negative trends developing in the behaviour of both Cook and Omai. The change in Cook's nature, so apparent at Ship Cove, continued but not for the better. His temperament, patience and tolerance all took a turn for the worse. Relatively little charting was done over this extended period and although Cook was told of the proximity of Fiji he had no curiosity to go and visit the island. His biographer suggested he was showing signs of inner tiredness.

The Tonga experience was not what Omai needed, although he did not know it at the time. He positively luxuriated in all the fawning attention he received from the Tongans who were excited by his extravagant tales of the power of *Pretane* and, by implication, his own importance. It is as though Omai was being led willingly up the slope of an escarpment with a tall cliff at the summit. He used some of his wealth to buy red feathers so cherished in Tahiti until he owned so many that they filled a large drawer in his cabin.

The *Resolution* was visited on 6 May by a chief not from the nearby island of Nomuka but from Tongatapu. It became immediately apparent from the obsequiousness of the trading natives, bowing their heads to their feet, that this was a bona fide ranking chief. He differed from the usual pattern of Tongan chiefs inasmuch as he was young, slim, fit, approximately thirty-five years of age, intelligent and handsome. He introduced himself as Finau, King of all the Friendly Islands. Omai, acting as Cook's interpreter, was so impressed that he proposed exchanging names with Finau, becoming his *tayo*, something that was done between people of equal rank. Observing that Omai was someone highly valued by Cook, Finau readily agreed, unaware how this agreement undermined his status.

A healthy trade in foodstuffs developed between Cook and the local Chief Tupoulangi who declined to deal with anyone other than Cook. His sensitivity towards rank was a common feature which went some way towards emphasising Omai's achievement in exchanging names with Finau. The Tongans proved no less accomplished in thievery than any others in the South Pacific. Cook punished equally those natives caught stealing and his own men in charge of whatever had been stolen. When a hatchet went missing from the galley, the impeccably behaved young man on duty at the time received six lashes of the cat-o'-nine-tails. As if to demonstrate his even-handedness, Cook awarded twelve lashes to a chief accompanying Finau for pocketing an iron bolt. Finau resented Cook's action in humiliating his colleague but kept his counsel. Cook held the chief on board, tightly bound, until his ransom of a large hog had been delivered to the ship. Anderson the surgeon had no problem with the lashing but took exception to the chief being 'confined in a painful posture for some hours after, or a ransom demanded after proper punishment for the crime had been inflicted I believe will scarcely be found consonant with the principles of justice or humanity upon the strictest scrutiny'.

It may well be that Cook believed it to be a sign of weakness not to deal effectively and summarily with wrongdoers; that was certainly the manner in which the local chiefs exercised discipline. But Cook was not a local chief and, more importantly, the man whose blood was now congealing on the deck of the *Resolution* was. 'After this', said Cook, 'we were not troubled by thieves of rank', who sent their subordinates to steal and run the risk of flogging. Clerke had an entirely different approach, half-shaving offenders' heads and beards before tossing them overboard. The animals all went ashore to feed upon the abundance of this idyllic island, which the sailors much appreciated. There were many women prepared to offer their services for goods in lieu. Some had been blighted by venereal disease, from which the inevitable conclusion must be drawn that it had been introduced to the island during Cook's previous visit. 'Wherever we go, we spread an incurable distemper which nothing we can do can ever recompense,' wrote King. Anderson now marked Tiarooa among those afflicted. Of food, there was an abundance, but it did not take long, ten days, for the young visitors and animals to eat through the island's reserves. There had been a noticeable improvement in the look of the animals, 'from perfect skeletons, the horses and cows were grown plump, and as playful as young colts'. Finau recommended Cook to move on, as though an *arioi* group, to Lifuka, the principal of five islands to the north-east of Nomuka. Finau came from Vava'u. Perhaps he decided to call at Lifuka rather than there after gauging the visitors' voracious appetites.

Omai chose to stay ashore at night with his *tayo* and New Zealand retainers – it was all to do with bonding. Although Finau and his people did respect Omai, there can be no doubt that his habit of babbling on was used by Finau as a source of intelligence. Fortunately, Omai's habit of gross exaggeration may have spared the visitors from what Finau had in mind for them. No doubt Omai told Finau of the massive firepower available to Cook, the embarked marines, and of King George III and everything available to him. This latter revelation had the negative effect of relegating Cook to the role of mere functionary in the eyes of the chiefs.

When Finau went ashore, he led Cook and Omai before a great assembly of the people of the island. After introducing Cook, Finau laid down the rules to be observed throughout the duration of his guests' visit. There was to be no theft, no molestation, but by all means they were encouraged to bring food in exchange for interesting curiosities. When Cook came ashore the next day, he witnessed Finau's capacity for organisation and his clear intention during the course of the day's activities not to be outdone by anything Cook had to offer. Lines of men and women entered the arena carrying hogs, turtles, chickens, fruit and sugar cane which they gathered in two piles, one larger than the other – the former for Cook, the latter for Omai, recognised as a person of importance in his own right. The show began in front of the three-thousand-strong audience with a fight between men armed with clubs, followed by boxing and wrestling. Two women came before the spectators and began to box. This was too much for one of the young gentlemen who stepped forward to stop the bout. The natives laughed at him for his trouble. At last light, a team of superfit-looking natives circled the arena lighting torches, to the haunting sound of calls from the conch shell. Some of the sailors accepted invitations to come forward to box or wrestle with the natives. A number did, but not one of them won. Almost too soon, sunrise ended the evening's entertainment. Cook examined the gifts which 'far exceeded any present I had ever received from an Indian chief'. The local people would not have been so delighted to observe five boatloads of their food making for the cavernous stores of the *Resolution* and the *Discovery*. The morning was the morning of 19 May, there being no entry for that day in Cook's journal.

Finau had special plans for Tuesday 20 May, for on that day he intended to kill Cook, his officers and crew and seize their ships. The initiative had originally begun among the island chiefs still smarting from the knowledge of what Cook had done to one of their number (Clerke had also imprisoned the son of a visiting chief), but principally they acted from mercenary reasons in expectation of what goods might be accrued once the British had been swamped by the weight of their numbers. The details of this plot emerged thirty years later when the chiefs involved confessed to an Englishman living among them. Finau had not been the driving force of this conspiracy but acted as adviser and consultant. First, the natives had to assess the potency and effectiveness of the marines as a fighting force. Finau asked Cook whether the marines might give a display on the morning of the 20th. What the natives saw of the sailor-soldiers in their egg-cosy hats gave them no cause for concern. Only one musket ball from a volley aimed at a canoe hit the target.

The islanders presented to Cook and his people a show worthy of the Edinburgh Military Tatoo. One hundred and five men entered the arena carrying 2-foot long paddles with which they described intricate movements to the accompaniment of two 4-foot-long hollow log drums. All the visitors had their attention fixed by the novelty and quality of the dance, ending with the paddlers singing a song in harmony. There could be no better moment for the assassins to move among their guests and kill them. Yet it did not happen. Finau had had second thoughts. Perhaps he had been worried by Omai's description of the visitors' potential for retaliation, which is why he had wanted the deed done in the open, in daylight. The island chiefs demurred, preferring to attack during the night – something Finau would not contemplate. Accordingly, he refused to countenance the attack. Oblivious to what had gone on behind the scenes, Cook returned to the *Resolution* for dinner, mightily impressed by the native performance which 'so far exceeded anything we had done to amuse them that they seemed to pique themselves in the superiority they had over us'. Accordingly, he instructed the gunners to prepare a firework display for the same evening.

The fireworks began on a night when both sides vied for supremacy in the quality of their respective displays. Lieutenant King judged that the firework display 'made us perfectly satisfied that we had gained a complete victory in their own minds'. The natives saw water rockets fired into the sea, the apparent destruction of which they could not comprehend until, to their amazement, the rockets emerged from beneath the surface, climbing up into a star-filled sky before unexpectedly exploding. King reported how these 'water rockets exercised their inquisitive faculties, for they could not conceive how fire should burn under water'. Omai interjected nonchalantly how it was a relatively simple matter for the British to destroy the earth, water and sky. No doubt a number of chiefs that night thanked their gods for the wisdom of Finau. No sooner had the fireworks ended than the natives presented a series of pulsating, rhythmic, balletic dances illuminated by flickering torches set before the backdrop of silhouettes of palm trees. Some of the female dancing could be described as risqué, yet even the unpopular Mr Williamson admitted his admiration for 'the most beautiful forms that imagination can conceive in the younger part of the sex'.

The prevalence of theft continued to cast a long, dark shadow over all that was good on the island. Cook retaliated by continuing to flog natives found stealing, and taking chiefs hostage. The captain's reaction began to stoke opposition ashore. Cook decided it was time to move on and, besides, he and his people had consumed the island's reserves of food. Finau protested and asked him to wait a while, for he wanted to go to Vava'u to collect red feather bonnets, one each for Cook and Omai to take to Tahiti, 'knowing their value among our Society Island friends'. Cook said he would go with Finau, an offer Finau declined on the grounds that there was alleged to be no suitable harbour at Vava'u. Finau promised to return in four or five days. There was a suitable anchorage at Vava'u but if time was a factor, the natives' canoes were far faster than Whitby cats. Instead of sailing away to Tongatapu, Cook repositioned his ships to the south of Lifuka where he heard that the king desired to come on board. Had not the king sailed off to Vava'u? wondered Cook. No, insisted the natives, this man, Paulaho, was the king of all the isles, senior to Finau. Cook found Paulaho to be an intelligent, sensible man aged about forty and grossly overweight, 'the most corporate plump fellow we had met with'. He was the paramount chief of the islands by virtue of being the descendant of the god Tangaloa and was therefore senior to Finau, the islands' political chief. If there was any doubt, that doubt was dispelled by the natives' display of obsequiousness and deference.

The news that a chief had emerged who was senior to his own was not something Omai wished to hear. Cook observed how he 'was a good deal chagrined at finding there was a greater man than his friend

Finau, or Omai as he was now called for they had from the first changed names'. Omai's reaction became worrying; he was juvenile and immature. 'Omai all this time was out of temper with Paulaho, and wanted to persuade us that he told lies in saying he was a greater man than his friend,' wrote Lieutenant King. 'It should be observed that these two had exchanged names, it was therefore impossible that Omai could consent to be degraded and he examined the fat King very closely.' Paulaho remained gracious, inviting Cook and Omai to join him ashore. Cook gladly accepted the invitation but Omai, in a fit of pique, declined.

At sea again, Cook threaded his ships through the coral, sometimes following Paulaho, at other times using best judgement: on one occasion Bligh came close to running the *Resolution* seriously aground. On 5 June the expedition's ships arrived off Nomuka, coinciding with Finau's arrival from Vava'u. Here Finau came face-to-face with Paulaho, his superior, his body language indicating that he neither enjoyed making his obeisance nor appreciated being denied a place at the same dining table as Paulaho. After four days, course was set for Tongatapu, the two cats struggling to make headway while the native canoes, the greyhounds of the sea, soon far outstripped them.

With time no longer a critical consideration, the three remaining factors which did impinge upon how long Cook stayed at any one place during this island-hopping phase were: the availability of food and water; the stage at which the level of theft became intolerable; and, to a lesser extent, when his own personal curiosity regarding the people, their manners and customs became sated. To some extent Cook, assisted by Omai, found himself compensating for his decision to exclude scientists from the voyage by conducting his own anthropological scientific investigations. These factors could come into play either singly or in combination. On the ships' arrival at Tongatapu, Cook and Clerke were whisked off to a *kava* ceremony presided over by Paulaho. Concurrently, to the consternation of the natives, the animals came ashore and the observatory's paraphernalia was unloaded, as were the tents. Clearly Cook envisaged staying on

Tongatapu for more than a few days.

While with Paulaho, Cook learnt of a man by the name of Maealinaki living nearby whom the king insisted was more powerful than he. In reality, Maealinaki, in his sixties, exercised a presidential role in the islands. Cook said he would be pleased to meet the wise old man, the 'father of Tonga'. A meeting would be possible, but only if Cook and Clerke stripped to the waist. They were having none of that; why, even when they came before their own king, an immensely more powerful man, all that was required of them was to doff their hats. Paulaho heard what they said and arranged an exemption. When the group went off to Maealinaki's well-appointed house in Mu'a they were kept waiting. A flunkey told Omai that the person they hoped to meet was either ill or had gone down to the ships. Immensely irritated, Cook stormed off. Next day, Maealinaki called on Cook and was shown the camp, the animals and the cross cut-saw producing planks. The old man appeared very interested and received presents befitting his rank. They had a kindly friend in Court in addition to Paulaho and Finau. Nevertheless, this counted for nothing among a people intent upon theft.

The ever-resourceful Omai set up a dwelling near the trading post, to which he brought his young lady. Stories began to emerge of his poor behaviour. John Rickman of the *Discovery* had made unflattering remarks about Omai's character before. Rickman suggested that Omai was unable to control his drinking:

> He set no bounds to his excess . . . At those times he out-acted the savage in every kind of sensuality, and when he could no longer act the brute, he would often act the drunken man; storming, roaring, brandishing his arms, and by contortions of his mouth and face, setting at defence, after the manner of his own country, the whole host of his enemies who were represented by the common sailors, with whom, upon these occasions, he was generally surrounded.

On this occasion there is corroboration of Rickman's assertions from someone recognised as a friend of Omai's – Jem Burney:

Shortly after our arrival, Omiah in a drunken fit took offence at one of the sentinels on shore and struck him, which the corporal, who was present, resented by pushing him away and threatening to beat him. Omiah, who among these islanders had always been looked upon as a great man, was so much incensed at this rebuff, that he immediately left the tent and repaired to one of the Indian chiefs, the two young New Zealanders with him, declaring his resolution to return no more to the ships.

Indeed, Omai had no theoretical need to return to the ships, for his *tayo* Finau offered him the chiefdom of the island of Eua. Burney possibly had in mind the eventual exposure of Omai's true identity when he wrote: 'had he been suffered to have accepted, his continuance in that station after the ships were gone, would have been very precarious.' Domestic politics in the islands were extremely powerful considerations. Would the Tongans accept Omai as a chief any more than his own people would? The debate is academic for Omai returned the next day. Omai's remaining on Tonga had been a matter which Cook regarded as being subject to his approval. His orders required Omai to be taken to the Society Islands. The captain declined to discipline the corporal as demanded by Omai because Omai had been drunk and struck a person on duty. He had brought his loss of face upon himself.

The chiefs invited their visitors to some native entertainment, dancing and singing, much of which had been seen earlier on other islands. These meetings enabled thieves to circulate and the sailors experienced an exponential increase in theft. Cook's response, as opposed to the more equitable Clerke's, was uncompromising, awarding thieves with upwards of four dozen lashes which shredded a man's back. Other thieves had their arms cut through to the bone so that they might be recognised in the future: there was no differentiation between natives and their chiefs except that the senior chiefs did not indulge in theft. This did not exempt them from being taken hostage until stolen goods had been returned. As the punishments increased both in number and severity, so too did the Friendly Islanders become less friendly. Whereas in the early days there had been large smiles and genuine welcomes, the natives became introspective, occasionally offering violence to the visitors. 'Scarce a day afterwards passed without some people being robbed and insulted on shore', wrote Burney. 'Instead of asking us into their houses which they had hitherto done whenever we passed by, the doors of their plantations were shut and fastened against us.' There were no senior civilians on this voyage available to act as a brake on Cook's excesses; Omai gave him every encouragement.

Rickman was among the officers to witness Cook's cruelty and disproportionate punishments: 'It is not to be wondered that after such wanton acts of cruelty, the inhabitants should grow outrageous; and though they did not break out into open acts of hostility, yet they watched every opportunity to be vexatious.'

The young gentleman George Gilbert, though still in his teens, was old enough to recognise what was acceptable, civilised punishment as opposed to something 'unbecoming of a European'. He provided examples of Cook's behaviour: 'By cutting off their ears; firing at them with small shot, or ball, as they were swimming or paddling to the shore and suffering the people to beat them with oars and stick the boat hook into him wherever he could hit them.'

Lieutenant Bligh and a friend out on a shooting expedition had their muskets and personal possessions stolen. On their return, fearing Cook's reaction, they asked Omai to approach the chiefs with a view to their weapons being returned. All that Omai's intervention achieved was to send Paulaho and Finau into the forest for fear of what Cook might do to them. They were only enticed out after being given reassurances that they were considered blameless. Cook despaired at Omai's behaviour and gave him 'a reprimand for meddling'. Omai and Tongatapu were beginning to frustrate, to get under Cook's skin.

But unless the object or thing we wanted to enquire after was before us, we found it difficult to gain a tolerable knowledge of it from information only without falling into a hundred mistakes; in this Omai was more liable than us because he never gave himself the trouble to gain knowledge for himself, so that when he was disposed to explain things to us his account was often very confused . . . Our situation at Tongatapu where we remained the longest (one month), was likewise unfavourable; it was in a part of the country where there were few inhabitants except fishers; it was always holiday with our visitors as well as with those we visited, so that we had but few opportunities of seeing into their domestic way of living.

An opportunity did arise for Cook to witness an occasion of local importance when Paulaho, believing that the support of the British visitors would strengthen his case to have his son accepted as his natural successor, invited Cook, Clerke, Omai and others to attend the preliminary social ceremony. What followed in effect mirrored Finau's entertainment at Lifuka, with dancing, boxing and wrestling. None of the visitors made any headway against the local champions. The next day the marines were unwisely called out to demonstrate their skill-at-arms, punctuated by music from a band found from among those on board capable of playing drums, fifes and French horns. Bligh witnessed the marines' *tour de force*: 'A most ludicrous performance, for the Marine Officer was as incapable of making his men go through their exercise as C. Cook's musicians or music was ill adapted.' Again, the gunners were called for to rescue the visitors' reputation with the tried and tested fireworks display.

Paulaho invited Cook to attend the ceremonial or *inasi* when the boy would be formally nominated as his father's successor. Paulaho's purpose in inviting Cook to be present was in order that his god could add to the importance of the occasion. This was only a partial invitation for aspects of the ceremony were taboo to outsiders. When ordered to strip to the waist, Cook refused until it appeared that harm would come to him if he disobeyed. He accordingly removed his upper garments and arranged for his hair to fall loose. Thereafter he consistently refused to do as he was bidden, to the extent that he came close to being killed. This was indeed strange, irresponsible behaviour, not least to his officers, aghast at seeing their commanding officer in the ceremonial procession in an unkempt, half-naked condition. He had compromised his position, dignity and authority in order better to understand one particular native ceremony, the ultimate success of which he had put at risk through his unreasonable behaviour.

Cook decided that he could best maintain security over his animals if he distributed the Tongatapu quota sooner rather than later. Omai announced that in the morning the chiefs would be presented with their livestock. For Paulaho there was a bull, a cow and two goats, a horse and mare for Finau and a ram and two ewes for Maealinaki, which he did not want and which were therefore redistributed. Although peeved that these animals had been distributed here, meaning there would be fewer available to distribute in Tahiti, Omai gave hints on animal procreation and husbandry. Cook had asked Omai to tell the chiefs to look after the animals and kill none of them until their numbers had greatly increased. He was to tell them that they are undemanding, requiring only grass, that cows' milk was good, particularly for children, and their meat was good. The horses were an excellent means of transport and their meat could also be eaten; the latter fact Omai refused to translate. Of all the animals, the sheep produced the best meat, the chiefs were told, and the voyagers showed them their coats made from sheep's wool.

Meanwhile the situation between the natives and their visitors became more tense. It became apparent that other chiefs had been unhappy at not having had a share of the animals. Two turkey-cocks and a kid were found to be missing. Cook went ashore determined to recover the animals as well as a number of tools stolen from the carpenters. In a foul mood, he called for Paulaho and Finau and had them imprisoned, not to be released until the missing items had been returned. After Omai conveyed this information to the chiefs it served to throw them into 'a great disorder'. Paulaho said he did not know where the missing items were, that only Finau could get them. Finau accordingly despatched a messenger. A number of iron wedges, axes and one turkey-cock filtered back. Meanwhile the chiefs' subjects were becoming restless, some arming themselves. Cook told Paulaho that if he valued his safety he should tell his people to disperse, which he quickly did. Finau told Cook through Omai that the kid and other turkey-cock had been taken away in a canoe and could not be returned until the next day. Satisfied, Cook released the chiefs, inviting them on board for dinner.

It was now time to go. Cook decided to wait until 5 July when he knew an eclipse of the sun would occur, something he intended to announce in advance in the expectation of enhancing his reputation among the natives. When the day came, cloud blotted out the sun and the opportunity was lost. Five days later, Cook took advantage of favourable winds to leave Tongatapu, taking course for Eua. Here Cook and his people were regaled with what they now recognised as the standard entertainment. Cook did not linger to overstay his welcome, having but one minor incident to deal with. On 16 July 1777 the *Resolution* and the *Discovery* set course for Tahiti to take Omai home.

Omai, prince in *Pretane*, with an offer of becoming a chief on an island now in their wake, where he had been an unknown, had as his next and final port of call an island where he was known. Etiquette would require the distribution of gifts among the priests and suitable sacrifices offered up to the gods. The chiefs would have the expectation of receiving presents of the highest quality as a prerequisite to smoothing the way for the accommodation of Omai in the manner he would wish. His best hope of success would be conditional upon winning the unqualified support of Tu or, failing that, moving on to another island where he and his considerable wealth might be used to mutual benefit. Omai's essential problems were his inflated ego and his delusions of grandeur. Success depended so much upon his behaviour among the native people, his capacity for compromise and the manner in which he shared his wealth.

Above all, there was the question as to precisely how he hoped to address his declared aim of removing the Bora Borans from his family property on Raiatea.

Over the past three years, Omai had blown hot and cold on the subject of the evil Bora Borans to the extent that some observers might reasonably have assumed his outbursts to be mere rhetoric. His challenge was of course to turn an intention into reality. Cook told him in no uncertain terms that he would endeavour to achieve the best he could in Omai's rehabilitation short of participating in armed conflict. Nevertheless, Omai now persisted in expressing in public his determination to right the wrong which had befallen his family.

On 12 August, a lookout aboard the *Resolution* sighted Vaitepiha Bay. Omai spent the day on the forecastle. As Tahiti drew nearer, tears welled up in his eyes. Whether these were tears of joy or trepidation, only he would have known.

CHAPTER 10

Return of the Native

Omai did well to survive the voyage. Now he faced the even greater challenge of surviving among his own people. Above all, he needed a strategy to win over and maintain the support of the chiefs. On this point, Cook was perfectly clear. Unfortunately, Omai was not. He was their first real experience of *nouveau riche*, someone who, despite an instinctive disinclination, they might consider treating politely out of deference to Cook. Rickman summarised too harshly what he thought Omai's problem to be, but what he said nevertheless contained an element of truth: 'Men sprung from the dregs of the people must have something more than accidental riches to recommend them to the favour of their fellow citizens.' What Omai brought in support of his aspiration to be accorded enhanced status were his eligibility, his wealth and his weaponry.

No mention would be made of his fourth wife who, after his four years of absence, had probably not bided her time as the chaste, loyal wife any more than he had been the chaste, loyal husband. Although there would be no possibility of Omai becoming a chief, there would have been an outside possibility of his marrying a chief's daughter. His wealth would have been an incentive not only to his new wife but also to her father who would anticipate a frequent supply of desirable gifts. Omai's challenge in such a situation would be to consolidate his position before the supply of gifts ran out. Another course open to those desirous of raising their status was through bravery in battle. Omai arrived with the tools of the trade, namely his force multipliers – his muskets – capable of turning defeat into victory. The latter course was not one which Cook favoured but Cook would have kept an open mind, aware of the options open to him, any one of which he could decide to pursue according to circumstances. Cook would be Omai's safety valve.

Cook had Omai's best interests at heart as well as the interests of the nation in establishing a partisan honorary consul within the islands. In addition to Omai, Cook had a responsibility to consider Omai's two New Zealand retainers. If Omai succeeded, so too would they; if Omai failed, so would they, becoming prisoners on a distant island. It was essential for Omai to consider and reflect upon Cook's wise counsel.

Perhaps the most important personal quality Omai had to develop was that of humility when he appeared before the chiefs, particularly Tu. That was easier said than done, for one prominent characteristic in the make-up of the Tahitian male is pride. Humility would go some way, but we must not underestimate the challenge this posed for Omai. As he stood at the ship's forecastle, only yards from the shore, he was returning to a structured society in which he had had no natural position of worth, yet he had mixed with the most sophisticated members of a foreign society pre-eminent in power, economics and culture. In telling what he had seen, heard and experienced (which the British encouraged), he had to take care that he neither denigrated nor humiliated the chiefs by inferring the relative insignificance of their own status. Some had forecast that it would be Omai's knowledge and enjoyment of the comfortable life that he had experienced in London which would condemn his rehabilitation to failure. If that were to be the case, mused Lieutenant King, it would have been due to 'his want of some useful knowledge that might have made him respected among his countrymen and would have counterbalanced his defect in rank'.

This part of the unfolding story has been described by McCormick as 'part social comedy, part social drama' with Omai as the central character and the crews of the two ships the 'absorbed and sometimes self-conscious spectators'. At the outset, the majority of the British, but not all, liked rather than respected Omai. As each event was played out, his friends took a view as to how best to succeed while Omai had a disconcerting and unhappy knack of invariably taking the opposite course of action. The first scene of the final Act began, as was so often the case, with a number of fishing canoes leaving the white sand beach at Vaitepiha Bay and making for the *Resolution*. Cook related how Omai took no notice of the occupants of the canoes as they were only 'common fellows'. Herein lies a dichotomy which bears repeating, for Omai was most at ease among 'common fellows' whose companionship he cultivated. What we have here is a confused young man, uncertain in this environment as to who he is or who he wants to be.

When the visitors came on board, they greeted Cook warmly but showed no interest in Omai and, although he fired off questions at them, they did not pause to consider why one of their own was aboard one of the visiting ships. Among those who followed shortly were a Bora Bora chief named Utae and Omai's brother-in-law who by chance happened to be in the area. Indifferent is the word which best describes the meeting between the two visitors and Omai. Omai's only possible interest in a Bora Bora chief, of all people, would have been as a means to an end. In view of Omai's treatment of his wife, the coolness between him and his brother-in-law could be readily understood. King wrote that many in England envied him and his friends being in Tahiti to witness the return of Omai to his people. What they saw at first was a deflated Omai – nothing to write home about. Unfortunately, Omai found himself unable to resist taking his brother-in-law and Utae down to his cabin where he opened the drawer overflowing with a king's ransom of red feathers. As Clerke explained: 'These people's extraordinary passion for red feathers has been before recorded; they look upon them the first of all human possessions.' Both men looked wide-eyed at what for them was a hoard of treasure. Their mood change was instantaneous. Utae immediately wanted to be Omai's friend, his *tayo*, to change names, a proposal to which the flattered Omai instantly acceded. To his new friend he presented a handful of feathers, to which Utae later reciprocated with a gift of a hog.

Omai's behaviour left Cook exasperated, it being obvious to everyone 'that it was not the man but his property they were in love with'. Cook reckoned that had Omai not shown off his collection of red feathers, 'I question if they had given him a coconut'. This first meeting with his countrymen did not augur at all well for the future. Omai spurned advice that he should foster respect among the islanders and stimulate curiosity and a desire among the chiefs to become acquainted with the newly returned prodigal son, 'but instead of that', continued Cook, 'he rejected the advice of those who wished him well and suffered himself to be duped by every designing knave'. Omai's stupidity particularly exasperated his friend Burney who observed the antics of the brother-in-law, 'a greedy rascal ever begging and never satisfied'. The brother-in-law, one of the many relatives on Tahiti, flattered to deceive and headed the long queue of islanders intent upon praising Omai, 'a large train of followers whose only motive was to profit by his profusion and carelessness'. Lieutenant King found he had no influence in the unfolding 'farce of flattery and vanity'.

The prospect of having their palms crossed with feathers loosened the tongues of the multitude who, but for the feathers, would not have given Omai the time of day. Among the intelligence passed to Cook came a report of two ships calling twice at Vaitepiha Bay since his last visit and that these visitors had also more recently landed animals for the benefit of the people as well as returning one of the four natives they had taken with them back to Lima. These visitors had been the Spaniards who had, over a ten-month period, gone through their own appraisal of the efficacy of establishing a Christian presence on the island. The news of the landing of Spanish animals left those who had suffered the extended presence of their own gift of animals deflated by the realisation that they had been pre-empted. Omai related to Cook how the people from Rema (Lima) built a prefabricated house on the beach in which lived four men – two priests, a servant and an official interpreter by the name of Mateama (Maximo Rodriguez). The same two ships eventually returned, evacuating the whole party but leaving behind the body of Boenechea, their leader, whose grave they marked with a conspicuous cross.

The news of the availability of red feathers aboard the ships (it was not only Omai who was aware of the value of red feathers among the Tahitians) spread like wildfire so that by early morning the next day, both ships were found to be surrounded by canoes carrying fruit and hogs for barter. 'Not more feathers than might be got from a tom tit', wrote Cook, 'would purchase a hog of 40 or 50 pounds weight.' During the course of that day, the value of feathers fell by 500 per cent. No longer were they the exclusive, privileged possession of the chiefs and aristocracy but, in a sweeping, egalitarian fall in the market, every native might aspire to own some; not a development that would have left the chiefs best pleased and, what is more, they knew who was to blame. In a stroke, beads and nails had become worthless while among the 'fine women' – as opposed to the usual run-of-the-mill women who associated with sailors – red feathers became such a highly desirable fashion statement that they 'have come on board the ship and would cohabit for nothing but red feathers. As soon as they had obtained a small quantity by cohabiting once – have disappeared and not been seen after by us either on board or on shore.'

After some delay in anchoring, the cattle went ashore and caulkers set about filling in the gaps which had begun to appear between planks. In the translucent sea below them, sailors peered down in perpetual enchantment as sharks and rays, highlighted by the white sand bottom, wove their endless balletic magic. Cook took the opportunity to check foodstocks as a preliminary to the next phase of the voyage in the Arctic. In that cold climate, grog would be more appreciated than here in Tahiti. Cook gathered his crew together and suggested stocks should be conserved. He proposed that grog be issued once a week, on Saturday, which would give them the opportunity 'to drink to their female friends in England, lest amongst the pretty girls of Otaheite they should be wholly forgotten'. Cook had a distinctly strange sense of humour, particularly since he permitted local girls virtually unlimited freedom to visit and even stay with their beaux on board. Cook and Clerke also apprised their men of the £20,000 reward on offer for completing their mission. That piece of information may have been instrumental in easing the ships' final departure from the Society Islands. When it came to Bligh's turn with HMS *Bounty*, there was no such incentive.

Just as Cook prepared to take Omai ashore, their departure became delayed by the 'extremely moving' arrival of Omai's sister. They went below to weep together in private. Omai took Cook directly to visit a disabled Bora Bora chief whom Cook at first assumed to be immensely important. He shared the name of the god Oro yet his real name was Etari. There were no obvious signs that Etari was in any way out of the ordinary. He sat under the type of small shelter chiefs had erected in their large canoes, with a scattering of plantains around him. Omai obviously rated the chief highly, showing deference and handing over a tuft of red feathers, talking in quiet tones. An old woman appeared by Etari's side, Omai's aunt, whose tears fell on her nephew's feet. Cook, having had a surfeit of the emotions of Omai's female relatives, and unimpressed by Etari, took his leave to find the Spanish house about which he had heard so much. He was no wiser as to how Etari fitted into the hierarchy.

Cook had heard that Tu, chief of Big Tahiti, was alive and well. Vehiatua II, the previous chief of Little Tahiti, had died, as some would claim due to the Spaniards' disregard of taboos but more likely to their influenza against which he had no immunity. His younger, twelve-year-old brother had assumed the title but was presently away. The most important person to have died was Oberea – news so significant that her obituary eventually appeared in London newspapers.

Turning back the calendar to 26 September 1774, the Spanish frigate *Aguila* accompanied by the packet *Júpiter* had sailed from El Callao harbour on the first ever missionary voyage to Tahiti. The *Aguila* was again under the command of de Boenechea. On board, he carried two Franciscans – Fray Geronimo Clota and Fray Narciso Gonzalez – of the order of Propaganda Fide, the true faith, the first clergy to establish a ministry on Tahiti. Also on board were the two surviving Tahitians, Thomas and Manuel, and the interpreter Maximo Rodriguez who would prove to be popular with the Tahitians. The packet, or storeship, carried the two-room prefabricated house, with loopholes in the wall intended to admit air and to provide firing positions for muskets. In addition, the packet carried a 3-metre-high cross bearing the inscription:

CHRISTUS VINCIT
CARLOS III IMPERAT 1774

The Spanish ships arrived at Vaitepiha Bay on 27 November 1774, from which point the establishment of the settlement and exploration commenced. Clota and Gonzalez, keen to learn something of the natives' religion and culture, seized the opportunity to investigate precisely what a visiting group of *arioi* did. The timing of the arrival of these people of sensitive disposition, coinciding as it did with the presentation at the *heiva* of the most pornographic dance in the *arioi* repertoire, left a lasting impression from which the priests never recovered. Moreover, to their surprise, it was they, the Franciscans with their black habits and tonsures, who became a sideshow, a situation which persisted even after their house had been assembled. They looked to Thomas and Manuel for help, but they had rejected their assumed Christian faith and gone home to their families.

The Spanish ships eventually departed from Tahiti on 7 January 1775, returning after a fortnight's sailing off the islands. It is possible that it had been their intention to allow time for the missionaries to find their feet. It is also possible that the imminence of de Boenechea's death caused the ships to seek out the Franciscans to administer the last rites. The captain died on 26 January and was buried at the foot of the tall cross. The friars officiated at the religious ceremony, watched with much curiosity by a crowd of natives. Two days later, both ships departed for El Callao under Lieutenant Don Tomás Gayangos. He had sailed on the *Aguila's* previous voyage to Tahiti, indicating a shared predilection for experience as evident in both the

British and Spanish navies. On board *Júpiter* were four more natives to be 'accorded the same welcome (by d'Amat) as to those who came up before'.

The *Aguila* sailed for her last round trip to Tahiti under Lieutenant Don Cayetano de Lángara on 27 September 1775 on what was thought to be a routine mission to replenish the supplies of the Franciscans and their support staff. On board was one of the four natives taken by Gayangos. Two had died in the intervening period and one declined to be repatriated. If Lángara expected to find a flourishing religious community at Vaitepiha Bay led by the zealous Franciscans, then he was to be hugely disappointed. The ordered life as practised by the two celibates and the libidinous freedom enjoyed by the natives proved irreconcilable. The natives would most certainly have propositioned the priests, including perhaps the *mahus*, men dressed as women, but as a genuine token of friendship.

The diary of Maximo Rodriguez, a marine by profession, who readily welcomed temptation, reveals that the natives showed no hostile intent, offering the friars nothing but warmth and affection. Clota's and Gonzalez's journals told different stories. In their nine months on the island they had developed a paranoid, siege mentality, resisting any attempt to go out among the '*gentiles y idolatras*'. On meeting Lángara, they demanded a detachment of soldiers to protect and defend them. When told their request was impossible to meet, they categorically insisted they be taken off the island and returned to Lima. Lángara had no alternative but to accede to their request and abandon the settlement, turning loose a bull, a ram, goats, dogs and pigs which had accompanied him. The *Aguila* sailed for Lima on 12 November on what would be her last voyage. Old and rotten, the Spanish navy scrapped their only frigate in Peru, a crumbled relic reflecting the state of Spanish power in the Pacific. The Spanish made no further attempts to introduce Christianity on Tahiti. The Viceroy wrote in anger: 'It is on record that missionaries deficient in catholic zeal on other similar occasions cried off through timidity and repining. They are like soldiers lacking in honour, or love for their King and

Fatherland.' All that remained to mark their presence was the cross, a small house and an assortment of animals foreign to Tahiti.

Standing there, surveying the Spanish house with its numbered planks, the thought may have occurred to Cook how simple a matter it would have been for carpenters to dismantle and reassemble the building elsewhere. That thought had not escaped Omai who appeared later on the scene. He found a vegetable patch in which the Spaniards had grown cabbages. There were still a couple there which the natives clearly neither recognised nor tried. It came as no surprise to find a neglected Spanish grapevine. Omai liked the idea of growing his own grapes to sustain his passion for wine long after the supply he brought with him had been exhausted. Apparently the natives tried the unripe fruit, found the grapes sour and assumed them to be poisonous. Cleverly, Omai took away a number of grafts. 'He had several slips cut off the tree to carry away with him', wrote Cook, 'and we pruned and put the remains to order, and probably with what Omai told them they may suffer the fruit to come to perfection and not to pass so hasty a sentence upon it again.'

The natives had built a thatched roof over the Spanish building to afford greater protection from the elements. They took their responsibility for the house seriously, obviously expecting the Spaniards to return one day. Each of the two rooms was 5 to 6 yards square. In one room there were a table, a bedstead, stools and some clothing. It was unusual that these items had not been stolen, but it was also significant that during the short period the *Resolution* and the *Discovery* spent at Vaitepiha Bay, there were no reported thefts. Omai believed the Spanish house to be ideal for his purposes. He offered the natives a generous incentive to encourage them to surrender the building but they refused, 'for it shows their firm belief that the Spaniards will return, for they said that if the cross or house was hurt or removed, that they should all be killed'. This sensitivity did not deter Omai from sleeping in the bed in the Spanish building for as long as the ships remained in the bay.

The cross annoyed Cook. To him, the reference upon it to 1774 implied that to have been the date of Tahiti's discovery by Europeans. The natives became exceedingly anxious when the cross came down but all Cook intended was to set the record straight. On the other side he had his carpenters carve 'Georgius tertius Rex Annis 1767, 69, 73, 74 & 77', the dates that British ships had visited the islands.

Initial signs that Omai might be accepted by the local people appeared favourable. Returning from viewing the Spanish house, Cook found Omai surrounded by a crowd of people hanging on his every word. A few days after arrival, he and one of the officers exercised the two remaining horses, not in itself exceptional other than that Omai rode in full body armour, carrying a sword and pike. The natives had seen nothing quite like this. If they gathered round ever closer to confirm what they were seeing, Omai would discharge a pistol over their heads to clear the way. Sometimes Omai let himself down by falling from the horse, it being no easy matter to pick himself up off his back from the ground wearing full body armour. Overall, these people of Little Tahiti were impressed by what one of their own had accomplished, although to what end they may not have been entirely certain. Relations between the inhabitants of the Bay and their visitors had rarely been more convivial. The natives presented a *heiva* which Williamson witnessed for the first time: 'the whole concluded with a very obscene part performed by the ladies, there are many customs in the entertainments of women, the relation of which though it might gratify curiosity, must offend modesty.'

The news of the arrival of the two British ships drew Thomas and Manuel, the two earlier returnees from Lima, out of their villages to refamiliarise themselves with civilisation. Clerke entertained one on board the *Discovery* assisted by Burney acting as translator. They attempted to engage in conversation but it appeared that their visitor's only Spanish was '*Si, señor*', which he repeated at regular intervals. Clerke made arrangements for the young man to return the next day in order that they might develop their conversation and talk about life in Lima. He did not keep his appointment. 'When he saw the great abundance of Omai's riches', wrote Clerke, 'he cursed the signiors very heartily and lamented much, that his good fortune had not given him a trip to England instead of Lima.' His friend went aboard the *Resolution* and no sooner had Cook sat down to interview him than Omai, hearing one of the returnees had come aboard, went to Cook's cabin.

I should not have known he had ever been out of the island had it not been for the congé he made on entering the cabin and some of his countrymen informing me who he was. I had scarce time to ask him any questions before Omai came on board, and while I was busy about some other matters, got him out of the ship and I never saw him afterwards; which I rather wondered at, as I had treated him with uncommon civility; but, I believe, Omai had treated him a little roughly, being displeased there was a traveller upon the island besides himself.

On 16 August word came that Vehiatua had returned to the bay through the pass, at the head of which are magnificent sculptures carved by the elements. Omai seems to have had difficulty deciding what to wear. His solution was an attire part-European, part-Tahitian and part-Tongan. The visitors assembled the pre-selected gifts to accompany them prior to the presentation to the twelve-year-old chief. Omai had made a *maro* or belt of red and yellow feathers, far superior to anything its intended recipient Tu had ever possessed and an item only the most senior chiefs were entitled to wear. Far back in Raiatean history an alliance of kings met at Opoa under the guidance of King Tamatoa who was entitled as his badge of office to wear a *maro*, there being no higher honour. There was an obvious disparity between this, the initial visit to Vehiatua, and Omai bearing an expensive gift not intended for the chief they were visiting but for his rival on Big Tahiti. Cook used all his powers of persuasion to encourage Omai to present the *maro* directly to Tu when he met him at Matavai, but to no avail. Omai had complete confidence in the honesty and fidelity of Vehiatua to deliver the *maro* on his behalf to the great Tu. Cook's words of caution proved apposite: 'whereas he highly disobliged the one without gaining any favour from the other for Vehiatua kept the maro and only sent to Tu a very small piece of feathers, not a twentieth part of what was in it.' Tu sent an angry message to Vehiatua demanding the return of his gift. The answer came back in the negative, accompanied by an unfortunate individual given by Vehiatua to Tu to be used as a human sacrifice.

Cook and Omai assembled at Etari's home where they were to meet the chief. The young chief arrived with his mother and two equerries who sat opposite Cook and Omai, their gifts laid out on the ground in front of them. Speeches criss-crossed the floor. The last to speak told of the final words of advice left by the Spaniards, denigrating the British and recommending that they be denied access to the bay and the island. The Spanish did carry weight, not least because the frigate *Aguila* was substantially larger than the Whitby cats; moreover, their officers were more formally attired in elegant uniforms than were the British who customarily relaxed their dress code in such obscure places as eighteenth-century Tahiti. The chief set aside these reservations, crossed over to Cook whom he embraced and exchanged names. That night they dined together aboard the *Resolution*.

On 19 August Vehiatua sent Cook a gift of a dozen hogs, some fruit and some cloth. Meanwhile, a message came from Tu asking why they had delayed visiting him at Matavai. That night the British did what they did best and arranged a fireworks display which 'both astonished and entertained'. Hardly a day had passed here when it had not rained, but the night of the firework display was the welcome exception. All agreed that the fireworks and the bringing of red feathers was something that the Spanish had never done. On the 23rd, Omai and Cook took their leave of the young chief, but not before being accosted by a deranged soothsayer, after which they took a course for the favoured Matavai Bay.

A favourable breeze from the east carried the *Resolution* to Matavai that same day but the wind was not as favourable for the *Discovery* which arrived on 24 August 1777. Before the *Discovery* anchored in Matavai Bay, Tu, accompanied by many canoes, came up from

Pare, landing at Matavai Point from where he conveyed to Cook his recommendation that they make rendezvous there. Obviously smarting from the natives' criticism of his and his men's dress when compared with the Spanish, Cook issued orders that a greater effort be made to impress their hosts. As the pinnaces left the *Resolution* they were seen to be flying silk flags and bunting. On landing, the delegation formed up behind the ships' band, marching to where Tu and 'a prodigious number of people had assembled'. Cook halted in front of his *tayo*, a more corpulent Tu than he had known before, saluted and handed over his personal gifts, a linen suit, a gold laced hat, some tools and the *pièce de resistance*, red feathers together with a feathered bonnet from Tonga. For that last valuable item alone, Tu reciprocated with the gift of ten large hogs. After the presentation of his gifts, Cook stood aside for Omai to come forward.

Omai had dressed conventionally for this his second public outing – conventionally, that is, for England, for he had put on his smart suit of English velvet, first worn at the Leicester civic dance all that time ago. Although he presented a striking figure, his suit was not the most sensible attire for Tahiti's tropical heat. Omai fell on his knees before Tu, embracing his legs. Tu ignored him. Cook said, 'perhaps envy had some share in it'. Nonplussed, the returning native took up his position to give Tu a summary of his experiences. The chief, impatient to hear his story, asked him a hundred questions before giving him time to answer one. Rickman's accounts were not always reliable but on this occasion it was true that Omai's effusive praise of George III annoyed Tu:

> Omai began by magnifying the grandeur of the Great King; he compared the splendour of his court to the brilliancy of the stars in the firmament; the extent of his dominions by the vast expanse of heaven; the greatness of his power, by thunder that shakes the earth. He said the great King of Pretane had three hundred thousand warriors every day at his command, clothed like those who now attended the Earees (leaders) of the ships and more than

double that number of sailors, who traversed the globe, from the rising of the sun to his setting.

In such a vein, Omai continued, describing the Navy, the massive guns, ('pooh poohs'), carried on each ship, some of which fired 'globes of iron' which, if 'thrown among the fleet of Otaheite, would set them on fire, and destroy the whole navy, were they ever so numerous'. Then there was a city, undoubtedly London, 'on the banks of a river far removed from the sea, there were more people than were contained in the whole group of islands with which his Majesty was acquainted'. Making Tu appear small and insignificant before his assembled people was not the wisest of acts from someone seeking favours. The chief, who 'seemed more astonished than delighted with this narration, suddenly left Omai to join the company that were in conversation with Captain Cook and the other officers'.

After the assembly broke up, Tu and his immediate royal family went with Cook to the *Resolution*, followed by several canoes heavily laden with sufficient provisions to last the crews a week – had they been able to keep everything fresh. The whole of the chief's family wished to be associated with the gift, which meant Cook having to give each one a present in return. Interestingly, when Tu's mother came on board – she had not been at the original reception – she divided her gifts between Cook and Omai. By this shrewd move, Tu's mother demonstrated that she recognised Omai to be a wealthy man worth cultivating. Perhaps she already saw Omai as a prospective son-in-law. Such a development would have pleased Cook for he intended to put Omai under Tu's protection, but there were few indications of a harmonious relationship between the two. Omai had been foremost among those responsible for the devaluation of red feathers, followed by the impertinence of having a devalued gift delivered through the hands of a lesser chief. Now, finally, Omai had called into question Tu's power and importance.

Cook persevered. He had had to suffer his ship becoming an ark carrying assorted animals halfway round the world. He wanted nothing more than to deliver the animals into Tu's care and thereby discharge his responsibility to George III. As a realist, Cook recognised that none of the natives had the faintest notion of animal husbandry, with the exception, that is, of Omai. He had already moved ashore, staying at the home of his sister and brother-in-law, one of the so-described *black guards* of the island, 'among those he squandered most of his red feathers and other articles'. After addressing the problem arising from his brother-in-law's influence, there was therefore merit in his staying here at Matavai not only to supervise the management of the animals but also because Cook believed he would be more respected the further he was from his home island.

After dinner, Cook and his senior officers accompanied Tu to Pare, being careful to include the smaller animals Cook intended to leave with the chief. First to go were Lord Bessborough's noisy peacock and hen, a turkey-cock and hen, one gander and three geese, a drake and four ducks. To the visitors' surprise, they saw at Pare the gander Wallis had given to Oberea ten years previously, together with several goats and the best specimen of a Spanish bull they had ever seen. The bull now belonged to Etari and was due to be moved to Bora Bora. Cook placed an immediate embargo on any intended movement of the animals. But the bull, in his splendid isolation, could not function as intended without a cow or two. Cook remedied the situation the next day by sending ashore at Matavai three cows, a bull, a horse and mare and a number of sheep. He could now breathe a sigh of relief having been able to carry out this particular aspect of his mission successfully: 'But the satisfaction I felt in having been so fortunate as to fulfil His Majesty's design in sending such useful animals to two worthy nations sufficiently recompensed me for the many anxious hours I had on their account.'

During Cook's absence at Pare, Odiddy, Cook's favourite, called at Matavai where the observatory had been resurrected in its usual place and to where the *Discovery's* mainmast had been brought for repair. Apparently Odiddy lived at Matavai under Tu's patronage, the same relationship Cook intended for Omai. The new officers and those who had been on the *Resolution*'s previous voyage were all well aware that Cook had rated Odiddy above Omai and it was for that reason that the visitor came in for close examination. Their overwhelming impression was one of acute disappointment, 'to find him one of the most stupid fellows on the island, with a clumsy awkward person and a remarkably heavy look'. Bayly considered: 'It does not appear that he would have made any figure in England if he had gone, for he appears to be one of the most silly fellows among them', an appraisal with which King concurred: 'the most stupid, foolish youth I ever saw'. A German among the two cosmopolitan crews was the only one to speak well of Odiddy: 'he spoke English no worse than Omai and would have benefited from visiting Europe where his natural intelligence and fine physique could have been developed to his advantage.' When Cook returned, he appeared delighted to meet his protégé, handing over the gifts he had brought from the Admiralty, and from Banks some clothes and tools.

Cook's immediate problem was the rehabilitation of Omai. The time had come to examine the promising marriage option. *Promising* because, if the marriage came to fruition, the problem of Omai's status would be nicely sidestepped and he would live at Matavai from where he could supervise George III's gift of animals. Tu had a sister who, not to put too fine a point on the matter, was plain – too plain for Omai. No sooner had they been reacquainted than Tu offered Cook the services of his sister but true to form he politely declined. This was no virginal Poetua; she came with a history which did not impress Omai. She also had an established lover. The lover told Omai that Tu was not to be trusted because he had designs on Omai's property. That night the lover and friends provided him with a lovely girl, said to be Odiddy's wife, in the expectation that they themselves might relieve Omai of some of his belongings during his sleep of exhaustion. Awakened during the night, Omai fired a pistol at one of the robbers, missed, and in so doing woke up the girl beside him. 'They all quarrelled', wrote Bayly, 'and the girl left him but not till she had in a manner stripped him of his most valuable things, and to crown all she gave him the foul disease.' All in all, therefore, not a propitious beginning.

Bayly believed Omai to have been ill-served by those who had equipped him for his new life in the islands 'by giving him a collection of the worst things that could have been procured'. There were 8-inch nails, sent out apparently accidentally, while the rest was said to have been rubbish, of no use for barter or any practical use. Bayly examined Omai's hatchets, finding them to be the cheapest and shoddiest available except for four or five which might have cost a shilling or fourteen pence each. Of the pound's-worth of glass beads, there was not one the natives would trade for a coconut. If that had not been the case previously, it was certainly the case in the days of the red feather revolution. Bayly believed Omai to have been equally responsible for having brought so much junk this far. Had he been less focused upon his own pleasures and checked what was being procured for him rather than leave the business to third parties, the problem would not have arisen. After examining his boxes and casks, 'he was very nearly going out of his senses, finding himself little richer, either in knowledge or treasure, than when he left his native country'. Bayly's assessment varied from that of Alexander Home, the master's mate, who wrote: 'He has arrived in his own country with such a fortune as none in it possessed comparatively speaking. Lord Clive's was a mere mite when compared to it.' The truth appears to lie somewhere between the two. Omai condemned Banks for providing him with nothing more than the electrifying machine, not even a useful hatchet. A number of officers took pity on Omai, exchanging his cheap hatchets for ones of better quality.

As day followed day, so Omai's failings became increasingly evident. His rejection of Tu's sister had not been diplomatic but Omai's insistence that Tu disband the *arioi* and send all Bora Borans on Tahiti packing were just causes for Tu and his relatives to treat the upstart Omai with disdain. Cold-shouldered by the aristocracy, Omai sought solace among the peasantry, lavishing upon them gifts which the chiefs themselves coveted. Cook felt slighted by Omai's refusal to accept his advice and for conducting himself in such a manner as not only to lose the friendship of Tu but that of every other person of note on the island:

> He associated with none but refugees and strangers whose sole views were to plunder him and if I had not interfered they would not have left him with a single thing worth the carrying from the island, this was what got him the ill-will of the principal chiefs, for many of these low people got from him such things as no one in the ships could give to them.

Elsewhere in Cook's journals is the observation: 'A great deal of unnecessary sentiment has been spent over Omai's return to Polynesia both in England and on shipboard; and now he was behaving like the vain and gullible fool that he was. He had given some trouble in Tonga already.'

Occasionally, within the accounts of Cook's voyages to and from the South Pacific, events arise as reminders that his wallowing Whitby cats were Royal Navy warships armed with cannon and each with its complement of embarked marines. On 27 August 1777, an incident occurred where Cook cleared the decks for action as a contingency operation, while concurrently among the Tahitians there formed the idea that the fortunate arrival of Cook and all the firepower at his disposal might usefully be channelled to their advantage in their oft-postponed naval intervention in Eimeo's (Moorea's) war of succession.

On that day, a self-declared messenger arrived from Vaitepiha Bay with the news that two Spanish ships with the marine Maximo aboard had arrived with the specific intention of attacking the British. Cook demanded evidence. The messenger replied that he himself had gone on board one of the ships where the Spanish gave him a piece of blue cloth, which he duly produced. With no reason to doubt this report, Cook ordered the ships cleared for action and guns placed in their firing positions. Lieutenant John Williamson, ordered out on an armed reconnaissance, had the task of verifying the Spanish presence in Vaitepiha Bay. Williamson returned on 29 August with the news that there were no Spaniards, nor had there been. Fortunately for the messenger, he was able to leap overboard before being dealt with in the ship's usual manner. Cook presumed the man's purpose to have been to encourage the ships to depart, thereby depriving Tu and his close friends of the seemingly laden conveyor-belt of gifts flowing ashore. No doubt Vehiatua believed that by this ruse he would be able to divert the visitors' largesse to Vaitepiha Bay. At that precise moment, Tu, his followers and people, took sanctuary inland. They were a people with long memories, mindful that the clearing of the decks had been the precursor to the *Dolphin's* subsequent action of firing upon the natives. They were also aware of another unwelcome development ashore.

After a welcome break, the spate of thefts resumed, this time at the observatory encampment. During the night, Bayly seized a would-be robber by the hair, calling out to the sentry to assist. The sentry responded by fleeing and was to be flogged for his cowardice. Bayly confided in Cook his opinion that the man he apprehended was none other than Tu. There had been other minor occurrences of theft. Tracking down the skulking chief, Cook reassured the man that he did not hold him blameworthy and relations were quickly restored.

As was so often the case, Tu had Moorea on his mind. The Tahitians knew that their Moorean allies had been forced inland into the mountains. The chief remembered how greatly impressed Cook had been with the Tahitian fleet on his previous visit in 1774. But Tu remained essentially a timid leader, preferring to operate only in a risk-free environment. Other chiefs pressed him to act. There was only one circumstance in which he would be happy to support naval operations against Moorea and that would be with the active support of Cook, his ships and their firepower. The chief would have remembered Omai's glowing reports of those ships' capabilities. By chance Cook had called on Tu, without Omai, at the same time as the Moorea debate in his home raged on between the chiefs. By this time, Cook had a reasonable understanding of the Tahitian language and was able to comprehend more than he could speak. What was his contribution to be, they asked? 'None,' he replied. Cook explained that he knew nothing of the background of the dispute and could not offer violence to those who had not offered violence to him. Cook's response would not have surprised Tu but he was none the less annoyed because he was unavoidably committed to providing a lead.

The hawkish Chief Towha of Arahurahu, given the nickname the 'Admiral' by the British, announced his intention to offer up a sacrifice at the important *marae* within his bailiwick. Human sacrifices were made in the hope of attracting the god's blessing upon a proposed warlike operation. Tu received from Towha what was in effect a summons to the ceremony at Oro's *marae*. Would Cook wish to attend? 'Yes', he said with enthusiasm. They left almost immediately, Cook, Anderson, Webber the artist and Omai. When they arrived at the small point of land close to the *marae*, which de Boenechea had also visited, the sailors received orders to remain where they were and the officers to remove their hats. The killing of the middle-aged sacrifice, probably a vagrant, had already taken place, the victim having been struck down from behind by a heavy instrument, his body bruised and tied to a pole. Many men and a few boys had been assembled to witness the event which excluded women. The attitude of the congregation resembled that of a group dragooned to attend obligatory prayers, the lack of interest being palpable. Anderson noted:

> that though a great number of people had collected on this occasion, they did not pay the least attention to what was doing during the ceremony, and Omai happening to arrive in the midst of it they flocked round him and were engaged the remainder of the time in making him relate some of his adventures, which they listened to with great attention.

The rhythm of sinister sacrificial drums throbbed across the clearing, echoing off the stepped walls of the *marae*. Skulls looked down through eyeless sockets upon the scene. The priest offered up prayers. Tu went through the motions of pretending to eat one of the victim's eyes. A sacred kingfisher looking down upon the ceremony cried out. 'It is Atua the god', explained Tu to Cook. Red feathers featured in the service, with the presentation of the entrails of a dog with some of the victim's hair. Men then came forward to dig a grave about 2 feet deep, 'when they threw in the body with an air of great indifference'. At the same time, a dog was brought in and had its neck broken. 'The hair was singed off and the entrails taken out,' wrote Anderson:

> The guts were burnt on the fire and the liver only roasted and the body of the dog after being besmeared with blood and dried over the fire was with the liver put on a *whatta* or scaffold about six feet high along with two dogs and two hogs which had lately been sacrificed and at this time emitted an intolerable stench.

With a great shout from the priests, the first day of the ceremony came to an end.

On the second day, the earthy manifestation of the god Oro was carried out for part of the proceedings. The priests refused Cook permission to come close to examine the bundle. Unlike at the *inasi* ceremony, he obeyed. Meanwhile Webber had been active, sketching the event, later to be completed as a painting. This one would be special for of all the paintings he executed, in England this one attracted the most adverse comment and notoriety. Its bloodiness and sheer nastiness sustaining, so they argued, all the objections of those opposed to the concept of the noble savage.

Cook accompanied Tu back to the ship, calling upon Towha en route to Matavai. The 'Admiral', concerned that he might not have a navy to command, pleaded with Cook to support his cause, for Cook's support was certain to swing the doubters behind him. Again Cook politely refused. Towha, now beside himself with anger, asked Cook how he had enjoyed the sacrifice. He replied, through Omai, that he disliked it extremely, from which point Omai continued into his own personal deprecation of the event, bringing the chief close to a state of apoplexy. Omai informed Towha that if he, as a chief in England, had put a man to death as he had done, he would have been hanged. Towha thereupon exploded in a high state of indignation, crying 'vile! vile!', refusing to listen to another word, 'so that we left him with as great a contempt of our customs as we could possibly have of theirs'.

The first two days of September 1777 which had begun with the ceremony of human sacrifice, flowed naturally into the third day and the volcanic meeting with Towha, after which substantive activities became beset by calm if not actual inertia. From 4 September onwards, there followed a week of entertainment and socialising. Little of practical benefit was being achieved, probably because Cook found himself in a real bind as to what was to be done with Omai. One solution was for Omai to host a dinner party to which Tu and his relatives came. The accounts of the meal of poultry, fish, pork and puddings, prepared with the assistance of six servants to which he was not entitled, were as favourable as ever. However, little progress seems to have been made in winning over Tu, Omai acting the part, according to Samwell, 'of a merry Andrew, parading about in ludicrous masks and different dresses'. Perhaps the chief thought the host wearing armour at dinner to have been over the top. The damage appeared too severe to repair. Omai continued to associate with the lower classes and so casual had he become in distributing his wealth among them that Cook decided to take control by impounding the residue of his possessions.

Omai's homecoming had not been a happy occasion. He decided he would not remain on Tahiti. Cook had orders to leave him on the Society Island of his choice but was disinclined to take him to Raiatea for fear of becoming embroiled in a civil war of Omai's making. Huahine therefore became almost the self-selecting final destination for Omai. Otherwise, minds were very much focused upon food and other inconsequentials. Not to be outdone, Odiddy also hosted a dinner party, serving fish, pork and fruit but not apparently extending to a proper pudding. For his part, Cook waxed lyrical on the subject of local puddings: 'we can make few in England that equal them, I seldom or never dined without one when I could get it, for they were not always to be got.' The food supply flowing out to the ships proved endless. But for the want of salt, the victuallers' stocks would have more than held their own. For the moment there was no requirement to draw on the sea stocks being conserved for the voyage into the Arctic. The food was essentially a *quid pro quo* in so far as it came in exchange for personal goods supplied from the ships.

As a result of the visits of a growing number of European ships, the quantity of personal belongings being accumulated by the island's aristocracy began to present new problems. Previously the natives had not stolen property from among themselves because no one had desirable personal possessions worth stealing. Now, a significant number of the island's notables had accumulated belongings that were attractive to others. The problem was one of the negative outcomes associated with European discoveries in Polynesia: it had become so bad that even Tu was not spared the need to take precautions against burglary. The worthies took their problem to Cook, together with examples of lockable chests and trunks abandoned by the Spanish. Cook set his carpenters to work to copy the examples given, although the chests made for Tu were so large that one or two men could sleep on top; perhaps they did.

Cook knew that his firework displays never ceased to enthral the natives. He told his gunners he wanted something a little special for Matavai, his most favoured port of call in the Pacific. On Sunday, 7 September, the natives foregathered as bidden to a display that Omai promised would be unforgettable. That was true. They would recall rarely having been more frightened. Most held their ground until the explosion of a table rocket, when 'even the most resolute fled'. Each day of this quiescent period, to the amazement of the populace, Cook and Clerke rode the two horses along the length of Matavai beach. Omai had not been invited to take part. He had not overcome his embarrassing habit of falling off; besides, Cook was endeavouring to convey to the natives the subliminal message of how relatively far advanced were the British in comparison with the Tahitians.

During the period of the phoney war, Cook spent more and more time with Tu at Pare. On 17 September, news came that Towha had launched an inconclusive attack upon Moorea. The 'Admiral' requested reinforcement from Tu's fleet, drawn up ready in the bay, but to no avail. The next day, Cook, Anderson and Omai returned to the royal seat at Pare to deliver a further collection of animals. Etari had arrived from the south-east and now claimed the Spanish bull. Tired of the so-called god changing his mind, Cook repeated his instruction that the bull was to remain where it was until the cows had been served. Cook is said to have remarked that 'instead of being a god he was the greatest jackass I ever saw in my life'. Omai sprang to Etari's defence: 'Ah, Captain Cook, he is a very good gog! A very good gog Captain Cook.'

By the end of the third week of September, Cook's ships were ready to put to sea repaired and fully victualled, the observatory had been dismantled and taken on board. Inquisitive as to the nature of Tahitian naval tactics, Tu satisfied Cook's curiosity by detaching two canoes from his fleet, still on stand-by to go to Moorea. By this time, Omai had soothed Towha's troubled brow with the gift of red feathers for which Towha reciprocated with the gift of a fully-crewed double canoe. Towha had come to like Omai, suggesting he should agree to come under the chief's protection. Omai declined this, the latest best available offer. The simulated fight had Omai in one canoe versus Tu in the other, with Cook and King aboard as observers. Both canoes went through cat-and-mouse manoeuvres before clashing head-on. The umpires judged Omai's canoe to have defeated that of the chief. Rather than accept his victory with quiet dignity, Omai put on his full suit of armour and stood up on one of the canoe's stages to be paddled the full length of Matavai Bay before an underwhelmed crowd.

Meanwhile, news came to hand that Towha, denied the benefit of the reinforcement of Tu's fleet, had been forced to sign an unequal peace. Threats and recriminations flew backwards and forwards, including a suggestion that Tu would be attacked by the combined forces of Vehiatua and Towha. For the first time, Cook came off the fence to advise that in such an eventuality he would side with Tu. As a consequence, Tu found himself invited to a peace conference. Cook, suffering acute rheumatic back pain, sent King as observer and deputy with Omai as translator. Meanwhile, Tu's mother, three sisters and eight unrelated women called upon Cook, told him to strip, and set about pummelling his body until, after four sessions, he was cured of his ailment.

The time drew near now for Cook to leave Tahiti, never to return. There were formal calls to be made to the royal cantonment at Pare and animals to inspect for the last time. Tu asked Cook whether Webber might paint him (Cook) for posterity. Cook agreed and presented the final product to Tu, the friend he had grown increasingly to like, though perhaps not entirely to trust. Tu took a tax off girls visiting the ships. When, just before the designated time for sailing, Tu complained about the number of local girls still aboard, Cook put them ashore – which was neither what Tu intended (he wanted a reward for allowing them to stay) nor what the sailors wanted.

During the course of his earlier visits Cook had never visited Moorea and decided that now was his opportunity to do so. He told Omai of his intention. Omai's acquisitive sister and brother-in-law said they would come too. Cook responded in the negative. Leaving his despondent relatives behind, Omai set out for Moorea on 29 September with both his New Zealand retainers on board his own flag-bedecked double canoe, the *Royal George*. The *Resolution* and the *Discovery* followed, but only after a formal farewell to Tu with the firing of seven guns, three loaded with ball to show Tu their range. With exquisite timing, Tu presented Cook with a carved double canoe to be delivered to George III, presumably via the Arctic. There was no possibility of Cook being able to take the chief's gift. He seemed not to be too disappointed, presenting instead his wish list of gifts for the next time a British ship would be sent out to Tahiti. Tu particularly asked that horses should not be overlooked; he quite liked the idea of having his own horses. Tu remained on board until 5 p.m., then lifted his great weight over the side and climbed gingerly down the ladder into his waiting canoe. The ships stood off the harbour overnight before following Omai to Moorea the next morning.

Early the next day the two ships took a course for the island of Moorea, clearly visible from Matavai, 11 miles distant. Moorea is 53 square miles in size, shaped like a triangle with the base uppermost to the north. It remains an island of outstanding natural beauty with mountains rising up to 4000 feet.

Cook's idea of sending Omai ahead was for him to reconnoitre a passage into one of the two harbours centrally sited on the north coast. A number of large canoes from Matavai followed behind the two British ships, maintaining a relative, fixed interval between the two groups. The canoes carried the crews' wives' club, the passengers being well aware of the ships' intended initial destination. The Tahitian women's eventual goodbye to their sailors would leave both parties deeply saddened. Strangely, there was a noticeable and marked difference in the beauty of the Tahitian women compared with those from Moorea, so strikingly different that Cook felt compelled to mention the fact in his diary. The Moorean women were 'low of stature, have a dark hue and in general forbidding features, if one sees a fine woman among them one is sure, on enquiry, to find she is of some other island'.

At midday on 30 September, Omai made rendezvous with the ships which he led into the western of the two harbours, Opunohu Bay. It is one of those idiosyncrasies that the bay forsaken by the ships is today named Cook's Bay. Formerly Paopao Bay, it lay within the territory of an ally of Tu's, while Opunohu Bay belonged to Tu's enemy, the warlike Chief Maheine. Cook appeared satisfied with Opunohu Bay, giving the place the name of its pass, Tareu, which he mistakenly called Taloo. Cook did, however, visit the bay which bears his name, albeit involuntarily while rampaging around on what became a notorious hunt to track down a stolen goat. The facilities of the beautiful, 2-mile-long Opunohu Bay offered a sheltered anchorage as good as any he had seen anywhere in the South Seas, where the wind could either take ships deep into the harbour or back out on to the high seas. Mountains rise above the bays from where clear, fresh water tumbles towards the sea. The great variety of trees provided bountiful supplies of fruit and wood (on Tahiti, all wood belonged to someone), and the flowering hibiscus became anchor points to which the ships were made fast by hawser. 'It is scarcely possible for nature to have formed a most complete harbour,' wrote Bayly. No sooner had the ships been brought close inshore to anchor at 7 fathoms than they were besieged by natives unfamiliar with European ships. The next day, the natives arrived prepared with the usual range of goods for barter, the offer of women politely declined because the sailors were about to be reunited with their girlfriends from Tahiti. An account in Samwell's journal of 1 October describes: 'Many of our old sweethearts arrived from Otaheite and we gave them a most welcome reception.' It is, on reflection, strange that two of His Majesty's ships, with little available space, should so readily be allowed by their captains to be used for amorous liaisons, few of which could have been satisfactorily conducted in private.

Being so close to shore meant that the few remaining animals could be released into the lush grass. Ropes ran from ships to beach to encourage the army of rats to abandon ship. It would not be long before covetous eyes would pass over the available animals with a view to making bids for ownership.

The old warhorse Maheine chose not to present himself during the first few days, being uncertain of what kind of reception he would get from Cook, known to be Tu's *tayo*, while he, Maheine, was Tu's sworn enemy. Eventually he made a tentative approach but initially was extremely reluctant to go aboard the *Resolution*. So much had been heard of this fighting chief that the British were keen to set their eyes upon him. When they did so, on 2 October, he came as a massive disappointment. The great fighting chief with the heroic reputation, now acting as regent to the eleven-year-old paramount chief, did not look the part. The British half expected a youngish, virile warrior but the person who eventually presented himself was judged to have been in his fifties, and had many wounds and blemishes. He came accompanied by what was described as a wife, a relative of Oberea. He stayed only half an hour, accepting and giving presents. On his way off the ship he no doubt cast his eye over the available grazing animals. Shortly, Maheine requested of Cook the gift of two goats, a request Cook felt unable to satisfy from the limited number of animals he had brought to Moorea. These were breeding goats required for other islands.

Cook differed from Wallis in so far as his curiosity to explore took him far and wide, including into Maheine's chiefdom where his party was able to see the damage Towha had wreaked upon homes and trees. Thinking it better not to follow through with the return courtesy call, Cook told Omai they would go back to the ships with a view to sailing for Huahine the next morning. The discovery that two goats had been stolen put that plan on hold. Cook sent an immediate message to Maheine to the effect that if the goats were not returned immediately, he would face extreme retribution. In fact, one of the goats had been taken by way of compensation by an individual incensed that Cook's men had taken his breadfruit and coconuts and refused to pay. Goat and worried native both found themselves brought back to the ship, the latter being released unharmed. The goat which remained unaccounted for was important since it was pregnant, but whether the matter was sufficiently important to excuse Cook's behaviour from this point on is debatable.

Informants told Cook that the goat could be found at Maatea which could be reached by boat and back on the same day. Two warrant officers were accordingly sent off for the said goat. To the amusement of the villagers, the sailors found themselves kicking their heels while the goat was being fetched. The natives had no intention of letting this happen. Thus it was, at the end of day, two angry warrant officers returned to report the failure of their mission. Cook felt that he could not back off with 'any tolerable credit', thereby stretching a point because the Royal Navy had no immediate intention of returning to Tahiti and its islands. Cook sought Omai's advice. He recommended forming a group of armed sailors to go out into the countryside and shoot everyone on sight. Cook adopted an alternative plan based on his leading a thirty-five-strong group of armed sailors in search of his goat. Omai asked Cook's permission to shoot the first man he encountered.

As soon as the group reached their destination, the sailors spread out in search of the goat but without success. Cook told Omai to tell the natives to gather round. Through Omai, he told them he knew they had his goat. If it was not surrendered, he would burn their houses and boats. They protested their innocence, whereupon Cook ordered the destruction of between six and eight houses together with three war canoes. Cook and his men then marched for approximately 8 miles to make rendezvous with the three armed, pre-positioned boats under Lieutenant Williamson, burning six war canoes they encountered on their way for good measure. The word spread before them, the villages having emptied except for a number of brave souls who pleaded for their houses or canoes to be spared. Cook's party arrived back on board, exhausted, at 8 p.m. to find no word of the goat. His punitive expedition had had no effect.

On the morning of Friday, 10 October, Cook sent one of Omai's men to Maheine with the threat that if he failed to return his goat he would commence destroying every canoe on the island, stopping only when the goat had been given up. The carpenters went to the head of the harbour where they disassembled three or four war canoes, the planks from which they took on board for the purpose of building Omai's house on Huahine. Cook then cut across to the eastern harbour, the one which now bears his name. The route which he took to avoid the perpendicular cliffs of the sacred mountain, Mount Rotui, probably went to the south via a tenth-century *marae*. At Cook Bay, he broke up and burnt a similar number of canoes to those destroyed and dismantled at Opunohu Bay. He reached the *Resolution* at 7 p.m. to hear that half an hour previously his goat had been returned.

Cook's extreme behaviour upset the majority of his officers. Williamson wrote: 'I cannot help thinking the man totally destitute of humility, that would not have felt considerably for these poor and before our arrival among them probably a happy people and I must confess this once I obeyed my orders with reluctance.' There had been an outbreak of jaundice among the two ships. Perhaps Cook was ill but his reaction had been disproportionate to the original act, something which on reflection Cook would have conceded. 'Thus this troublesome, and rather unfortunate affair ended, which could not be more regretted on the part of the natives than it was on mine.' Clerke stood by and supported Cook's action yet the majority of the junior officers found Cook's behaviour difficult to accept. 'I doubt whether our ideas of propriety in punishing so many innocent people for the crimes of a few', wrote King, 'will be a very strong motive not only to these islanders, but to the rest, to give a decided preference to the Spaniards, and that in future they may fear, but never love us.' Omai's behaviour, which 'was very officious in this business', stood out among the small number of hard-liners. He had accumulated as a result of this business two additional canoes and sufficient timber to build his dream house at Huahine. The damage caused to the natives would be felt for years, although thankfully none suffered physical injury. They had lost twenty houses, twenty-seven large war canoes and three others cut up for their timber. Under different circumstances, Cook would have arrested the chiefs, refusing to release them until the stolen goods had been returned. This procedure, which invariably succeeded, was never attempted. Now, the pressure was on to get away before anything else untoward happened.

At noon on 11 October, both ships departed Opunohu Bay on a languid voyage northwards, led by Omai in his canoe which had a pilot on board. At three o'clock the next morning, musket fire was heard ahead of the *Resolution*. The watch thought Omai to be signalling that land had been sighted. In reality, his canoe almost overturned in a squall and the firing was intended to be an SOS. Unbeknown to Cook, a stowaway had come on board the *Resolution* and was found in possession of stolen goods. Cook ordered the man's head to be shaved and his ears removed. Lieutenant King arranged the token removal of an ear lobe, tossing the man overboard as the ships entered Fare Harbour, Huahine. Omai watched the ships enter harbour from his canoe. He had returned to the same point from where his adventure had begun over four years earlier.

CHAPTER 11

A Case for Two Blue Beads

The lack of preparation for Omai's return, his own weaknesses, not least an ambition tempered by his apparent preference for being among the common people, his tunnel vision, and the strategic intention to invade Bora Bora without making the necessary preparations to do so, are among his many failings. Although, ultimately, the often intractable Omai was misunderstood, wronged even, in the end he was in a position to help himself. This was not the case for his two New Zealand retainers, every bit as much the casualties in this strange story as Omai himself.

Cook's orders were to drop Omai off at the Society Island of his choice. Omai remained intent upon repossessing his land on Raiatea. Cook was not unsympathetic to that aim; they just could not agree on the means to achieve the end. Cook felt that he could negotiate the surrender of Omai's land by the Bora Borans, a course Omai did not favour. Huahine therefore became the self-selecting home of last resort for Omai.

Unfortunately, Cook's good friend Oree had been deposed in favour of the young eight- or ten-year-old Chief Teriitaria, 'a mean looking boy'. Oree had gone into exile on Raiatea but his two sons were at Huahine and were among the first to welcome Cook. The next morning Cook and Omai prepared to call on the youthful chief. Omai dressed himself soberly and selected a number of presents of bark cloth and red feathers to hand to the chief and the gods at an audience crucially important to his future. Word of Cook's arrival at Huahine – comprising, as with Tahiti, one large and one small island totalling a surface area of 28 square miles –

soon spread throughout the community, the chiefs hastily making their way to the principal settlement of Fare.

As soon as the young chief and his mother had arrived, the presentations began, first with those to the gods. Presents were laid out at the feet of a high chief, the names of British notables spoken as each gift was added to the pile with a prayer: George III, Sandwich, Cook and Clerke. At the end of the presentations, the priest collected the gifts and sent them off to a *marae* some miles distant. Then it was the turn of the young chief to receive presents, to which he reciprocated by giving presents of his own. Once finished, Cook set about establishing his terms for the visit to Huahine. There was to be no repetition of the thefts they had experienced on the previous visit. If there were, the thieves would be punished severely.

Then came Omai's turn to tell the young chief of his experiences in *Pretane*, just as he had done with Tu, adding that he had returned with many gifts and curiosities which would be put to the island's advantage. Then, in Cook's name, Omai requested of the young chief a plot of land for his own use where he could build a house and live with his retainers. If that were not possible, Cook would remove Omai and settle him upon Raiatea. Suddenly the chiefs became interested and excited; settling Omai on Raiatea appealed to them, which is not what Cook intended. Unbeknown to him, Omai had earlier schemed and discussed his intention that he and the warriors of Huahine, supported by Cook, should drive the Bora Borans out of Raiatea. After the plan had been explained to Cook, he said there and then that he would neither assist nor allow operations to be launched against Raiatea, and if Omai were to go there, it must be as a friend and not as an enemy of the Bora Borans. Any potential difficulty disappeared with a statement from a chief to the effect that the whole island and everything upon it was Cook's, therefore he could apportion to Omai whatever land he wished.

This apparent *carte blanche* appealed to Omai whose naïvety never ceased to amaze Cook, for Omai 'like the rest of his countrymen seldom sees things beyond the present moment'. If Omai believed he could rely upon Cook to make generous provision, then he was wrong. Cook wanted the land grant delineated out on the ground. After some discussion, the chiefs went outside, pointing out an area of land adjoining the house in which they were sitting. The plot measured 200 yards along the shoreline with a depth up to and including a nearby recognisable hill. In reality there was no gift of land. The property cost fifteen axes, some beads and other trifles. With this important matter settled, Cook could now turn his attention to the establishment ashore of a camp and the observatory. The carpenters of both ships set about building Omai's house, a one-room building 24 feet by 18 feet by 10 feet high, with a small attic. Nails were used sparingly so as not to be an incentive for others to destroy the house. Not all the crew enjoyed what they were having to do for Omai. Some resented his airs and graces. According to one of the crew:

> Omai was not well satisfied with his house which we had built for him and said His Majesty the King of England had promised him a house with a second floor and that this was only a one storey structure such as was used for housing pigs in England. Captain Cook laughed and said he did not deserve anything better.

Undeterred, Omai decided that in time he would build a large native house over his British-built house with its lockable door which he intended to use as a strongroom. Others prepared a garden. Cook himself planted a shaddock tree (*citrus grandis* or pomelo, related to the grapefruit) to which were added vines, pineapples, melons and other fruit and vegetables, all of which were flourishing by the time of Cook's departure.

As had happened on Tahiti, relatives of Omai came forward to declare themselves – a brother, a sister and brother-in-law – but unlike in Tahiti, these relatives were not grasping and acquisitive. Cook had the preservation of Omai's possessions uppermost in his mind, advising him as a precaution to distribute a number of the more desirable and removable items among the chiefs for safekeeping. If the lesser items were stolen it would not be the end of the world. If that were to happen, warned Cook, on his return they 'would feel the weight of my resentment'. Elsewhere, ships' administration focused upon the next stage of the mission. They took the bread out of the bread store to remove vermin but the swarms of cockroaches resisted all efforts to dislodge them.

Cook's warnings to potential thieves appeared to have paid off until Wednesday, 22 October, when Bayly's observatory, as in Tahiti, again attracted a thief. Someone carried off a sextant. An angry Cook sent ashore for Omai to tell the chiefs he wanted the sextant returned. When they received Cook's message they were watching a Raiatean *arioi* performance and took no action, not wishing to be disturbed during their enjoyment of a *heiva* led by a beautiful young woman. Cook was not one to have his wishes ignored. He stormed into the large building where the performance was taking place and demanded they stop and turn their attention to the important business of returning the sextant. He held aloft another sextant so that there should be no misunderstanding of what was missing. Then, and only then, was their attention turned away from a comedy act to the immediate determination of who the thief might be. He was in fact sitting nonchalantly among them. Omai pointed the man out but so strong were his denials that Cook at first gave him the benefit of the doubt until Omai persuaded him that he was indeed the culprit. In the process of containing the man, the whole audience fled, despite Cook's reassurances they had nothing to fear. The sailors took the alleged thief on board the *Resolution* for interrogation, the man apparently telling Omai where the instrument had been hidden.

The next day normal relations between the natives and the visitors had been restored. For his impudence and audacity and to set an example, Cook imposed the severest punishment he had ever previously awarded, sending the Bora Boran felon on his way without his ears. As he left, the man threatened retaliation. He began by wrecking Omai's garden, declaring that once Cook had gone he would kill Omai and burn his house. Cook responded by bringing the troublemaker on board and having him clapped in irons with a view to carrying him off and abandoning him on some remote island en route. Huahine lived up to its reputation as the most troublesome island Cook had experienced. There were Bora Borans ashore, ready at any moment to assist their friend. Cook found no one with whom he could liaise effectively. There was a token boy chief with an ineffectual mother. Cook greatly missed the former chief, his friend Oree, a wise head in a field of turnips.

As the house neared completion, on 26 October, Omai had his furniture, pots, pans and cutlery sent ashore. The removal had the effect of bringing out the curious, among whom were the young chief, most of the other chiefs and a multitude of natives. Of the items considered 'useless' by Cook was the box of toys discussed at Streatham in what must have seemed an age ago, but which 'when exposed to public view seemed to please the gazing multitude very much'. His pots, kettles, dishes, plates, drinking mugs and glasses stimulated no interest at all, to such an extent that Omai re-evaluated their true worth in his new environment, deciding to trade them in among the ships' companies for hatchets and other useful tools. As part of the housewarming celebration, on 28 October a firework display from Omai's stocks generated among the great crowd of natives a mixture of pleasure and fear. Unfortunately the show did not live up to the usual high standard due to many fireworks supplied by the Woolwich arsenal malfunctioning.

For a while, relations between natives and visitors were convivial and orderly but on this island such matters existed uncomfortably, as if on top of a sleeping volcano. While the volcano still slept, Omai entertained Cook and his officers ashore on a number of occasions, assisted by his large staff brought from Tahiti and supplemented by the two New Zealand boys. Among Omai's possessions were two good drums, the electric machine and a portable organ which he used to good effect to entertain the chiefs and their wives. 'We have nothing but mirth and good humour subsisting among us at present,' wrote Bayly, but how accurate was that impression? The British attempt to emphasise Omai's importance had been an overplayed hand since his relatively humble origins were well known to those on Huahine. As King wrote in his journal: 'he seems not to have known, or forgot the customs and manners of his own countrymen, otherwise he would have known that there is perhaps not a single instance where merit or abilities have raised a low man to a high rank amongst them . . . he ever supposed that from his first appearance all would bow to him.' The chiefs appeared willing to go along with the masquerade for as long as it remained to their advantage but at some stage Omai's supply of presents would be exhausted. 'The chiefs, while they partook of his entertainments', observed Rickman, 'paid him little or no respect, and, had it not been for their deference to Captain Cook, would probably have treated him, amidst the splendour of his banquets, with the utmost contempt.' This therefore was a most unsound foundation upon which to build the repatriation of an individual envied, perhaps despised, rather than respected.

Early on the morning of Thursday, 30 October, Omai came on board to bring Cook some distressing news. The Bora Bora man had escaped during the early hours of the morning. He could not have absconded without the active assistance of one or more of the crew of the *Resolution*. In a round of demotions and lashings, Cook upheld naval discipline. One negligent marine had the misfortune to accumulate three separate charges against him and as a result received twelve lashes on each of three consecutive days. Cook and Clerke both offered ten hatchets for the return of the prisoner or for information which would lead to his arrest. There was a thought that one of the midshipmen had released the prisoner. Some on board believed he had been 'set up' by Omai as part of his ongoing battle against Bora Bora.

When an event such as this occurred on an island it tended to hasten Cook's departure. That was again the case now. Omai appeared to have been reasonably settled. A carpenter chiselled out on one side of his house the inscription:

Georgius tertius Rex 2 Novembris 1777

Naves ⎰Resolution. Jac. Cook Pr
⎱Discovery. Car. Clerke Pr2

For his protection Omai had a musket with bayonet, a fowling piece, two pairs of pistols, two or three swords and his suit of armour. Cook remained consistent in his opinion that 'he would have been better without fire arms than with them', but nevertheless left Omai with 20lb of powder, musket cartridges and musket and pistol balls. To help sustain him, Cook left a stallion, a pregnant mare, a pregnant goat, an English boar and two sows to supplement his own sows.

King believed that the possibility of Cook returning would act to deter the chiefs from taking advantage of Omai: 'At Huahine I have observed that his conduct was prudent, and if he does not fall a sacrifice to his resentment against Bora Bora, he may yet be comfortable.' However, while the ships were still in harbour Omai had already fired at a group intent upon stealing his property and, on another occasion, the Bora Bora miscreant led an attempt to burn down Omai's new house. Cook must have pondered Omai's prospects for survival as the time for departure drew ever nearer. He would have much preferred to have left Omai at Tahiti. Omai had become more responsible in the management of his wealth, yet Cook had difficulty in determining what benefits Omai would bring to Huahine. Apparently not many: 'We are therefore not to expect that Omai will be able to introduce many of our arts and customs amongst them or much improve those they have got. I think however he will bring to perfection the fruits we planted which will be no small acquisition.' To the fruit, Cook might have added the benefits perceived to be derived from the animals they had brought to the islands. Both fruit and animals proved to be spectacular failures for want of a peaceful environment in which to flourish. Irrespective of how the diversion to bring Omai home might be assessed in terms of time, cost and effort, it was nevertheless an act of faith.

For want of a written language or of anyone capable of putting more than two English words together, an emergency alarm system was devised. If all went well after the ships had left, Omai was to send to the ships at Raiatea two white beads, if indifferently, two brown beads, but if in trouble or difficulty, he was to send two blue beads.

A great number of natives pressed Cook and Clerke to take them to England. Equally pressing was Omai who did not want challengers returning to undermine whatever legacy he had been able to achieve. As Cook said, 'he frequently put me in mind that Lord Sandwich told him no more were to come'.

The problem arose about what to do with the New Zealand boys, reference to whom had been largely omitted from Cook's journal. They had been paid for by Omai and were part of his retinue. Nevertheless, they obviously pricked Cook's conscience: 'If there had been the most distant probability of any ship being sent again to New Zealand, I would have brought the two youths of that country home with me, as they were both desirous of coming.' The boys, both of whom had been assimilated among the ship's crew, wrongly assumed that to be the case. 'They flattered themselves', wrote King, 'that we should have carried them to England.' When the truth dawned upon them their reactions were different. The sensible, unflappable elder of the two, Tiarooa, saw that, on balance, with the choice lying between his barbaric home and these relatively placid islands, the islands represented the lesser of two evils. Cocoa had become the ship's mascot, the sailors delighting in his sense of fun and his ability to mimic 'the witty sayings of Wapping and Saint Giles'. He most definitely did not want to leave friends who had become foster family and, if made to do so, he would not go quietly.

Omai's farewell was only ever going to give rise to some localised sorrow. Aware of his celebrity status as the crew were, many had grown tired of him, considering him too big for his boots. Only two days previously one of their number had been put in irons for insulting him although, to his credit, Omai pleaded for the sailor's release the next day.

What the judgements passed on Omai thus far have in common is their origin, exclusively from the West. When Omai is examined within the context of his place of birth and among his own people, the situation is less black and white. The key consideration here is something described as *mana*, which essentially means prestige but which also has an almost magical, undefinable, additional meaning. There are two kinds of *mana*, both of which generate respect and influence. The first, inherent *mana*, is concerned with prestige derived from birth and relates to the chiefs. The second kind of *mana* is that which is relevant to Omai and is classed, understandably enough, as secondary *mana*. Secondary *mana* is also derived from rank but more precisely the manipulation of rank. We have seen Omai's persistent quest at each port of call to become the *tayo* – equal in friendship as brothers – with the local chief. He was so successful because of his close position to Cook, the British connection: the chiefs assumed that someone who appeared to be Cook's right-hand man must be a man of high status. The other course open to those of low rank eligible to qualify for secondary *mana*, deliberately or involuntarily, was by proving themselves in conflict. The ultimate decision whether to recognise the attainment of secondary *mana* in this way remained the gift of the chief.

Omai was a proud man, but pride (*teo teo*) could be used selectively as a pejorative term to encompass the new, upwardly mobile, perceived to be using material possessions to prove their worth. This came at a time of change when few natives, including many of the chiefs, owned possessions of consequence and accordingly adopted hostile attitudes to those who did. Such a reaction was founded upon envy and greed (*nau nau*), resulting in there being a co-ordinated effort to cut down to size those who got too far ahead or who had become too self-important. They coveted iron. To witness one of their commoners prepared to appear before them on a sweltering day riding a stallion, discharging pistols and wearing a bespoke metal suit, head to toe, was more than they could endure. Jealousy in these days was certainly a Tahitian concept. The chief's eyebrows would have been raised by Omai's appearance with two foreign retainers, but for a *manahune* then to recruit six Tahitian servants for his personal use was not only considered presumptuous but also unacceptable. One way a person with possessions could avoid sanctions was to redistribute wealth among the less fortunate. Omai's possessions were of such originality and novelty, however, that they were cherished by the chiefs who became infuriated when they saw this largesse being distributed by Omai to his low-class relatives and other *manahune*. They bit their tongues, for they valued the British presence and respected Cook.

Maintaining friendship with the British had become the keystone to the diplomacy of the tribes living in the area of Matavai Bay. Their influence, reputation and standing had been significantly inflated by the British connection. Prior to that meeting, they had been a run-of-the-mill, ordinary tribe, their new-found power derived from the muskets and technology the British had introduced. Again, jealousy among the tribes became evident. It was for that reason Cook found himself the subject of a cunning ruse to draw him away from Matavai Bay back to Vaitepiha Bay. Central to the development of Omai's advancement had been his assumption that he could tap into the British connection so as to enhance his own *mana*, to use the British association to improve his lot, thereby erasing the stigma of his having been a defeated person. He hoped to build his powerbase upon this British connection and to acquire support through the generous distribution of gifts. Omai failed in his aim because he overstepped defined boundaries but there were also three peculiarly local reactions which caused his best efforts to be frustrated.

The first was his gaining a reputation for dishonesty. The natives would listen to his account of *Pretane* but what he had to say was so far beyond what they were capable of comprehending that they branded him a liar. While Omai may have been a success among English ladies, the fact remained that his Negroid features set him apart from his own people who genuinely desired the aspiring leaders they had about them to be good-looking. (This was a society that was significantly bisexual and homosexual, and a proportion of the latter dressed themselves permanently as women.) Finally, Omai had a real problem as a Leeward Islander returning to settle on Tahiti, one of the Windward Islands. The arrogance so obvious in his attitude to Tu and his people was founded not only upon ignorance but also upon deep-seated inter-island rivalry. One of a number of reasons for Omai's rejection of Tu's sister may have been due to the hope that he might do better on the Leeward Islands.

Having said all this, it seems a reasonable assumption that Omai did have more favourable prospects of living out his life in a manner he felt appropriate on the Leeward Island of Huahine. His first error of judgement was not to select the plot of land upon which he chose to live from a 'smart' area; this was not the place for an aspiring chief. Moreover, he had no social following in Huahine, he generated no respect, experienced a fragile existence and failed to court the friendship of those he approached. That his home and property were pillaged were not unexpected consequences for a man who found himself isolated.

It would have been incomprehensible to Omai that he did not make headway, was rejected and scorned by his own people. Had he not been royally treated in London, sought after by the nobility, painted by Dance and Reynolds, virtually cocooned in the white *tapa* of the Tahitian aristocracy? But that was all now behind him. Evidence shows that Tahitians who have been abroad do revert to their former life and lifestyle. That was true of Omai who, with one or two exceptions, did not live out the remainder of the short time left to him in the European tradition, nor did he follow British mores. His initial impulsiveness had run entirely to form; it is said to have been a national trait. Too much is sometimes expected of Omai. He had no formal education, no culture of learning. Certainly, he held his own in English society but that was due not only to his pragmatism and overweening confidence but also to other national characteristics, namely grace and the skill of mimicry. He watched carefully what was done, copied it superbly and found himself duly applauded. This was his great game. He experienced checkmate where he least expected it, among the home islands he so loved and where he so much wanted to succeed.

Taking advantage of an easterly breeze, Cook took the *Resolution* out of the harbour with a large number of friends still on board. He had five guns fired in their honour and to indicate the range achievable, which, wrote Bayly, 'struck them with great terror'. Omai remained on board until taken ashore by King, whose task was to collect part of a hawser cut through by rocks during the process of leaving harbour. He had made his farewell to his officer friends aboard the *Resolution* in a manly manner until, finally, he came to Cook, 'when with all the eloquence of sincerity he expressed his gratitude and burst into tears'. Williamson observed that Cook also 'was much affected at this parting'. Had the Omai experience been worthwhile? Williamson thought not: 'I believe had he gone to England again (which was greatly his wish and desire) he would have acted the same part over again being extremely fond of a gay life and being thought a great man.' Omai had begun his farewell on the *Discovery* where Bayly saw him in an emotional state: 'He was very much affected so as to cry much as did most of us who were his acquaintance, he kissed us and bid us a long farewell.' Burney wrote of his friend's 'tears of real and unaffected sorrow'. The parting had such a deep emotional impact upon Omai he was still weeping when he went aboard his canoe for the final farewell.

A number of the officers wept for Omai but what happened next, while they stood silently, unable to intervene, left the officers and crews of both ships with tears welling in their eyes. The two New Zealand boys 'who showed the most violent and poignant grief at parting from us' had gone out in separate canoes. Samwell recalled the distressed Cocoa being nearby in Omai's large canoe, close enough to shout out, 'to plead to his friends on board to take him with them'. He endeavoured to jump out of the canoe to swim after the ships, only to be restrained by those aboard the canoe. A violent struggle could be seen going on in Omai's canoe, a jumble of arms and legs, as a result of which the diminutive Cocoa wriggled free, jumped overboard and swam as best he was able to catch the ships now well under way. The canoe overtook him, the crew hauling him aboard where the struggle was resumed with the same intensity and, as a result, the determined

Cocoa again broke free, diving out of the canoe and swimming after the English ships. Visibly weakened, the small boy was once again dragged back into the canoe where the occupants tied him up, securing him inside with ropes. He continued to cry out, 'and called to his old shipmates for assistance which we were so inhuman as to deny him. I was upon the deck and saw all this and if I ever felt the full force of an honest heart ache it was at that time.' In the other canoe, in a mature display of *noblesse oblige*, Tiarooa shed silent tears. In the failing light, Omai could be seen standing in the bow of his canoe, rigid as a statue, illuminated by the reddish glow of the setting sun, his arms held high.

Almost a week later, a single canoe from the nearby island of Huahine, with two men on board, entered Haamanino harbour, Raiatea. They paddled to the *Resolution* where they asked for 'Toote'. When Cook arrived, one of the natives placed into his hand two white beads.

Looking back, it would seem on reflection that the disappearance of a goat would feature at the lower level of a scale of stress generation when compared to Omai's frustrating, self-induced, self-indulgent sabotage of Cook's best efforts to see him settled on Tahiti. Cook's different reactions to both situations are of interest. Settling Omai formed a crucial part of the mission given to Cook by Omai's sponsors. Yet Cook faced the histrionics with quiet, measured patience. He conceded that Omai 'was not a man of much observation' and, whatever his faults, Cook put on public record his opinion that they were more than offset by 'his great good nature and docile disposition'. Notwithstanding two different approaches to different situations, neither came to a successful conclusion.

Maheine never forgave Cook for his treatment over the matter of the goat and, in the fullness of time, took his revenge. He attacked Tu at Pare, slaughtering every one of the animals and progeny left by Cook that he encountered. On the other hand, Omai spurned an opportunity that might have worked for one which would not. Huahine was an anarchic society which owed the self-important

Omai and long-suffering Cook nothing. His prospects would have been more favourable on Tahiti under the patronage of Tu – something the chief might have undertaken if only out of deference to Cook.

After sailing from Huahine, Cook spent a month at Raiatea, visible from Huahine 12 miles away, his actions entirely compatible with those of a commander with time to kill, not wishing to arrive at the Arctic until the summer of 1778. He sent back to Huahine a male and female goat to replace Omai's goat which had died giving birth to its young, the effort taken to recover the said goat from Maheine thereby having been counter-productive in more ways than one. Among his visitors, Cook was surprised to meet the Bora Boran who had previously been prisoner on board the *Resolution* and who had threatened to terrorise Omai after Cook's departure. The man told Cook he and Omai were now the best of friends. Perhaps a number of axes or red feathers had contributed to resolving the problem or perhaps the Bora Bora man merely wished to know when Cook had left the region. The residents were taking full advantage of Omai's wealth, asking extortionate prices for the basic requirements of life to support him, his two retainers and six Tahitian staff. In a matter of months, Omai would have no remaining means of support.

There are core truths which tell of Omai's demise and two different versions purporting to explain the circumstances surrounding his death. The consensus is that in 1780, within thirty months of Cook's departure and still only in his twenties, Omai died, probably of natural causes, possibly Spanish influenza, possibly from no longer having the will to live. The two New Zealand boys died, 'pined themselves to death', at approximately the same time, there being doubt only as to the sequence in which they died. The house was destroyed. One report said it had been pulled down, another that it had been burned down. The seeds and plants were all gone. All that remained was the shaddock tree planted by Cook.

The first substantive account of the passing of Omai came from William Bligh, former master of the *Resolution* and now in Tahiti for five months in 1789 in command of HMS *Bounty*. Bligh reported that shortly after Cook's confirmed departure from the islands, there was an opportunity for Omai to make the residents of Huahine indebted to him. A dispute had arisen between Huahine and the people of Raiatea supported by warriors from Bora Bora. The chiefs of Huahine, conscious of Omai's armoury, asked him whether he thought it practicable to confront Raiatea. Perhaps it was the Bora Bora association which gave Omai cause to give the chiefs every encouragement to fight Raiatea and a band of mercenaries. Omai and his weapons played a battle-winning part in a victory which left many dead Raiateans and Bora Borans on the field of battle. It had been a close-run thing. So intense had been the rate of fire required for victory that the supply of flints soon became exhausted. Omai improvised, lighting the powder in the musket chambers with burning tapers.

In this society it would have been usual either to reward the hero or to elevate him to a higher rank, that is, to apply secondary *mana*. Omai received neither reward nor promotion, remaining but one grade above the lowest possible within the lower class. How Bligh was able to achieve such a high level of comprehension of the language to report all of this is unclear. There is even a plausible account from the *Bounty* to suggest that Omai 'had been killed for the sake of his property'.

The alternative version comes from a missionary, William Ellis, whose book *Polynesian Researches* was published in 1829, forty years after the Bligh account. According to Ellis, Omai soon abandoned his English dress, 'and adopted the costume, uncivilised manners and indolent life of his countrymen. Weakness and vanity, together with savage pride, appear to have been the most conspicuous traits of character he developed in subsequent life.' In reality, the Ellis description is a close fit to the Omai we know. There is also evidence that he did not entirely abandon his English dress. He continued to wear riding boots, 'so', wrote Bligh, 'it is evident that he did not immediately after our leaving him, lay aside the Englishman'. Ellis tells how Omai rode his horses occasionally with the intention of inspiring either terror or admiration in the minds of the natives. Ellis then went on to contradict Bligh comprehensively, telling us that the 'King of the island' had been so grateful to Omai for putting his weapons at the king's disposal that he 'gave him one of his daughters in marriage and honoured him with the name of Paari (wise or instructed)'. Unfortunately, the account does not ring true. The 'King', Teriitaria, would have barely reached the age of ten, hardly time to have had a marriageable daughter.

Ellis mentioned how the natives spoke Omai's name 'with execration rather than respect', pointing the finger of blame at his experiences in England and suggesting 'he might perhaps have returned with very different sentiments and principles, had he fallen into other hands during his visit there'. Among the 'other hands' Ellis had in mind would have been the clergy. That Omai had left his mark in Huahine is borne out by the fact that the site of his house is still known as *Beritani* (Britain) by the islanders. Unlike the animals landed at Tahiti, those left at Huahine were not subject to attack, but all but the goats and pigs had died.

Ellis went on to describe in his book the residual evidence of Omai's presence on Huahine. On the wall of the house where Omai's house had once stood hung parts of his armour, including his helmet, together with several cutlasses. One chief had the habit of bringing out as a special treat Omai's jack-in-the-box, 'a kind of serpent that darts out of a cylindrical case when the lid is removed'. Of his organ and electrical machine there was no sign. Ellis found in the possession of a chief on Tahaa, Raiatea's twin island, the large quarto English Bible with many coloured engravings given to him by Granville Sharp. In one or two generations, all trace of Omai would have gone.

Unlike Aoutourou and Tupia, and his friends James Cook (killed in Kealakekua Bay, Hawaii) and Charles Clerke and William Anderson (both of whom died of tuberculosis on the voyage), Omai did return home. His achievements and lionisation in England cannot be simply dismissed. It had been a glittering performance by a man of humble origins. He had the sense to see what was required to sustain interest, to keep himself in demand. He took London by storm to such an extent that people in Britain and France discussed and wrote of him long after his death. The young man in the Reynolds portrait was able to survive and live out a sham where he was a stranger. He should have known that this was a process that could not be repeated on his home islands, but so imbued had he become with his own opinion of himself that he became blinded to that self-evident fact. It fell within Cook's gift to negotiate a satisfactory deal with Tu, drawing upon Omai's strengths, his experiences, his wealth and his weaponry. If he had spent his time in London more usefully he could have been an even more attractive prospect. Believing he knew best, Omai stupidly frustrated every one of Cook's initiatives.

What the spoilt Omai proved was the wrongness of Rousseau's theory of the noble savage. London had its Johnsons and Lord Chesterfields in the same way that the islands had their Tupias and Omais. The situation is placed in a nutshell by reference to Tinker in Thomas Blake Clark's *Omai.*

> What the age learned from its test of man in the savage stage was precisely what every age must learn about its fellows in another state of existence – that they are, *mutatis mutandis,* very like ourselves, good and bad, glorious and inglorious, and that the state of perfection is placed before man for his inspiration and not as a beautiful dream of what existed long ago or perchance still exists in some unsuspected isle of the far seas.

Over a short period the philosophy of the noble savage, the *bon sauvage,* had given way to pragmatic thinking. With both Britain and France poised to embark upon systematic colonial expansion, there could be no logic in supporting a theory which insisted that those about to be colonised were in a preferable situation to that enjoyed by the colonisers.

What is left unsaid is the desirability of the crossing of different cultures, of bringing 'civilisation' to a people living contentedly in a state of innocence and beauty. It was Omai's lot to contract his second experience of 'veneral distemper' on Tahiti and the virus believed to have killed him had probably been brought to the islands by the Spanish. Obviously the Polynesians could never be protected indefinitely but Cook spoke idealistically as one of those who sorrowed at having been numbered among those who brought harm to paradise. As he left Tahiti for the last time, he wrote:

> I own I cannot avoid expressing it as my real opinion that it would have been far better for these poor people never to have known our superiority in the accommodations and arts that make life comfortable, than after once knowing it, to be left again and abandoned.

Select Bibliography

Alexander, Michael, *Omai, Noble Savage* (London, 1977)

Auckland City Gallery, *The Two Worlds of Omai* (Auckland, 1977)

Beaglehole, J. C., *The Life of Captain James Cook* (London, 1974)

—— (ed.), *The Journals of Captain James Cook*. The Hakluyt Society. Vols I–III (London, 1955–67)

Bligh, William, *The Log of the Bounty*, 2 vols (London, 1936)

Boswell, James, *The Life of Samuel Johnson*. Vol. III (London, 1820)

Bougainville, L. A. de, *A Voyage Round the World*, J. R. Forster (London, 1772)

Burney, Frances, *Memoirs of Doctor Burney*, 3 vols (London, 1832)

Chisholm, Kate, *Fanny Burney. Her Life* (London, 1998)

Clark, Thomas Blake, *Omai. First Polynesian Ambassador to England* (Hawaii, 1969)

Colman, G., *Random Records* (London, 1830)

Cook, J., *A Voyage towards the South Pole*, 2 vols. (London, 1777)

Cook, J. and J. King, *A Voyage to the Pacific Ocean*, 3 vols (London, 1789)

Corney, B. G., *The Quest and Occupation of Tahiti by the Emissaries of Spain 1772–1776*, Vol. I (Cambridge, 1913)

Cradock, J. *Literary and Miscellaneous Memoirs*, Vols I–IV (London, 1928)

Curley, Thomas M., *Samuel Johnson and the Age of Travel* (Athens, Georgia, 1976)

Ellis, Annie Raine (ed.), *The Early Diary of Frances Burney 1768–1778*, 2 vols (London, 1889)

Ellis, W., *Polynesian Researches* (London, 1829)

Fairchild, Hoxie Neale, *The Noble Savage. A Study in Romantic Naturalism* (New York, 1961)

Furneaux, Rupert, *Tobias Furneaux. Circumnavigator* (London, 1960)

Hawkesworth, John, *An Account of the Voyages Undertaken by Order of His Present Majesty for Making Discoveries in the Southern Hemisphere* (London, 1773)

Hibbert, Christopher, *George III. A Personal History* (London, 1998)

Hough, Richard, *Captain James Cook. A Biography* (London, 1994)

Howarth, David, *Tahiti. A Paradise Lost* (London, 1983)

Langdon, R., *Island of Love* (London, 1959)

Lascelles, Edward, *Granville Sharp* (London, 1928)

McArthur, N., *Island Populations of the Pacific* (Canberra, 1967)

McCormick, E. H., *Omai, Pacific Envoy* (Auckland, 1977)

Moorhead, Alan, *The Fatal Impact. The Invasion of the South Pacific 1767–1840* (London, 1966)

National Library of Australia, *Cook and Omai. The Cult of the South Seas* (Canberra, 2001)

Oliver, D. L., *Ancient Tahitian Society*, 3 vols (Honolulu, 1974)

Prince, Jan, *Tahiti and French Polynesia Guide* (Cold Spring Harbor, New York, 2002)

Rickman, John, *Journal of Captain Cook's Last Voyage to the Pacific Ocean* (London, 1785)

Rodger, N. A. M., *The Insatiable Earl. A Life of John Montagu, 4th Earl of Sandwich* (London, 1993)

Russell, Alexander, *Aristocrats of the South Seas* (London, 1961)

Salmond, Anne, *The Trial of the Cannibal Dog. Captain Cook in the South Seas* (London, 2003)

Skelton, R. A., *Captain James Cook – After Two Hundred Years* (London, 1969)

Stanley, David, *Tahiti. Polynesian Handbook* (Chico, California, 1992)

Warner, Oliver (ed.), *An Account of the Discovery of Tahiti from the Journal of George Robertson, Master of HMS Dolphin* (London, 1955)

Index